TEILHARD DE CHARDIN:
In Quest of the Perfection of Man

An International Symposium
Edited and Compiled by

Geraldine O. Browning

Joseph L. Alioto

Seymour M. Farber, M.D.

TEILHARD DE CHARDIN:

In Quest of the Perfection of Man

Rutherford • Madison • Teaneck
Fairleigh Dickinson University Press

Associated University Presses, Inc.
Cranbury, New Jersey 08512

Library of Congress Cataloging in Publication Data
Main entry under title:

Teilhard de Chardin: in quest of the perfection of man.

Papers presented at a symposium held in San Francisco, May 1971, jointly sponsored by the University of California's medical campus in San Francisco and the city and county of San Francisco.

Includes bibliographical references.

1. Teilhard de Chardin, Pierre—Congresses. 2. Man—Congresses. I. Browning, Geraldine O., ed. II. Alioto, Joseph L., ed. III. Farber, Seymour M., ed. IV. California. University. Medical Center, San Francisco.
B2430.T374T393 128 72-9596
ISBN O-8386-1258-X

Extracts from Teilhard de Chardin's *The Phenomenon of Man,* translated by Bernard Wall, 1965, and *The Future of Man,* translated by Norman Denny, 1964, are reprinted with the kind permission of Harper & Row, Publishers, Inc.

Printed in the United States of America

Contributors

MAJOR PAPERS

Joseph L. Alioto	Mayor of San Francisco
J. Ralph Audy, M.D., Ph.D.	Professor of International Health and Human Ecology Director, Hooper Foundation University of California, San Francisco
Theodosius Dobzhansky, D.Sc.	Professor of Genetics Rockefeller University
Mark F. Ferber, Ph.D.	Vice President for Student Services University of Santa Clara
Robert T. Francoeur, Ph.D.	Associate Professor of Experimental Embryology Fairleigh-Dickinson University
Ralph R. Greenson, M.D.	Clinical Professor of Psychiatry University of California, Los Angeles
L. S. B. Leakey, D.Sc., F.B.A.	Honorary Director, Centre for Prehistory and Palaeontology, Kenya

Teilhard de Chardin

Christopher F. Mooney, S.J.	President, Woodstock College
Emil Mrak, Ph.D.	Chancellor Emeritus University of California, Davis
Conor Cruise O'Brien, Ph.D.	Member of the Irish Parliament
George Gaylord Simpson, Ph.D.	Trustee of the Simroe Foundation
Bernard Towers, M.B., Ch.B.	Professor of Pediatrics and Anatomy University of California, Los Angeles
N. Max Wildiers, Ph.D.	University of Louvain University of San Francisco
The Honorable Pearce Young	Judge of the Superior Court Los Angeles County

CHAIRMEN

David P. Gardner, Ph.D. (Welcoming Address)	Vice President—Public Service Programs University Dean of University Extension University of California
Albert R. Jonsen, S.J.	President University of San Francisco
Philip R. Lee, M.D.	Chancellor University of California, San Francisco Professor of Medicine and Ambulatory and Community Medicine
Thomas D. Terry, S.J.	President University of Santa Clara
Robert A. Thornton, Ph.D.	Professor of Physics University of San Francisco

PANEL MODERATORS

Mrs. Allan E. Charles	Vice President, Board of Trustees Stanford University

Contributors

Professor Carl O. Sauer	Professor of Geography, Emeritus University of California, Berkeley

PROGRAM COMMITTEE

Cochairmen

Joseph L. Alioto	Mayor of San Francisco
Seymour M. Farber, M.D.	Dean, Continuing Education in Health Sciences

Members

Mr. John Anderson	Assistant Deputy for Development Office of the Mayor San Francisco, California
Mr. Robert Bainbridge	Executive Director, Northern California Phenomenon of Man Project, Inc. Northridge, California
Mr. Edgar H. Barber	Business Manager Department of Continuing Education in Health Sciences University of California, San Francisco
Mr. A. Bernstein	Extension Specialist Department of Continuing Education in Health Sciences University of California, San Francisco
Mrs. Geraldine O. Browning	Homemaker, Community Citizen
Cornelius M. Buckley, S.J.	President St. Ignatius College Preparatory San Francisco, California
Mrs. Sheila McD. Cooley	Homemaker, Community Citizen

Teilhard de Chardin

John Dillenberger, Ph.D.	President Graduate Theological Union Berkeley, California
Ruben Dixon, Ph.D.	Extension Specialist Department of Continuing Education in Health Sciences University of California San Francisco
Miss Marilee E. Fisher	Administrative Assistant Department of Continuing Education in Health Sciences University of California San Francisco
Albert R. Jonsen, S.J.	President University of San Francisco
L. S. D. Kimbrough, M.D.	Associate Director Department of Continuing Education in Health Sciences University of California San Francisco
Philip R. Lee, M.D.	Chancellor University of California San Francisco
Professor Lloyd D. Luckmann	Dean, Colleges of Liberal Arts and Science University of San Francisco
Piero Mustacchi, M.D.	Associate Director Department of Continuing Education in Health Sciences
Mrs. Edwin Rosinski	Homemaker, Community Citizen
N. Max Wildiers, Ph.D.	Professor University of Louvain, Belgium University of San Francisco

Contributors

INTERNATIONAL ADVISORY COMMITTEE

M. Claude Batault	Consul General of France San Francisco
M. Hubert De Schryver	Consul General of Belgium San Francisco
Prof. Theodosius Dobzhansky	President The American Teilhard de Chardin Association New York, New York
Monsignor John Tracy Ellis	Professor of Church History University of San Francisco
Robert L. Faricy, S.J.	Carroll House Washington, D.C.
Dr. Harry N. Olsen	Secretary-Treasurer Phenomenon of Man Project, Inc. Northridge, California
Sister Providencia, S.P.	Professor of Sociology College of Great Falls Great Falls, Montana
Professor Harry J. Rathbun	Professor of Law, Emeritus Stanford University
Mr. Frank R. Stong	President Phenomenon of Man Project, Inc. Northridge, California
Charles W. Wagley, Ph.D.	President American Anthropological Association Washington, D.C.

Editor's note:

Each of the papers in this book was written independently and without prior knowledge (other than scholarly reputation) of what would be said by the other contributors. The reader who is looking for an even and cohesive whole and a grand conclusion following a carefully established premise will perhaps be disappointed, but will understand one of the difficulties in editing a compilation of this sort. One is sorely tempted to relate one discussion to the next, to infer and cross refer, and to sequentially deduce. Fortunately, these temptations were resisted and the original academic spontaneity of the individual contributions has been left intact. For the panel discussions the actual transcriptions of the proceedings were used, with only minor editing to insure clarity and continuity. May the success of the finished product rest in part on its capacity to be the catalyst for each reader to speculate in his own way on the exciting possibilities of extensive debate on the many viewpoints here recorded.

Geraldine O. Browning

Contents

Preface

Throughout history two forces have contended for prominence and popularity in men's minds: a movement toward unity and another toward multiplicity. Perhaps the most outstanding characteristic of Teilhard de Chardin's thought is his effort, first to explain these apparently conflicting themes in human and cosmic development, and then to find a basis for synthesis and reconciliation between them.

The intellectual audacity of this attempt lies in the fact that the synthesis is made in terms of all reality: from the atomic level, through cellular combinations into man, the development of human institutions, and ultimately, into what Teilhard sees as a "planetisation" of man's potentiality —"the growth and biological perfection" of man.

Philosophically, Teilhard's work is the expression of an idea that has ancient antecedents in both East and West. But the focus of Teilhard's argument, his intellectual *modus operandi,* is completely contemporary; Teilhard is nothing if not multidisciplinary in his approach.

This approach is a 20th-century development *par excellence,* and has been manifested in science, technology, and in attempted solutions to social dilemmas. In Teilhard's work it involved not only philosophy and religion as might be expected from a Jesuit scholar, but it also draws upon numerous other specialties including paleontology, anthropology, cosmology, and cellular biology. These scientific disciplines are tugged, shaped, and fitted into a vision of reality with which specialists in these various fields may disagree; but it is a vision whose possible implications for the future cannot be ignored.

It is particularly fitting that the interdisciplinary thought of Teilhard should be presented and discussed at a modern center for health care, training, and research. For it is in the health sciences preeminently that a multidisciplinary approach to man's physical health and complete well-being has taken root. The comprehensiveness of this methodology could not be more fitting to the spirit of Teilhard's work. To this degree at least, health scientists and Teilhard are at one in appreciating that the nature of man and his future are determined by forces infinitesimal and macroscopic—both the elusive genetic particle and the all-too-palpable ecology of which these particles and man are a part.

Man, his institutions, and his future are the products of these forces, as Teilhard says. The disciplines represented at this symposium are involved in studying these forces in order to understand them, and, hopefully, to assist man in his quest for fulfilled potentiality—for the achievement of excellence in peace.

A. Bernstein
—from the Symposium Program

Introduction

Seymour M. Farber, M.D.

It is something of a truism in academic circles that the age of great philosophical systems is dead. On secular university campuses, at least, the vast cosmological and ethical constructs of a Spinoza, Descartes, or Kant are generally looked upon as historical curios—testimonies to man's intellectual energy, but of questionable relevance to today's problems.

One may speculate that these broad and encompassing visions of reality were engendered by a belief that the fundamental questions of knowledge and man's fate were at heart answerable, if not simple; and because of this, hope was both rational and possible.

By contrast, modern man's attempt to create a unified,

Dr. Farber is Dean of Continuing Education, Health Sciences, University of California, San Francisco. While continuously teaching and practicing medicine, his broad career has also encompassed original research on lung cancer and pulmonary emphysema; past presidency of The American College of Chest Physicians; and membership and chairmanship roles in national and international societies and advisory boards in the fields of medicine, social welfare, education, and the arts. He has published extensively in medical science, social science, and the humanities.

systematic, and comprehensive philosophical doctrine has foundered on complexity and despair.

The effects of relativity on science and society, Dachau, Hiroshima, a pervasive and apparently irresistible technology, dangerously high overpopulation, violent social movements of international dimensions, ecological disasters, biological engineering, the knowledge "explosion," and the continued cruelties of modern war have made it difficult for many to believe seriously in the possibility of sweeping philosophical systems that can provide either useful answers or hope.

In this context, Teilhard de Chardin is an anomaly: a system builder in an era of specialization, an optimist in a time of turmoil. To his many followers throughout the world, he is the scientist-philosopher-priest who has given us a unifying vision of reality. On both geological and philosophical grounds, he has contended that fragmentation and divergence in human history are but transient and imperfect forms of a synthesis that is leading to a state of perfection, both in individual men and in their institutions collectively. And in Teilhard himself, his adherents see a life that was dedicated to the belief that reconciliation of strife was not only possible, but inevitable.

Fundamentally, of course, this is a philosophy of hope, which according to Teilhard is based on scientific facts as manifested in an evolutionary trend toward human fulfillment, world unity, and peace. "Instead of seeking, against all evidence to deny or disparage the reality of this grand phenomenon," says Teilhard, "we do better to accept it frankly."

Not unexpectedly, there are scholars to whom the injunction has not been convincing. On biological, psychological, and political grounds, they feel that the evolutionary trend toward the perfection of man and his institutions seems questionable.

While appreciating Teilhard's sincerity, these critics have pointed out that the facts can be interpreted to show that individual alienation and social dissolution are far from decreasing in the world; and that the perfection of man and the amity of nations is more of a will-o'-the-wisp, more threatened, and perhaps less achievable today than it has ever been in the entire history of man's development.

Proponents of both points of view were invited to participate in the symposium of which this volume is a printed record. However, in so doing, the intent was not to present an ideological confrontation in which one side was to be politely judged right at the expense of the other. Quite the contrary.

As originally conceived and continuously supported by Mayor Joseph Alioto of San Francisco, the minimum and immediate purpose of the symposium was to provide the attending audience with an opportunity for gaining what was best on both sides. But something much more important was, and is, hoped for from this symposium on Teilhard de Chardin.

In the ensuing months and years, hundreds of thousands of people in this country and abroad will have seen or read about the proceedings through such means as this book and direct and delayed television coverage in this country and abroad. For all of these peoples, it is hoped that this symposium can offer a model, however imperfect and tentative, by which fundamental issues can be discussed by opposing sides—calmly, rationally, and with mutual respect.

Whatever one's own vision of the good, these qualities, so characteristic of Teilhard de Chardin himself, are absolutely essential to solutions of the grave problems that we as individuals, as nations, and as a planet must face. The scholars at this symposium, hopefully, have given us some of the facts and insights that will help to make these solutions more possible. Above all, it is hoped that symposia such as this one can help us to achieve these solutions in peace, based on a respect for each person's own vision of perfection and his perhaps unending quest to achieve it.

Symposia of this magnitude, involving scholars from several continents, cannot be presented without the devoted efforts of many people. It is impossible in an already too long Introduction to name all the volunteers who contributed to the success of this venture. However, at least formal, if inadequate, appreciation must be extended to members of the Program and International Committees, who are listed elsewhere in this volume.

Needless to say, the valuable guidance and advice received from these committees had to be implemented by diligent and persistent staff work. In this connection, special mention must be made of Mr. John Anderson of Mayor Alioto's office, who provided essential liaison between the University of California and official agencies of the City of San Francisco.

Similarly, from the Office of Continuing Education in Health Sciences of the University of California, San Francisco, the efforts of key members of my own staff must be acknowledged: Mr. A. Bernstein, who designed the program as finally presented and saw it through all stages of planning and preparation; Mr. Ruben Dixon, who provided invaluable guidance and practical assistance in many important ways; and Miss Marilee Fisher, who together with Messrs. Bernstein and Dixon, saw to it that a thousand practical details were attended to at the right time and place.

Appreciation must also be extended to Mrs. Geraldine O. Browning for her extraordinary skill, energy, and good cheer in editing this volume for publication. The videotaped version of the program was made possible through the cooperation of educational television station KQED in San Francisco, with a special note of thanks to Mr. Robert Hagopian, who was producer-director for the original live telecast.

The efforts of all of these and many other people were finally realized because of the generosity of the City of San Francisco and the International Brotherhood of Teamsters, without whose financial support the symposium could not have been presented.

In this connection, I must add my personal thanks to Mayor Joseph Alioto, who served as the distinguished cochairman of the symposium's program committee, and who provided us all with the practical inspiration upon which the symposium was based.

Seymour M. Farber, M.D.
Dean, Continuing Education
in Health Sciences
University of California,
San Francisco
Cochairman, Program Committee
Teilhard de Chardin Symposium

The Words of the Tribe

Conor Cruise O'Brien, Ph.D.

You have done me the honor to invite me to deliver here the opening address of this Symposium on Teilhard de Chardin, in which some remarkable and varied minds from many different disciplines will take part.

I think you won't expect me on this occasion to attempt anything like a panegyric, even if that were necessary, on the great pioneer and prophet round whose work we are gathered. It was not panegyric he ever wanted, but the discussion and criticism of his ideas and of other ideas sparked off by his. This was what was to a great degree denied him during his lifetime, by his being unfortunately forbidden to publish the work that perhaps meant most to him and that, I take it, is what we shall be meeting here to try to accord to that work.

As statesman, educator, and author, Dr. O'Brien has been both a participant and observer of major world events during his tenure as Director of the United Nations Secretariat, as Representative of the Secretary-General to Katanga, and previously in the Irish foreign service. His many academic distinctions include positions as Vice Chancellor of the University of Ghana, the Albert Schweitzer Professorship of Humanities at New York University, and in 1971 a Regents Professor of the University of California at Berkeley. Dr. O'Brien is currently a member of the Irish Parliament.

I should like to take as my text this evening two passages from the fourth book of Teilhard de Chardin, *The Phenomenon of Man,* which is the book I will be mainly concerned with in this address.

The first passage in Bernard Wall's translation runs as follows:

> Now to the degree that—under the effect of this pressure and thanks to their psychic permeability—the human elements infiltrated more and more into each other, their minds (mysterious coincidence) were mutually stimulated by proximity. And as though dilated upon themselves, they each extended little by little the radius of their influence upon this earth which, by the same token, shrank steadily. What in fact do we see happening in the modern paroxysm? It has been stated over and over again. Through the discovery yesterday of the railway, the motorcar and the airplane, the physical influence of each man, formerly restricted to a few miles, now extends to hundreds of leagues or more. Better still: thanks to the prodigious biological event represented by the discovery of electromagnetic waves, each individual finds himself henceforth (actively and passively) simultaneously present, over land and sea, in every corner of the earth.[1]

The second passage is a little later in the same book:

> In order to avoid disturbing our habits we seek in vain to settle international disputes by adjustments of frontiers—or we treat as "leisure" (to be whiled away) the activities at the disposal of mankind. As things are now going it will not be long before we run full tilt into one another. Something will explode if we persist in trying to squeeze into our old tumbledown huts the material and spiritual forces that are henceforward on the scale of the world.[2]

Teilhard, of course, does not assume optimistically that we are not going to run full tilt into one another. Speaking of

[1] Pierre Teilhard de Chardin, *The Phenomenon of Man,* trans. Bernard Wall (New York: Harper & Row, 1965), p. 240. Quoted by permission of Harper & Row, Publishers, Inc.

[2] *Ibid.,* p. 253.

the evolutionary past, he has said that "like Tolstoy's grasshoppers, life passes over a bridge made of accumulated corpses." He calls this "groping profusion." And in speaking of man's future progress toward "Point Omega," he allows for the possibility (and this is sometimes overlooked in his thought) of an "abyss," a final paroxysm of evil, and he writes:

> But there is another possibility. Obeying a law from which nothing in the past has ever been exempt, evil may go on growing alongside good, and it too may attain its paroxysm at the end in some specifically new form.
>
> There are no summits without abysses.
>
> Enormous powers will be liberated in mankind by the inner play of its cohesion: though it may be that his energy will still be employed discordantly tomorrow, as today and in the past. . . . A conflict may supervene. In that case the noosphere, in the course of and by virtue of the process which draws it together, will, when it has reached its point of unification, split into two zones each attracted to an opposite pole of adoration. Thought has never completely united upon itself here below. Universal love would only vivify and detach finally a fraction of the noosphere so as to consummate it—the part which decided to 'cross the threshold' to get outside itself into the other. *Ramification once again, for the last time.*[3]

This hypothesis, he observes, would be "more in conformity with traditional apocalyptic thinking" than the other hypothesis he envisages, the optimistic hypothesis perhaps more generally associated with his name, which states that:

> evil on the earth at its final stage will be reduced to a minimum. Disease and hunger will be conquered by science and we will no longer need to fear them in any acute form. And, conquered by the sense of the earth and human sense, hatred and internecine struggles will have disappeared in the ever-warmer

[3] *Ibid.*, pp. 288–89.

radiance of Omega. Some sort of unanimity will reign over the entire mass of the noosphere. The final convergence will take place *in peace.*[4]

Those are the two hypotheses. Whatever the relative probabilities may be—and Teilhard does not try to assess them here—he tells us that the hypothesis of a convergence in peace expresses the hopes toward which we ought "in any case to turn our efforts as to an ideal."

In what manner, then, ought we to turn these efforts; or, in what direction are these efforts evolving? The two formulations are in Teilhard's system essentially the same, and Teilhard does not help us here with the answer. There is no reason, in terms of his vision and his system, why he should. But there is every reason, both within and without his system, why we must do so. In an adaptation of Teilhard's language, it is toward this area that the leading shoot of evolution in the noosphere must now move. To put it another way: If we are thinking at all, we must think about this.

It is not easy to think about it now. Suppose we look at the world around us—we being the educated part of the rich West, the group to which Teilhard himself belonged and which has a certain pride of place in his system—and the world around us being the world of the poor, which we call by euphemism the underdeveloped countries. Looking at that world, it may well be easier at the moment to believe in Teilhard's apocalyptic hypothesis than in convergence in peace.

We speak of the population explosion, but the concept is too vast, and the nightmare turns into a mere *cliché* like the generation gap. Instead of talking in generalities about it, let me say something about the underdeveloped country I know best, which is Ghana, formerly the Gold Coast in West Africa. The population of Ghana at the time of the last census in 1965 was about seven and a half million. If the rate

---

[4] *Ibid.*, p. 288.

of increase continues as it ran between the two last censuses, there will be 240 million before the middle of the next century; that is to say, within the lifetime of children now being born. From seven and a half million to 240 million.

Most of these children (and Ghana is in many ways typical of tropical Africa) will grow up unskilled, unemployed, and unwanted, *unwanted* being generally a new feature, a new and sinister feature of a tribal society. Many of them have already been coming down from the arid regions of the north to ring the coastal cities with slums at a rate, to quote the *New York Times*, April 30, 1971, of 10 percent per annum. Coastal people, forest people, Savannah people, and their subdivisions struggle in vastly increasing numbers for resources that increase much more slowly, if at all.

The first to go are the foreigners; not the rich foreigners, who are needed, but the poor ones with small skills: the men from other parts of Africa or Asia whose jobs or small trades are needed. I just had a letter from one of these, a Nigerian turned out of Ghana. He is back in his village in Eastern Nigeria. There is cholera there in the wake of the Nigerian civil war. Tribally speaking, he is on the winning side in that war, for he belongs to the Rivers people. He lives not far from the losers, the Ibo. Scores of thousands of those, apart altogether from the war and its aftermath, are in essentially the same position as the man who wrote to me. They were turned out of Northern Nigeria because local people needed their jobs. Those who stayed were killed. A stationmaster's job is a prize worth killing for. This is the way profusion gropes at present—profusion of people—and if any of you may perhaps think I am exaggerating or overstressing the dark side of this particular picture, I would invite your attention to an article by William Border that appeared in the same issue of the *New York Times* quoted earlier. Among other things, he makes the point that in Nigeria, because of the vast expansion in unemployed population and therefore in crime, the government had instituted public execution of thieves. This is an example of the kind of panic measure that we may expect to find in these conditions.

What to do? Three main sets of answers are offered, none of them, I think, wholly satisfactory: a meliorist set, a *laissez-faire* set, and a revolutionary set.

The meliorist set, which is perhaps associated above all with the United Nations and UNESCO, consists in its essential parts of relief and technical aid. All are necessary, and yet relief by itself expands the dimensions of the problem. There is a horrible dilemma here, which was felt acutely very recently by missionaries and others who tried to help the Biafran people during the Nigerian civil war. I was associated with those people during that war through two visits there, and saw their dilemma. Was it right, they were asking themselves, to bring food to the hungry even at the cost of prolonging a war which was bound to end in mass starvation anyway? Might it not have been better either to give the Biafrans no help at all, making for a shorter war and less resentment after, or to give them the full help they asked for (including political recognition and military aid), thus enabling them to survive as a nation? There is no clear answer to questions like that. I mention them here merely to suggest the types of problems that in real life today underlie such an apparently simple concept, such a simple humane, humanitarian concept as relief.

Relief, then, as everyone realizes, needs to be supported by technical aid or it leaves things worse than before in terms of the needs of the survivors. And even with technical aid it often still leaves things worse than before, though not necessarily worse than they might have become.

I am not trying, I should say here, to decry the effort of aid, which I believe to be very necessary. But I am trying to situate the enormous difficulties within the framework of our concerns here. We are apt to say to ourselves, "well, with a little more aid and industrialization these problems will be cleared up." It is not so simple as that.

The multiple forms of technical aid—including investments, price supports, loans and grants, expert advice—depend for their effectiveness on the effective receptivity of the society to which they are offered. Unfortunately, the more a society looks for such aid, the less likely it is to be capable of absorbing it effectively, or at least with any major general benefit to its citizens. Aid can in certain frequent circumstances become little more than a slush fund at the disposal of a ruling elite, helping to perpetuate its grip on power and frustrating the potential creative forces within the society itself. This is especially true of the phenomenon euphemistically known as "military aid."

There is a Gresham's law about aid. Those forms of aid which are supposedly in the direct national interest of the donor country by keeping its supposed friends in power are the most likely to be continued, even though they are the least likely to benefit the recipient country. But the knowledge of how alleged aid in this sense actually works engenders cynicism about aid in general. And this cynicism tends to operate at the expense of those forms of aid which, being least in the direct interest of the donor country, are on the whole most likely to benefit the recipient countries.

It is reasonably clear, I think, that meliorism (relief and aid from the advanced countries), however desirable, however necessary—and it is both—is unlikely in itself to avert the catastrophe that threatens most of humanity and that, if we count misery as catastrophic, already does engulf it.

The second set of answers offered are the *laissez-faire,* or Malthusian ones. These answers are indeed not often offered explicitly, but they are present in the thinking and practice of various sets of people who exercise authority over the world's economy and resources. The governing idea, usually the unspoken idea, is that the solution will be supplied by natural checks on population. Curiously enough, I heard that idea most clearly formulated by a priest in Ireland. He was arguing, as most of the Irish clergy still vehemently do, that contraception was contrary to the natural law and therefore could not be necessary. The population explosion being of course invoked against him, he answered to the effect that the God of the Old Testament was likely to find the solution to this problem through the operation of war, famine, and pestilence. This surely is a classical example of what Teilhard calls "traditional apocalyptic thinking." I wonder, in passing, what Teilhard would have thought of the Encyclical *Humanae Vitae,* which my apocalyptic acquaintance was defending.

I have wondered to myself whether he would have considered *Humanae Vitae* an example of what he called noogenesis: thought being born. Perhaps in obedience he might, but I suspect that his arguments in favor of such a proposition would, as usual, not have been publishable in his lifetime.

The Malthusian or apocalyptic solution is more likely, in that the advanced economies feel no particular need of the new populations in the third world. Potentially, no doubt, these represent a vast market; actually they don't. To speak of the advanced capitalistic world as exploiting the peoples of the poor world is now a loose figure of speech, true only indirectly and marginally. It is true in the sense that the advanced world took off by exploiting the resources of the rest of the world, including its human resources ruthlessly through the slave trade and in other ways. But a reserve of manual labor on anything like the scale now available is economically not now needed. Some tropical countries have resources that are needed and that are bought cheap: bought cheap by the West and sometimes even cheaper by the East, as is the case, for example, with Senegal's groundnuts. Where the commodities in question are important, or where the territory is strategically significant, and in certain other more specialized cases, the advanced countries will seek to manipulate and control the economic and political life of the poor country concerned. Neo-colonialism in that sense is much more than a figure of speech in certain areas, notably perhaps Latin America.

But there are other areas, and these are probably growing in number, where the advanced countries, or at least their economic rules, have simply ceased to care what happens. In the heyday of the Cold War this indifference was in a sense compensated by competition: The need at all costs, as it was felt then, to get in before the other fellow does. But painful experience sharply diminished that kind of competition in most areas. Indifference took its place. For example, I have heard it said that the grimmest threat today throughout vast areas of tropical Africa is not neo-colonialism but the absence of anything to interest neo-colonialists.

It may, I fear, be taken as reasonably certain, then, that the natural checks (again a euphemistic and veiling phrase) will be left to supply a large part of the solution. But there are some checks even on the natural checks. In presence of a great visible disaster—and disasters have become more visible than ever—the more advanced countries will try to help. Unfortunately, altruism, in the present state of man's evolution, can only be counted on for marginal effects.

But there is more than that. The biosphere is indivisible. Two of the natural checks, war and pestilence, cannot be relied on to remain within the limits of the poor world. They threaten all of our lives. However callous the rich world may be, and it is calloused enough, it cannot quite afford just to let nature take its course. The *laissez-faire* answers are not, by themselves, adequate even on their own terms.

Remains then the third set: the revolutionary ones. A great variety of Marxist, neo-Marxist, and post-Marxist schools agree on the basic assumption of world revolution: social revolution on a global scale assuming finally a global unifying character. The international operation of capitalism will make, they think, resistance to it also international. The imperialist forces will be overextended and worn down by the implementation of Che Guevara's slogan, "two, three, many Vietnams." Maoists have asserted that the world revolution will take place in a manner analogous to the Chinese Revolution, with the advanced countries representing the cities (according to Lin Piao's famous formula) and being cut off and forced into submission by the revolutionary "countryside"—the poor world at large.

Others, like Mr. Ronald Segal in *The Race War,* see the same global confrontation primarily in racial terms; with the nonwhites of the world uniting against the arrogant whites in a kind of *Götterdämmerung.* Franz Fanon, combining class and race in his system, presents a similar picture in his *Wretched of the Earth.*

There are, I think, obvious weaknesses in such predictions and analogies. Although the invasions of Laos and Cambodia may have seemed to corroborate Che Guevara, it is, I hope, far from certain that there will be many Vietnams. "The bourgeoisie," Antonio Gramsci said, "can learn from Marx, too." They can certainly learn from their own mistakes and from the declared strategies of their enemies. America stumbled, lurched, and slid into the insane horror of the Vietnam War, not because it was a clear capitalist interest that this should happen, but because internal American politics worked that way. Precisely because of Vietnam, it is unlikely to work in precisely the same way again. As for Lin Piao's analogy about the cities, its most obvious weakness is that whereas the Chinese countryside could starve the cities out, the advanced Western countries (Lin Piao's cities) actually export grain to the world's countryside, including China. The "Race War" theory in its white versus nonwhite form is equally vulnerable. There are few signs of an incipient union among nonwhite peoples against whites, and many obvious cases where for a nonwhite people the enemy is another nonwhite people—as well as cases such as we have in my own country, where for the white people the enemy is another white people. And for many nonwhites, the whites are remote and not a very relevant category. Indeed, the whole concept of a division of mankind into white and nonwhite is a white idea, and the only nonwhite people who in their own way share it are those who have lived in some form of fairly close contact with a white community. For that very reason, these are the nonwhites of whom the whites are most conscious and from whom they hear most.

All great revolutions have been universalist in ideology and rhetoric but national in practice. And where revolutions have succeeded in different countries under the signs of an identical ideology, the ideology has then ramified into divergent and often hostile national forms. The revolutionary forces that shake the third world need not be expected to be uniformly convergent. More than that, the struggle of masses of men for scarce resources is taking forms that are not only not easily recognizable as class struggle, but are not even recognizable as national. Men clump and congregate and fight in response to their actual feelings and not by reference to what the Harlem schoolchild called the way it "spozed to be." Class solidarity has so far proved for human beings in advanced or advancing societies, a less potent bond than the national bond. But in other societies, and in certain pockets within the advanced societies, too, both class and national bonds are weaker than other more traditional bonds, such as linguistic, religious, cultural, and tribal bonds. Conflicts between such groups can be analyzed or at least talked about in class terms, since in a comparison of any two tribes, one is likely to be found at any given time to be at least a little better off than the other. This phenomenon has led some Western classifiers into the tortuous blind alleys of vicarious tribalism, identifying in Nigeria, for example, now with the progressive South against the feudal North, and at another time with the underprivileged Northerners against the Southern bourgeois stationmasters. Or, in Ireland, being *for* the Catholics in the North, where they are in the minority, but *against* them in the South, where they are in the majority but are, of course, the same people.

Sympathies and antipathies of this same kind copiously

becloud advanced discussion of processes of change in more traditional societies. And in certain conditions, as we know, the identification of peoples as "part of the world revolution of international communism" has led the most advanced nation to make war on these peoples to no good purpose. If this counterrevolutionary effort could have been sustained and generalized, as men on both the extreme right and the extreme left have hoped (as Guevara hoped, for example), then it might conceivably have welded the divergent and polymorphous revolutionary movements of the world into one world revolution directed against the United States as world policeman. But as matters have evolved in the last few years this outcome seems at present rather unlikely.

Thus we contemplate meliorism, laissez-faire, tribalism, revolution, and counterrevolution; the interactions and instabilities of all of these; a world in flux, spawning new forms of conflict and confusion through enormous numbers of short lives; a world increasingly crowded, polluted, and angry, finding makeshift and often brutal local solutions to parts of the universal problem; a bloody, messy, hungry world; a world unbearable for the young to contemplate without the illusion of an early, dramatic, and triumphant denouement—the millenary hope.

We may seem to have strayed a long way from Teilhard but that, if Teilhard is right, would be rather hard to do. I have been trying to describe, in an appallingly summary way, some aspects of our present "groping confusion." It has seemed to me necessary to do that before we can approach the question: Toward what can we now see the profusion as groping?

In general, of course, this is the question to which the whole of *The Phenomenon of Man* is a poem in answer. This also is the question on which we hope that our discussions here will shed light, making use of vast perspectives in time and space and inspired by the example of the courage in generalization and synthesis that the great Jesuit scientist left to our specialized and analytical age.

In this opening address I want to dwell on just one aspect of the enormous question, an aspect enormous in itself but limited in the perspective of the vast Teilhardian vision. This is the question of a phase in the evolution of humanity and of what Teilhard called the noosphere, the thinking layer, in our own historical period from now to the end of, say, the next century. Teilhard himself seems to see this evolution in terms of the westernization of mankind. He writes in the last paragraphs of the chapter "The Deployment of the Noosphere" in *The Phenomenon of Man* as follows:

> In truth a neo-humanity has been germinating around the Mediterranean during the last 6,000 years, and precisely at this moment it has finished absorbing the last vestiges of the Neolithic Mosaic with the budding of another layer on the noosphere, and the densest of all.
>
> The proof of this lies in the fact that from one end of the world to the other, all the peoples, to remain human or to become more so, are inexorably led to formulate the hopes and problems of the modern earth in the very same terms in which the West has formed them.[5]

Now, I think there is something wrong with that. Furthermore, what is wrong with that is what is wrong with us—us as Westerners and more generally, us as human beings. Something is wrong: not racism, certainly, with the cruel and vicious connotations that that word has won for itself; not racism, but what I shall call ethnocentric inertia. Now the word *inertia* may startle here, as applied to certain words of this unwearying traveler and thinker. Yet for this aspect and limitation of his thought, it is, I think, the appropriate word. Note that it is not ethnocentrism itself that I object to here. It is always well, I think to be aware of one's tribe—and one's position in it, even if one thinks of the awareness extending to so diffuse and heterogeneous an entity as "The West."

[5] *Ibid.*, p. 212.

No, what goes wrong, or rather what has to be surpassed, is not the tribal sense but the closings out caused by tribal sense—the social callouses, the anesthesia of sympathy in the contemplation of the stranger: "Since he is not quite like us, he is not quite human."

It is interesting, and I think strangely moving, that the peroration to the deployment of the noosphere constitutes in itself a classic unconscious example of the main obstable to this deployment.

You may say, of course, and some of you, I'm sure, are saying in your minds: "But Teilhard is right. Western civilization has been the prime source of human progress for centuries. Western ethnocentrism has a right to exist because this great and varied ethos is in fact, the center, being the creator of modern science and technology."

In a sense that would be hard to refute, nor is it enough to answer—though it is true—that this progress has been achieved at the expense and on the backs of non-Western peoples as well as of the Western proletariat. Equivalents of that are true of all evolutionary development, and Teilhard is writing in an evolutionary perspective.

I believe that the weakness in Teilhard's formulation here, and also in many other passages (because this is not an isolated passage), is not that he emphasizes the West's advantage, but that he gives a privileged, permanent, and quasi-sacred character to what may be a quite temporary and brief advantage. Teilhard implies that to remain human all peoples must formulate the hopes and problems of mankind in the very same terms in which the West has formulated them.

I must say I get here a touch of the atmosphere of the colonial schoolroom where, over the generations, children of Asia and Africa were told in effect, "you must be exactly like us—and you know you can't be."

The hopes and problems of the modern earth are not everywhere the same, and for non-Western people to try to formulate theirs precisely in Western terms is surely a recipe for stagnation and frustration. Please do not misunderstand me. I am not arguing in favor of Slavonic biology, or Nkrumahist algebra. Nor am I arguing that the non-Western peoples can remain or have remained immune to Western political and social ideas. What I'm saying is that the hope of the non-Western peoples lies not in formulating their hopes and problems in the very same terms as some particular set of Western ideas, but precisely in changing and adapting these terms to meet the very different demands of their local conditions and modes of discourse.

Thus, insofar as India, for example, has loyally and literally adhered to a Western political model—that of parliamentary democracy—the result is an additional form of ritual stagnation. Again, when the Chinese revolutionaries attempted to apply Marxism in the very same terms that reached them through the West through Russia, the result was frustration and defeat. But when a Chinese revolutionary genius took from Marxism as much as he saw would work in Chinese conditions and added other elements to form a new system, the result has been an earthshaking one of which Teilhard indeed saw the beginning: nothing less than the regeneration, political regeneration, of Chinese society.

By a strange irony, the Maoists on the international plane repeat the very same kind of error that they took care to reject within their own country. They, too, offer the same terms: a philosophy worked out to meet one set of conditions and claiming to be, in its essentials, valid in all. Chinese ethnocentrism is quite as stubborn, arrogant, and apparently impenetrable as is that of the West.

For Teilhard de Chardin, Frenchman as well as Jesuit, it was, I think, hard emotionally (as it was for Charles Péguy and many others of the noblest minds of France) to separate altogether the idea of Christianity (*Christianisme*) from that of Christendom (*Chrétienté*) : the historical community that professed Christianity throughout the Middle Ages and into modern times. It is an identification that has to some extent warped his system; I would at least offer this as a thought to be shot down. It certainly renders it largely unacceptable to most minds from outside of the world of historic Christendom and its offshoots. He was not, in fact, I think, addressing himself mainly or often to such minds, and this is logical enough. If indeed there is only one set of terms, the terms cannot be adapted; it is for minds formed outside of Christendom to adapt themselves to the terms in order to come in from the cold. "Psychic permeability" thus becomes a one-way system. It is for them to be permeated by us and to be permeated precisely in our terms.

The vision of the deployment of the noosphere, of the striving for convergence in peace, of an eventual unity in diversity: these are majestic and inspiring ideas and must leave their mark on any reader of Teilhard, no matter to what tribe or cult that reader may belong. But I suggest that any development of Teilhardian ideas, if it is in fact to move toward convergence in peace, unity, and diversity, must strive to shake off the specific ethnocentric inertia that the conditions of his time, obedience, and allegiance left in the work that Teilhard actually bequeathed to posterity.

Assuming—as at the moment seems reasonable although perhaps it is a precarious moment—that organized human societies will survive the time of troubles now opening before the world under the sign of the population explosion, then some of our descendants and some of the descendants of other people will come at some long-future date to know conditions in which the population of the planet becomes stabilized (as a result in the first instance of natural checks and ultimately by the generalization of deliberate birth control) at a level proportionate to its developed resources. Starvation, homelessness, illiteracy, human redundancy will be eliminated, and with them the more obvious and rationally assimilable incentives to intergroup violence, fear, and hate. The examples of such affluent societies as we already have, however, warn us that affluence in itself is no guarantee of convergence in peace. A further condition of such convergence is the development of a far more sensitive, delicate, and resourceful system of intertribal communication than anything we have yet possessed.

By tribe I mean here any group conscious, over generations, of an emotional bond uniting its members in conscious differentiation from another group or groups. In that sense, I firmly believe that we are all living in tribal societies.

By the refinement of intertribal communication I mean going beyond the mere conveying to Tribe A of what Tribe B thinks and feels. In its raw form that type of communication is often no more than the opening of an attack. What is needed, rather, is the development of intertribal antennae, making possible the systematic avoidance of what Teilhard calls "running full tilt into one another," so that we are *aware* at the moment of being about to run into another full tilt and can begin to draw back. To put it another way (still playing with Teilhard's terminology), in the chinks of our diversity there must develop an interpretive flora that will be our unity: a system that will be able to interpret not just the language but the assumptions and prejudices of Tribe A in a form that will be comprehensible, without evoking undue disgust or rage among members of Tribe B, so that the interpreters of Tribe B in their turn will become able to respond in a creative and adaptive way.

We may hope and I do in fact believe that interpretive diplomacy of this kind will develop to a depth and in a range of subtlety not yet imaginable and will form the filaments of what Teilhard called the noosphere. It will not, of course, be a radical and new thing. From the leopard-skin priest of Africa to the shrine of Delphi and to the courtly formalities of Eighteenth-Century Europe, societies in contact have in the past developed elaborate and partially successful rituals, prayers, and protocols for survival in contact. These procedures never totally broke down, but they became badly blunted and in part apparently atrophied in our modern age —the age that opened with the French Revolution and may now be ending.

Ideological revolution and counterrevolution are obviously destructive of communication, interpretation, and diplomacy. This is the Manichean world in which the tribe locks itself into its inner righteousness and has no truck with the abominations of the others. Ideology encouraged such an attitude, but the attitude once encouraged reverted to its tribal base. *La Marseillaise* and *L'Internationale* became national anthems; *la grande nation* and the Worker's Fatherland took shape. Democracy, where it appeared and in the forms in which it did appear, on the whole encouraged the Manichean trend, and so did communication in democratic conditions. In these conditions it became all too easy for the tribe to lash itself into a frenzy on occasion and normally to maintain a condition of paranoid sulks in relation to other tribes, alternative systems, and possibilities. Propaganda, nominally addressed by Tribe A to Tribe B, became in practice a device for keeping the self-righteousness of Tribe A at a high level. The tribes, in fact, were encouraged thereby to talk to themselves more than to one another, which is always their tendency.

The process, no doubt, followed necessity: "What would we do without our enemies?", Teilhard asked himself. There can be no doubt, either, that the process is now continuing and holding millions of people in its grip. But man's capacity to learn, when he has to in order to survive, is never to be underestimated. The pressures of survival in the times that are coming will require of the survivors (and it is always of survivors that we're talking when we're talking of evolution) gestures, rituals, and language that must become more economical and precise and that must also become in an increasing proporton more a means of intergroup communication and less a means of collective self-indulgence.

"To love the little platoon to which we belong in society," wrote Edmund Burke, "is the first, the germ as it were of public affections." Yes, but transposed to a larger scale the problem becomes that of bringing about the germination. Burke himself did not solve that. His military metaphor is in itself ominous. It is, I think, the poet Mellarmé who points the way of germination when he defines the poet's task: *"donner un sens plus pur aux mots de la tribu"*—not the abandonment of the tribe or its words, but the giving of a purer meaning to the words. Only thus can diversity be combined with unity. Only thus can there be, in a future time and after multiple convulsions, a convergence in peace.

The Testament of a Friend of Father Teilhard

Jeanne-Marie Mortier

Translated from the French and edited by Geraldine O. Browning; verified by Professor N. Max Wildiers

My contribution to this symposium cannot be placed at the same level as that of a scientist or theologian. Rather, it is the simple testament of a friend of Father Teilhard who, wishing to help him in his work, served as his voluntary secretary during the years 1939 to 1955, and then, as his heir, worked to insure the publication of all his writings.

In order that Teilhard's most enlightening thought might radiate over the whole world, I created in perpetuity the Foundation Pierre Teilhard de Chardin at the Library of

Miss Mortier's relationship to Teilhard is described in her paper. As legatee of his philosophical and theological writings, she insured their publication and dissemination. For this the world owes her a debt of gratitude. She is also the coeditor of *Album Teilhard de Chardin*.

the Museum of Natural History in Paris. The Association of the Friends of the Father, whose membership is representative of all seven continents, was organized as an international auxiliary for the Foundation. Each summer at Vézelay, the ancient and famous city on the Yonne River, these two groups jointly sponsor a one-week seminar under the direction of world-renowned scholars.

I am very happy and deeply honored that your kind invitation to participate in this symposium has given us an opportunity to extend our efforts to the United States for the first time.

Now, let me take you back to the time when my path first crossed that of the great thinker whose memory we are now honoring.

In order to meet Father Teilhard in a truly comprehensible manner, it is necessary to have undergone a long and progressive preparation. Then, when that moment of meeting arrives, one's thoughts find immediate harmony with his and one can join him in his *milieux divins.*

All my life the need to find a philosophical and theological "Unity" grew and intensified. Father Teilhard had also searched since his earliest youth for this same unity, which he called the *Inalterable.*

I had dedicated myself to help any and all efforts that sought to unite the religious and human conditions; and, in order to do this, a vision of ultimate synthesis was indispensable to me. I had to conceive of the point where the world and God, the natural and the supernatural, matter and spirit could all converge.

In 1938 I was deeply immersed in this research, but, at the same time, felt a despairing certainty that the unity I sought could not be achieved. Many years of philosophical and theological study had convinced me that official Christian doctrine would always be characterized by duality, due to its medieval strain of Augustinian--Aquinism, which rendered a definite synthesis impossible.

Thus, I waited in spiritual darkness for a way out from my ordeal. The way suddenly presented itself in the book *The Divine Milieu,* Teilhard de Chardin's principal work of philosophical symbolism. I read one of those copies, bound in green, which had been mimeographed by the Countess Bégouën, the first friend of Teilhard to publish his philosophical writings composed during the years spent in China.

Reading this brilliant book, I was shown at last a clear road toward unity. From that moment onward, everything that was going to happen was the process of achieving my life's goals, which had become bound irrevocably to those of Teilhard.

Now, after thirty-two years of uninterrupted service to the world of ideas created by Teilhard de Chardin, I believe, at last, that I can completely perceive the thought and personality of the author. I have traveled an almost infinite distance since that day in March 1939 when Father Teilhard received me for an interview on *The Divine Milieu* at the headquarters for the magazine *Études* (15 *rue Monsieur*), which served as his Paris home between his long trips to China.

The kindly religious man I encountered then was transformed little by little through the years into the saint, whose stature (a stature built on the firmest foundaion) will only be truly measured by humanity at some future time. Let us learn how he himself describes his humility:

> the more time passes, the more I begin to believe that my role will have been to be, rather like a smaller image of John the Baptist, the one who announced to the world and told about what was *going to happen*. . . . I think that when God wants something truly momentous to occur, He causes it to come from our simplest and least calculated endeavors without our even knowing it ourselves. This is the history of all great religious movements and of all great discoveries.[1]

---

1 Pierre Teilhard de Chardin, Letter to Jeanne Mortier, April 15, 1940.

This humility, accompanied by a love of God's will, which he preferred above any personal desire, is the explanation of his unwavering religious obedience and his ability to transcend rebellious sentiment. When he returned from Rome, where he had been denied any hope of publication, he said simply, in a spirit of total self-abnegation and limitless faith: "If my writings come from God, they will live on. If they are not from Him, they should be forgotten."

Complete self-sacrifice was the condition for success, and Father Teilhard accepted this premise in advance.

> I have offered myself to God as a test case where he can experiment on a small scale in fusing together the two great loves: the love of God and love for the world . . . without this coalescence, I am persuaded that the reign of God is impossible.[2]

This fusion that Teilhard described could be realized only by a great fiery clarification of spiritual values. By vocation Teilhard was dedicated to this illuminating and purifying fire:

> I yearn for You [God] as Fire, and it was as Fire that I understood You at our first intuitive meeting.[3]

And, at the end of his life, he prayed: "Your Universal Presence springs from diaphaneity and flame simultaneously, Christ, ever greater!"[4]

Teilhard, like St. Paul, was a witness to Jesus reborn. The glory of his vision mystically burned into his eyes and gave him the insight and inspiration to undertake the awesome mission of establishing the universe in the place of the Church as the unifying force of apostolic doctrine.

In this doctrine (promulgated through the centuries by the

---

[2] Pierre Teilhard de Chardin, Letter to Father Valensin.
[3] Pierre Teilhard de Chardin, *The Heart of the Matter* (unpublished, 1950).
[4] Pierre Teilhard de Chardin, *The Christic* (unpublished, 1955).

Eastern Church and then in the West by Duns Scotus, Cardinal de Bérulle, and finally Teilhard de Chardin), the incarnation of the Son of God was foremost in the creative design and continued to be the essential keystone of all Creation. This principle bound the whole of the universe to the Creator, and consequently guaranteed the triumph of Mankind through the rebirth of Christ. Redemption was a reality that first Easter morning. And, with this belief, Christianity was fundamentally optimistic and victorious.

How then did the Western Church drape itself in mourning? Simply because Thomas Aquinas, under the influence of Saint Augustine, gave Evil such a magnified role that the *need* for salvation assumed a preponderant position.

In chapter 3 of his *Summa Theologica,* Saint Thomas judged that the Incarnation of Christ was necessary, due to man's need for salvation because of his sins. From a Christian point of view, this judgment knocked out the keystone of the world. It would no longer be a world inhabited by souls preordained for a divine life, but rather, it became a world of the guilty.

Mankind began to sink down and settle itself under the shadow of the Cross. It was losing sight of the dawn of the Resurrection. From this time onwards, pessimism was a characteristic of the Christian religion. And, as this pessimism spreads, it will generate a vast process of repudiation. Atheism will grow, manifesting itself first in philosophical theory, which will then give rise to new political and sociological trends and thus reach the everyday world of man.

As a wicked universe is essentially absurd, one inevitably ends up with rejection such as Sartre expresses in *Nausea* and Camus in *The Rebel.* Just as inescapable will be the loss of all joy of life when this kind of revolution is recognized as being powerless.

Confronting this derivation of Christian thought and the abyss into which it was leading, Father Teilhard's work opens a road to salvation. He describes this work as ". . . an attempt to *see* and *to make others see . . . Seeing.* We might say that the whole of life lies in that verb."[5]

Teilhard's vision offers Youth exalting dreams. He gives Mankind back his ennobling origins, pursuits, and destinies.

He gives Matter dignity by reintegrating it back into the synthesis of the world:

> Blessed be you, universal matter. You I acclaim as the inexhaustible potentiality for existence and transformation wherein the predestined substance germinates and grows.
>
> [you are] limpid crystal whereof is fashioned the new Jerusalem.
>
> I acclaim you as the divine *milieu,* charged with creative power, as the ocean stirred by the Spirit, as the clay molded and infused with life by the incarnate Word.[6]

Teilhard then outlines the greatly enhanced position held in the universal plan by the Son of God. By developing the traditional apostolic message, he gives to our time a christo-cosmic conception of the world, which tomorrow will become that of a reunified Church:

> By the Universal Christ, I mean Christ the organic centre of the entire universe.
>
> *Organic centre:* that is to say the centre on which every even natural development is ultimately physically dependent.
>
> *Of the entire universe:* that is to say, the centre not only of the earth and mankind, but . . . of all realities on which we are physically dependent, whether in a close or a distant relationship.
>
> *Of the entire universe,* again, that is to say, the centre not only of moral and religious effort, but also of all that effort implies—in other words of all physical and spiritual growth.[7]

5 Pierre Teilhard de Chardin, *The Phenomenon of Man,* trans. Bernard Wall (New York: Harper & Row, 1965), p. 31.

6 Pierre Teilhard de Chardin, *Hymn of the Universe,* trans. Simon Bartholomew (New York: Harper & Row, 1965), pp. 69–70.

7 Pierre Teilhard de Chardin, *Science and Christ* (New York: Harper & Row, 1968), p. 14.

In studying the Universal Christ we do more than offer the world, whether believing or unbelieving, a more attractive figure. We impose upon theology (dogmatic, mystical, moral) a complete recasting.[8]

The unique business of the world is the physical incorporation of the faithful in Christ. . . . This major task is pursued with *the rigour and harmony of a natural process of evolution.*

Et Verbum caro factum est. That was the Incarnation. By this first and fundamental contact of God with our kind, by virtue of the penetration of the Divine into our nature, a new life was born, an unexpected enlargement and "obediental" prolongation of our natural capacities: Grace.

Christ is the instrument, the center, the end of all animate and material Creation.

And since the time when Jesus was born, when he finished growing and died and rose again, *everything has continued to move because Christ has not yet completed His own forming.*

In the pursuance of this engendering is situated the ultimate spring of all created activity.[9]

In fact, from the beginning of the Messianic preparation, up till the Parousia, passing through the historic manifestation of Jesus and the phases of growth of his Church, a single event has been developing in the world: the Incarnation, realised in each individual through the Eucharist.[10]

With the road clearly mapped, Father Teilhard then accelerates the march of humanity toward its destination:

---

[8] *Ibid.*, p. 16.

[9] Pierre Teilhard de Chardin, *The Future of Man*, trans. Norman Denny (New York: Harper & Row, 1964), pp. 304–5. Reprinted by permission of Harper & Row, Publishers, Inc.

[10] Pierre Teilhard de Chardin, *The Divine Milieu* (New York: Harper & Row, 1968), p. 124.

> The Age of Nations is past. The task before us now, if we would not perish, is to shake off our ancient prejudices and to build the Earth.[11]

To "build the Earth" is to participate in all its many disciplines and activities with increased knowledge and ardor; to have a clear vision of the goal, and a firm resolve to effectuate universal interchange and rapprochement. This implies:

> Development of each one in sympathy with all. Graduated organization of spiritual energies in place of the mechanical balance of material forces. Law of teamwork replacing the law of the jungle.
>
> We are still far from having performed this delicate but vital transformation on the scale of individuals. Is this a reason why we should not hope that it will finally be realized between nations?
>
> The future thinking of the earth is organically bound up with the transformation of the forces of hatred into forces of Christian love.[12]

And Teilhard, the prophet, sees and describes the splendor of the city of the future built by the unanimity of man:

> Jerusalem, life up your head. Look at the immense crowds of those who build and those who seek. All over the world, men are toiling—in laboratories, in studios, in deserts, in factories, in the vast social crucible. The ferment that is taking place by their instrumentality in art and science and thought is happening for your sake.[13]

---

11 Pierre Teilhard de Chardin, *Build the Earth* (Wilkes-Barre, Pa.: Dimension Books, 1965), p. 54.
12 Pierre Teilhard de Chardin, *Vision of the Past,* trans. J. M. Cohen (New York: Harper & Row, 1966), pp. 213–14.
13 Teilhard de Chardin, *The Divine Milieu,* p. 154.

the organization of research is developing into a reasoned organization of the earth. Whether we like it or not, all the signs and all our needs converge in the same direction. We need and are irresistibly being led to create, by means of and beyond all physics, all biology and all psychology, *a science of human energetics.*

It is in the course of that creation, already obscurely begun, that science, by being led to concentrate on man, will find itself increasingly face to face with religion.

Thus Renan and the nineteenth century were not wrong to speak of a Religion of Science. Their mistake was not to see that their cult of humanity implied the re-integration, in a renewed form, of those spiritual forces they claimed to be getting rid of. When, in the universe in movement to which we have just awakened, we look at the temporal and spatial series diverging and amplifying themselves around and behind us like the laminae of a cone, we are perhaps engaging in pure science. But when we turn towards the summit, towards the *totality* and the *future,* we cannot help engaging in religion.

Religion and science are the two conjugated faces or phases of one and the same complete act of knowledge—the only one which can embrace the past and future of evolution so as to contemplate, measure and fulfill them.[14]

Hence, with the author of *The Phenomenon of Man,* we have arrived at a synthesis that simultaneously embraces all evolution and the summit of man's destiny. "The past showed me the future," he stated. Teilhard had submerged himself in the past and a geological study of almost the entire planetary surface in order to understand the very structure of the world. From this base of knowledge he could then thrust out his thoughts to comprehend the very limits of time and space.

This spectrum of the past, infinitely broader than that of biology alone, was the indisputable foundation of Teilhard's work. Because of this comprehensiveness, the College of France welcomed him and proposed creating an Academic

[14] Teilhard de Chardin, *The Phenomenon of Man,* pp. 283–85. Reprinted by permission of Harper & Row, Publishers, Inc.

Chair for "The Future of Man." This occurred in 1939, before Teilhard even entered the French Academy of Science; but at that time, he could not abandon the administration of the Geobiological Institute of Peking. This Chair at the College of France was the highest teaching position offered to the Father during his lifetime, but, when it was presented a second time, Teilhard obeyed the orders he had received from Rome and refused.

God led his servant Teilhard through years of heroic self-sacrifice and religious obedience; He led him through the exhausting work and physical hardship of his desert studies and explorations; He led him to a vantage point from where, fifteen days before his death, Teilhard perceived "The Promised Land." Such is the title of the conclusion of his last essay, *The Christic:*

> Energy itself is becoming one with the Divine Presence. It would seem that a single ray from a source of such light, no matter where it fell on the Noosphere, would, like a spark, cause an explosion strong enough to almost instantaneously encompass and renew the whole face of the earth.[15]

Already in 1919, Father Teilhard sensed "the Supreme Being in all things yet apart from them—superior to their substance within which he drapes Himself." For Teilhard, "God was shining forth from the summit of that world of matter whose waves were carrying up to Him the world of spirit.[16] And Teilhard saw himself, like matter, carried up to God in a "fiery chariot."

On Easter Day, 1955, Father Pierre Teilhard de Chardin left this life in the living "fiery chariot" symbolic of Christ, the Redeemed.

He invites us to break away from the structured life as he did, and follow in his footsteps along the road of light and purifying flame.

---

15 Teilhard de Chardin, *The Christic* (unpublished, 1955).
16 Teilhard de Chardin, *Hymn of the Universe,* p. 68.

He wants to introduce us to the universal harmony that he listened to with such ecstasy, in order that we, too, can understand that the music of the universe is not a series of chance discordant notes, but rather a symphonic composition revealing the hand of the All-Creative Genius.

The life and the thought of Teilhard exemplify for the youth of this last half of the century a synthesis of moral values and intellectual knowledge of the highest order. The importance of the genial saint and the great legacy he left us can only continue to grow with time.

To conclude, I would like to repeat the words of Teilhard used to express his own great desire: "May God always let me hear and make heard the profound music in everything!"[17]

---

17 Pierre Teilhard de Chardin, *Letters from a Traveler* (New York: Harper & Row, 1962), p. 123.

Teilhard and Political Determinism

Joseph L. Alioto

Sir Julian Huxley, as you know, wrote the Introduction to the English translation of *The Phenomenon of Man* and noted that "Teilhard de Chardin's most important contribution to thought is undoubtedly *The Phenomenon of Man*—a notable and I think a seminal work which has now been translated into English." This was written in 1955, and nothing in the events of the past fifteen years has diminished that appraisal.

Teilhard was not permitted to publish this work or many of his philosophical writings during his lifetime. Two of the participants in this symposium played an important role in their eventual publication, and I would like to recount this background.

Joseph L. Alioto is San Francisco's thirty-third Mayor and one of the nation's foremost antitrust attorneys. Beyond his accomplishment in law, public service, and politics, Mayor Alioto has an abiding interest in the arts and letters, and in education. He is past president of the San Francisco Board of Education and a member of the National Advisory Council on Extension and Continuing Education. He has lectured extensively on English literature as well as jurisprudence, and was instrumental in bringing to San Francisco the most valuable oriental art collection in the Western Hemisphere.

In 1948 Dr. Wildiers, while studying biology in Belgium, became fascinated by some of the basic scientific writings that had been published by Teilhard. He secured permission from Mademoiselle Mortier, who held Teilhard's documents while he was traveling, to examine these documents. Included was a typewritten copy of *The Phenomenon of Man*. In 1952 Dr. Wildiers published an analysis of the thought of Teilhard with Teilhard's approval. Then in 1955 at the time of Teilhard's death, Mademoiselle Mortier, to whom Teilhard willed his papers, in consultation with Father Wildiers and with the covert cooperation of some very distinguished members of the Jesuit Order, published *The Phenomenon of Man* with an introduction by Dr. Wildiers.

I cannot help but feel a sense of loss that *The Phenomenon of Man* was actually written in 1939 but not published until after Teilhard's death in 1955. Had Teilhard published during his lifetime, he would have had an opportunity to meet objections that were raised, particularly by Jacques Maritain, for example, and we might have had one of the great polemical discussions of all time.

Julian Huxley said further of Teilhard that his ideas are beginning to bring about a rapprochement among biologists, theologians, and philosophers. Huxley was, of course, no undeviating follower of Teilhard. He acknowledged that Teilhard's hypotheses as to the increasing convergence of human variety and the resulting increase of the psychosocial pressure which in turn would increasingly direct the course of man's further evolution, were more radical than his. And Huxley, true to the tradition of his famous grandfather, was quite unable to follow Teilhard in his approach to what he believed was the ultimate goal of evolution's march, his so-called Point Omega, in which natural and supernatural were combined in a mystical and, to Huxley, an incomprehensible manner.

What is significant to me is that a man of such totally different theological background should be impressed by Teilhard. Yet Huxley thought him a very remarkable human being. He recognized Teilhard as a leading paleontologist with unusually good knowledge of the geology of large regions of the world. He recognized that Teilhard's paleontologic work gave him a consuming interest in the general problem of evolution, while his experience of human societies at different levels, and particularly from his vantage point as a Jesuit Priest, gave him insight into a new approach to the problems of man and to the problems of his evolution. And despite their difference on matters of theology and metaphysics, Teilhard and Huxley found themselves in agreement and, indeed, in active cooperation over the subject of the future of mankind and its transcendant importance for the thought of our times. Huxley stated that the important thing they could both agree upon was to study the problem of mankind as a phenomenon and to look at it *sub specie evolutionis* (under the aspect of evolution) confident that increasing understanding would gradually bring about a reconciliation of theoretical differences as well as lead to practical improvements.

The rapprochement between the Jesuit and the famous agnostic was paralleled, in my own mind, by the apparent acceptance of Teilhard by significant Communist leaders, and by the fact that he is published in the Soviet Union. The Frenchman Roger Garaudy (the leader in the Christian-Marxist dialogue in France) quotes at length Teilhard de Chardin's evolutionary exposition of original sin, pointing out its dynamic-process dimension as the key reason why he, as a Communist philosopher, finds this view of mankind's original sin not only acceptable, but completely compatible with his own Marxist interpretations of the nature and future of man. Of course, it was Teilhard's ideas on original sin that sparked the original controversy between Teilhard and his superiors in Rome. It is of some significance that the whole question of original sin is being reexamined now throughout the Catholic world as a result of a special commission appointed by Pope Paul VI. But Marxist Garaudy saw this interpretation of original sin as completely compatible with his own Marxist interpretation of the nature and future of man. He saw the story of the Garden of Eden, as most of us do, as an allegory that expresses the invasion of the transcendent into man's life, expressed in the language of imagination in the terms of each epic's conception of the world.

This fact, then, that the thought of Teilhard appeals to so many of such diverse views, particularly diverse theological and philosophical views, is of great interest to me—both personally and as a politician. The basic acceptance of Teilhard by atheists, agnostics, Marxists, and eminent churchmen is the basis for my belief that Teilhard may well be an instrument for unifying many in the world who have lived in antagonism to each other and who suddenly discover that maybe they are all riding in the same boat. That so many men of diverse philosophical and theological differences can find common comfort in the basic thought of Teilhard gives hope that Teilhard's own strong belief that the world tends toward unification can be applied in a practical political framework to the resolution or mediation of those volcanic antagonisms which mark the society of our day and of which the urban crisis, the crisis of our big cities, is a conspicuous example.

What are the implications of Teilhard to a practical politician? To begin with, a practical politician deals with the world *as it is,* in the hope of either solving or, more exactly, of managing problems of conflict between human beings with some attempt to assuage the impact of man's inhumanity to man. Our society has wounds that burn. We apply ourselves to immediate palliatives but hope to set in motion—*hope* to set in motion—programs in the directions that will lead ineluctably to progress in the broadest terms of human betterment compatible with a changing world.

There is an evolutionary concept here. I think it is important whether a political leader accepts an evolutionary image of man, or whether his image is of man as fixed and changeless. I think that's important. It affects his own actions. There is a considerable difference in a political leader who will deal with political problems in terms of a dynamic process rather than in terms of a fixed, static world. A central city with its marked proclivities for hatred and injustice, and with pervading stubborn pockets of poverty, could very well be the principal laboratory of our times for dealing with mankind's persisting problems.

Those who are sitting on the cutting edge of the revolution of our day proceed very differently, depending on whether they see society as fixed and unchanging or whether they believe that change is not only inevitable but also highly desirable. To be discontented with things as they are, and to strive always for things as they ought to be is a concept of dynamic movement; not that change will be accomplished by some magical transformation. Nobody believes that. But change can be effectuated by setting things in directions that ultimately, though often painfully and slowly, lead to progress in our cities, in our nations, and in our world. Since the pace of evolution is glacial and the pace of political activity is rapid, and even feverish, there is admittedly a limited relevance of evolutionary theory to practical politics. Nevertheless, inasmuch as both depend on trends and directions—and I think this is clearly true—considerable utility can be gained by practical politicians from the philosophical insights of evolutionists and philosophers.

I guess I really should have said that the pace of evolution *was* glacial. There is increasing evidence in our day that the slow and tedious movements of evolutionary developments are about to accelerate geometrically. Man now doubles his knowledge every 10 years instead of over spans of centuries, as has been true up to this point. Take one important realm alone for example: there are more active geneticists living in the world today than have existed in the whole space of mankind's recorded history. That has to tell us something.

The work that is going on in genetics, some of which is generally known and some relatively obscure, could well justify the notion of Teilhard that the big difference in our day with respect to evolution is that man is now in a position to mold, to direct, and somewhat to influence his own evolution.

But again, what does this have to do with the practical politician? Man lived for many centuries with the image of the world as fixed. He believed that the earth was the very center of the universe. The medieval image of the universe as portrayed by Dante, for example, was a harmonious complex of concepts drawn from the physical sciences, philosophy, and the theology of the day. The Renaissance man began to explore the world and to push forward. A great turning point was the publication by Galileo of his famous work, the *Dialogue Concerning Two Great Systems of the World*. This work, controversial at the time, was rejected by the earth-centered followers of Ptolemy but accepted by Christians everywhere. It advocated the new sun-centered system proposed by the Polish priest Copernicus at least a century before.

The image of the world proposed by Copernicus and Galileo had its impact not only on theological and philosophical thought, but on political thought as well. The dramatic change from a fixed static cosmos with everything tidily placed in order, to a new image of the universe as a changing evolving system, seriously influenced political philosophy. The concept of extremely slow changes occurring with the passage of time, the concept of evolution itself, was first applied to the heavens. Only gradually and after many struggles among scientists and theologians was this perspective applied to the geological history of the earth, and then to living organisms, and, finally, within the last 100 years, to man himself. Considering the fact that man is a Johnny-come-lately to the universe, just a kind of flash in the order of time, we are only at the beginning of this concept, and it has a lot to do with the way political figures administer the world.

In the beginning of the nineteenth century, Jean Baptiste Lamarck proposed the first scientific explanation of the evolutionary development of plants and animals. His efforts were vital for preparing the ground for Charles Darwin. Darwin applied the dimension of time change and evolution to the history of life on this planet in his now famous *Origin of Species.* And 20 years after *Origin of Species,* Darwin made the vital step in revolutionizing our image of the world from a fixed and static to a dynamic evolutionary image when he published *The Descent of Man.* For the first time in the history of human thought, the dimension of time and the evolutionary perspective was applied to man himself.

We come by change with great difficulty. It remained for the Americans, you know, to stage one of the great circus courtroom trials of all times in the so-called Scopes monkey trial. We look back on that and think it difficult that it really could have happened as late as 1925. Scopes, you remember, was a high school biology teacher in Dayton, Tennessee. A state law made it a criminal offense to teach evolution in public schools. Scopes violated that law in an act of civil disobedience for the purpose of testing it. William Jennings Bryan, three times a candidate for the President of the United States, and Clarence Darrow, the famous agnostic criminal lawyer locked in bitter court debate. They were prosecutor and defense attorney in the trial. It makes us blush when we consider that it had to be held, and was in fact held, in our own generation.

That things are not fixed but are subject to change has an application to the realm of ideas as well. Darwin's contemporary, John Henry Newman, wrote a very arresting but much neglected essay called *The Development of an Idea,* which delineates in exquisite prose the strong evolutionary process at work at the very heart of an idea. He said that ideas acquire new meaning and accumulate growth by constant and continuing contact with changed social realities that may appear, disappear, and reappear in the broad sweep of history. There is a dynamic movement even in the realm of ideas.

It was Thomas Aquinas, incidentally, and not some latter-day empiricist, who wrote in connection with the positive law (the law that we administer on a daily basis to run the affairs of mankind) that this law could rightly be changed on account of the changed condition of the times. And we sometimes forget that a whole chapter of the *Summa Theologica* is devoted to the subject of changes in our law.

An idea by a political figure ought to be regarded as current equipment and not some kind of museum piece. Education should consist in part at least—and I emphasize "in part at least"—in the transmission of durable ideas from one generation to another, with these ideas under constant reexamination in the light of the proliferating knowledge of our times.

New ideas do not spring, as you know, full-blown from the sea. They are the product of a dynamic evolutionary growth as they are applied generation after generation to new social conditions. And the old idea itself grows to assume a somewhat different shape and appearance though it remains unchanged in its essence.

I think a comparison of Teilhard de Chardin's ideas with the writings of Newman at the time of the Darwinian controversy would give us a philosophy that could well guide the role of political leaders in our country.

Now, is there an actual practical application of the philosophy we are talking about and the life as we see it, particularly in our cities today?

For good or evil, many world movements of the last fifty years have originated in the great cities of Paris, London, or San Francisco. This applies whether we are talking about an existentialist movement or whether we are talking about a new youth movement, or whether we are talking about a new form of music, a new form of poetry, a new form of poster art, a new form of journalism. And there is very, very much that originates in San Francisco. Take, for example, the ecology movement. San Francisco was the center for the Sierra Club for a long, long time, when this drive to save our environment was first being urged. Now it comes full-blown on the world itself.

Let me deal for a moment specifically with the city I know best. San Francisco has within its borders large communities of Orientals, of Blacks, of Europeans and Latins. I think we can develop in San Francisco a Teilhardian concept of the unification of mankind. In that respect, we don't ask that everything be turned into some kind of an amorphous mass. We ask, on the other hand, that there be a constant development of the individual ethnic cultures and customs of those who live in San Francisco within a broad unity of American citizenship, or a framework of unity in terms of a common affection for the city.

And as we deal with the problems of poverty, we should recall the notion of Teilhard that man, in time, will ultimately solve the problems of hunger and the problems of disease. In this respect, the record of America is not quite so good as the record of some other countries, but I see a practical application of these Teilhardian ideas at work, particularly in the solving of the tensions between the Blacks and the Whites.

It takes a great deal of patience when you are dealing with volcanic tensions, and you can't push too quickly. This is no plea for gradualism; there is no gradualism in a city. But I think race relations are good in San Francisco because we have made significant strides in dealing with the problems that create those tensions.

Just fifty years ago there was a man who ran for Mayor of this town on a platform that "the Chinese must go." Our schoolchildren were reading poems then by Bret Harte, including *The Heathen Chinee,* which from the standpoint of racial injustice would be incredible today. And yet over the years the Chinese have developed as an integral part of San Francisco life, and today they contribute a very strong luster to the personality that is San Francisco.

There is no reason to believe that we can't continue making these strides that are so compatible with the Teilhardian notion of convergence. On a larger scale there is no reason why there cannot be a great rapprochement between the one quarter of the people who inhabit the globe in China and the rest of the world. The recent signs of thaw that are developing should be encouraged. We in San Francisco have always encouraged rapprochement between the East and the West, with one terrible exception. In what was probably the worst constitutional aberration in our whole history, we took American citizens, drove them from their homes, despoiled them of their businesses, and put them into concentration camps only because they were of Japanese ancestry, even though they were American citizens. They came back not in rancor or in hatred, but determined to rebuild and rejoin the community. Here was an example of the truth of the Teilhardian philosophy.

Teilhard, on his mother's side, was a collateral relative of Voltaire; on his father's side a collateral relative of Pascal. What Pascal called the variant by-paths of the human heart were fully explored by Teilhard in his philosophical and his theological reflections. Teilhard talked of unification and optimism. He condemned the pessimist and the coward and the individual who thinks only of himself. There is nothing inconsistent with Teilhard's or Newman's notion that in the development of an idea it is quite possible to have a unification while there is simultaneously a strong assertion of individual qualities. The resulting unification will be a better unification because of this.

There are those who speak of abandoning our great cities, saying that they are hopeless. Yet we know that the great advances of our civilization come from our cities—our trouble-racked and turbulent cities: cities like Jerusalem and Athens and Rome and Paris and London and New York and Florence and, I like to think, San Francisco. Teilhard encouraged us to work with our problems, manage our problems, with the belief that there will come a time in an evolutionary development when they will be a little bit better than they have ever been. And there will come a time in the evolutionary development when there can be a unification of mankind in accordance with the common problems it seeks to solve for a common humanity.

World Picture and Culture

N. Max Wildiers, Ph. D.

The work of Teilhard de Chardin has many aspects and invites us to discuss many problems. In the present paper I would like to consider his work from the viewpoint of the philosophy of culture and to propose some considerations on the relationship between world picture and cultural activity. Teilhard himself was very interested in this question and on various occasions he discussed the importance of his world picture for the cultural development of humanity. Considerations on this interaction between world picture and culture constitute a large part of his writings. By choosing this topic —from among many others—I have the impression of being faithful to the general theme of the Symposium, which is concerned with the quest for man's perfection. This perfection indeed will depend in large part on our cultural activity,

---

Professor Wildier's early studies in philosophy, theology, and biology are reflected in his lifelong interest in the ultimate issues affecting man's fate. He has published several scholarly works, including *An Introduction to Teilhard de Chardin* and *The Meaning of Technology*. A member of the Franciscan Brotherhood, Dr. Wildiers holds senior faculty positions with The University of Louvain (Belgium) and The University of San Francisco.

and this activity will be influenced by the way we conceive of our place in the world.

The culture of a people at a certain moment of its history always contains a wide variety of facets and all kinds of expressions. Ethics, political and social structures, arts, science, technology, and so on are all parts of one and the same human activity. But all these different elements are not disconnected or isolated. A true culture possesses an organic unity in the sense that all the different elements that constitute this culture are linked together by one and the same principle, by one and the same inspiration, by one and the same vision of the world. A commonly accepted understanding of the world indeed unifies the different cultural activities and imposes on them a similar shape and structure.

This relationship between world picture and culture has been described by Alfred North Whitehead:

> In each age of the world distinguished by high activity there will be found at its culmination, some profound cosmological outlook, implicitly accepted, impressing its own type upon the current springs of action. This ultimate cosmology is only partly expressed, and the details of such expression issue into derivative specialized questions of violent controversy.[1]

In order to create unity and coherence and to play its part in the building of a culture, each world picture needs two fundamental properties: first of all, it has to propose an acceptable explanation of a reality we observe in the Universe, and second, this explanation has to express in an exemplary way some general principle, some ideal of perfection able to inspire and to guide our human effort. These two aspects are not really distinct. The second is already contained in the former. They show us two moments in our understanding. Logically we discover first the general shape of the world, and once this task is accomplished we try to

---

1 Alfred North Whitehead, *Adventures of Ideas* (New York: Cambridge University Press 1961), p. 19.

discover the practical consequences and implications indirectly contained or suggested by this world interpretation.

The world picture first of all should be a true and believable representation of the facts of our experience, or at least according to the famous expression of Plato: "Save the appearances." The credibility of a world picture depends, of course, largely on the historical circumstances. What seems to be acceptable at one moment of history can be completely unacceptable at another moment. The credibility need not extend to every aspect and detail of the proposed cosmology. In fact, there can be disagreement and difference of opinion on secondary questions. It is important only that the general shape and features of this cosmology are accepted as indisputable. From this viewpoint we have to distinguish the world picture of a cultural period and the more sophisticated cosmologies of particular scientists.

The second, and no less important, aspect of the world picture concerns its practical implications. It is not sufficient that a world picture possess a certain degree of credibility. More important, from the viewpoint of culture, are the general principles or ideas suggested by the world picture that are able to influence our action. The function of a world picture is not to give practical solutions to concrete problems, but to supply us with a viewpoint from which we can approach and solve them. It aims not at a particular field of human action but at all kinds of action without exception, giving them a common shape and orientation. Its importance consists precisely in the fact that it suggests to us a general principle or ideal appropriate, in an analogical way, to the different fields of cultural activity.

The origin of such a world picture is very complicated. It has its roots in man's desire and need to understand himself and to situate himself in a meaningful way in the world to which he belongs. Our relationship to the world is an essential dimension of our existence. In all cultures, the most primitive as well as the most sophisticated, we discover a world interpretation that gives unity and strength to the culture. This world picture is not realized at the beginning. Sometimes it takes a long time before it reaches its definitive shape, but once realized by the combined effort of observation and imagination it becomes the ever-present paradigm of all human action. From that moment on, man will try to conform his life and to build his world in conformity with the image he projects on the Universe. It seems no exaggeration to say that the creation of a world picture constitutes the most central and basic part in the whole process of culture building.

No world picture however is everlasting. When the old world picture is challenged by a new interpretation of reality, a period of confusion and uncertainty, a period of crisis will set in. The existing type of culture will still try to survive for some time as light persists for some time after sunset. The old structures resist as long as they can, but their decline is inevitable. The old world picture loses gradually its credibility and the new one is not yet sufficiently established to be accepted without hesitation. Nobody wants to leave his home, even when it becomes old and uncomfortable, before the new building is ready. And world pictures are hard to kill. Even when they are rejected intellectually, they survive as a kind of archetype in the subconscious of communities. It takes a long time before the new representations are really accepted and it takes much more time before all the implications contained in the new interpretation of reality are discovered.

The general theory outlined up to this point will receive a more concrete content and justification in the following pages. It will be the aim of this contribution to analyze the function of the world picture in our Western tradition, not only as far as the past is concerned, but more explicitly in regard to our present situation.

I

The building of a commonly accepted outlook on the cosmos is, as I said, a very complicated phenomenon. In

Greek antiquity, for instance, we find initially very differing concepts concerning the universe. Geocentrism as well as heliocentrism were represented. Besides the static outlook of Parmenides, there was the dynamic view of Democrites. How did it happen that geocentrism soon got the upper hand and drove back both heliocentrism and atomism? Several explanations have been offered for this phenomenon. The triumph of geocentrism would be attributed by some to the fact that only this theory was worked out mathematically and was therefore of better use for navigation and time calculation (A. Koyré). Others, however, have proposed a psychological explanation. Mankind, they say, has two different spiritual families which find expression in the classical and in the romantic types. The classical type is more inclined toward order, balance, harmony; the romantic type, toward action, change, and adventure. Greek man was a more classical type and thus would give priority to a more orderly and static explanation of the cosmos (A. Koestler). A third solution is offered by sociology and this one deserves perhaps a little more of our attention than the two preceding ones.

In this theory, which was very strongly expressed by Peter L. Berger, the appeal to a cosmic order is explained by the human desire to give a firm foundation and a greater durability to his culture. Man is a being who shows great uncertainty and helplessness as compared biologically to the animal. The animal possesses from his birth a behavior pattern: it *knows* by instinct how to behave to maintain itself under the different circumstances it encounters. In this case education plays little or no role. The animal enters the world already equipped for life; from a biological point of view, it appears as a completed creation. Man, on the contrary, comes into the world as an incomplete being, totally incapable of maintaining himself by his own means. He does not have his life pattern at birth but has to acquire it: partially through education, partially through self-creativity. His biological incompleteness has, however, a positive side: it gives him an openness toward the world that offers unlimited possibilities. Where the animal always repeats the behavior pattern of its species, we encounter in man an endless diversity, which manifests itself by the great variety of forms of culture that he has created over the ages. Because of his biological incompleteness, man is condemned to freedom and creativity. From the beginning he was given the task of creating his own world—a world that did not exist before, but that man had to invent and realize himself.

However, the creation of a personal world is a difficult and never completed venture. Groping and searching, one must find his way, uncertain of which direction to follow. Is there no one or nothing around him to serve as a measure or support in this dangerous enterprise? The order of things which he has so painstakingly contrived, the institutions which he has built up step by step, are constantly threatened with destruction, sometimes by dangers from without, sometimes by divisions from within. The fear of constantly threatening chaos, the concern for the unstable order which he has built, leads him to seek co-believers and to question whether his concept of order can find support in the vast and astounding world that surrounds him. His imagination makes him discover in the cosmos a higher, eternal, and intangible order—an order which is the work of the Creator—of which the order man has himself created appears to be only an imitation and reflection. The so-unstable order created by man and the eternal order of nature then melt together in such a way that the latter gives to the former something of its eternal and sacred character. Thus the culture conceived by man acquires a firm foundation and is, as far as its basic pattern is concerned, no longer subject to human arbitrariness and man's own will. It acquires the outlook of a high and holy obligation to which he has to submit unconditionally. The order that he has himself projected on the cosmos comes back to him as a divine law and a paradigm to be constantly followed.

This process of "cosmisation" can be traced back in many cultures. In a striking way this appeared in our Western culture from Plato until the beginning of modern times. For almost two thousand years Western man has justified his culture by appealing to a cosmic order that was considered perfect, unchangeable, and hierarchic. This world picture, implicitly accepted by all, gave unity and stability to the old and medieval culture and produced the basic principles for Western man's ethical, political, theological, and aesthetic ideas. It gave him self-confidence and peace of conscience, and inspired him to all sorts of creations, which even today compel our admiration and which are all marked by one and the same pattern of thought.

The semantic evolution of the word *cosmos* is in this case very instructive. From the Greek, this term originally referred only to phenomena in the sphere of human society. In this sense, *cosmos* means order, balance, usefulness. To act: *kata kosmon* means to act in the right way. One should find *cosmos,* order, in the army and in the state, the *polis.* Tools should be designed and used *kata kosmon.* If this is not done, one encounters *akosmia*—disorder, chaos. Therefore this term fully belongs to the cultural world of man. But at a certain moment in the semantic history of this term an important shift occurs. This concept of order is transferred to the universe and is used to indicate this universe. The moment at which this happened can be determined quite accurately and can be situated during the life of Plato and Xenophon. It is striking how the word *cosmos* as meaning universe is used continuously only in the later writings of Plato. In his earlier writings it appears in this sense only twice, and each time he indicates specifically that it concerns an expression used by philosophers. As an example, let us look at the following quotation:

> The wise men argue, Callicles, that heaven and earth and Gods and people are kept together by civic sense, friendship, sense of

> order (kosmioteta), wise temperance, sense of justice. Therefore, my friend, they call this universe *kosmos* and not chaos or debauchery. [Gorgias 507e–508a][2]

In this text one immediately notices that Plato attributes this manner of speech to the "wise men," the philosophers, and thus insinuates that this is not the case with the common people. Particularly striking, however, is the fact that he describes the universe by means of concepts derived from human society. The universe is a *koinonia,* a community of heaven and earth, gods and men; and this community is being kept together by love, steadiness, and justice—a procedure that still clearly recalls the former meaning of the word. Only in his later writings, and especially in his *Timaeus,* does Plato use the word *cosmos* continuously in its technical meaning and describes the universe according to its physical properties.[3]

Thus Greek man projected his desire for order on the world surrounding him. From this originated an outlook on the world which, indeed, did not correspond with reality, but nevertheless lived up very well to the expectations: to give support and a justification to a painstakingly built culture. From then on, this picture of a perfectly ordered universe was the model and touchstone toward which all human effort should be directed. The human society had to be an extension of the order that was supposed to be present in the cosmos. Thus the institutions and behavior pattern were forever withdrawn from human arbitrariness and instability, and a permanent basis was found for cultural activities in every field.

Until the appearance of Copernicus (and also for quite some time thereafter) the geocentric world picture influenced the Western mind. The earth is the center of the universe and

---

2 W. Kranz, "Kosmos," in *Archiv für Begriffsgeschichte. Bausteine zu einem historischen Wörterbuch der Philosophie* (Bonn, 1955), 2:1.

3 A. P. Orban, *Les dénominations du monde chez les premiers auteurs chrétiens* (Nijmegen, 1970).

is formed by four elements: earth, water, air and fire, each, by nature, pursuing its own place. Around it are the seven spheres made from invisible matter and bearers of the seven planets. All this is then surrounded by the heaven of the fixed stars, the *caelum stellatum* to which later on two more heavens are added: the *crystalline heaven* and the *empyrean heaven.* In this cosmos exists a perfect hierarchical order: the most worthy stands above, the least worthy below. Each movement finds its origin in the highest sphere and is gradually passed on from sphere to sphere. The function of the seven planets (the moon, Mercury, Venus, the sun, Mars, Jupiter, Saturn) consists in keeping the four elements on earth together and thus producing the mixed bodies. All physical phenomena that occur on earth, especially birth, illness, and death, find their origin in the movement of the planets. Whether the human will was also influenced by the movement of the planets is a question about which endless discussion took place. Within the framework of this general pattern, more complicated scientific and philosophic systems were worked out, which led to numerous disputes but never to the questioning of the general picture.

This concept of the universe has dominated the Western spiritual life for about two thousand years. During the Hellenistic period, as well as during the Middle Ages, man looked up to the cosmos in order to find in it a guideline for his own existence. With this compass he could sail safely. What could man do better than follow, in all his undertakings, the great example set by the Creator Himself for the ordering of the primitive chaos? Therefore, the purpose of all study and research has to be directed, according to the word of Aristotle and his medieval followers, to reflect in our minds as perfectly as possible the great world order: *totus ordo universi.*[4] This firm belief in a perfect, unchangeable,

[4] "The ultimate perfection which the soul can attain . . . is according to the philosophers to have delineated in it the entire order and causes of the universe." St. Thomas Aguinas, *Truth* (de Veritate), trans. Robert W. Mulligan, q.2.a.2.

and hierarchical world order was part of Western man; it gave his culture a firm basis and his endeavors a never-failing orientation. This gave birth to a form of culture that was characterized by a great organic unity.

In three fields especially, the old world picture has exercised a profound influence: in the fields of ethics, of organization of the State, and of religion.

From antiquity the observation of world order was considered to be an ideal preparation for an orderly way of life; ethics were nothing else but the transposition of the world order into the behavior of man. Following the great teachers who had preceded him, Ptolemy learned that nothing can urge us on to a better way of life than the study of the firmament which confronts us with balance, harmony, and order.[5] Seneca, and with him the whole Stoa, teaches us that the philosopher has to try to acquire the same serenity as is present in the superlunary.[6] Cicero shows us in *The Dream of Scipio* how the contemplation of the universe can impel us to a greater devotion to duty.[7] We find again the same conception in the Middle Ages: an act is good or bad depending on whether or not it is in harmony with the order that is present in all things; sin is by definition "disorder which is offensive to the Creator" (*deodinatio injurians Deum*, Thomas Aquinas) ; our acts are virtuous when they are in harmony with the order wanted by God. On the basis of this principle the Scholastics have built up an extensive moral system in which all human behavior is tested according to the concept of order. This moral system therefore has an obvious cosmological background.

Also, as far as the political structures and social life were concerned, the cosmic order was taken as an example and yardstick. Human society is not possible without authority and order. How could man invent a better ordering than

---

5 *Almagest* I, 7, 17–24.
6 Epist. LIX, 16.
7 See William H. Stahl, *Macrobius' Commentary on the Dream of Scipio* (New York, 1952) .

the one put into His work by the Creator? Since the cosmos knew a perfect hierarchical order, where the lower was constantly guided and governed by the higher, human society had to be built after this model. Feudal government structure can be considered as an effort to take the cosmic concept of order as a guideline in building the community. Therefore, there had to be someone at the top of the community in whose hands all wisdom and power were united and who passed on his commands to the next links, who in their turn gave their orders to the lower members. A reversed movement from bottom to top and a participation of the people in political matters would completely contradict this concept of order. The people at the bottom did not have any rights as such, but they could acquire privileges and favors that were not derogatory to the general structure of the state. Dante, as well as Thomas Aquinas, refers to the cosmic order to justify this concept of government. Raymond Lulle divides nobility into seven groups by the analogy of the seven planet spheres. By thus connecting the order of government with the cosmic order, it at once acquired a sacred character. The *Imperium* became a *Sacrum Imperium* (the Holy Roman Empire of the Germanic nation). Man had thus found a support and justification for his political order and the latter was withdrawn from human arbitrariness.

As far as the religious views are concerned, these too were strongly influenced by cosmological concepts. This was already the case during Hellenism, which was characterized by a cosmic religiousness. This religiousness of the late-Greek-culture period was strikingly expressed by the well-known epigram of Ptolemy:

> Mortal though I be, yea ephemeral, if but a moment
> I gaze up to the night starry domain of heaven,
> Then no longer on earth I stand; I touch the Creator
> And my lively spirit drinketh immortality.[8]

[8] Trans. Robert Bridges.

In the medieval interpretation of Christianity, the cosmic concept of order plays an important role. Although the concept of order is completely foreign to the Bible and the word does not even appear in it, the medieval theologians, following the steps of their predecessors, attempted to interpret Christianity in the framework of the prevailing world picture. The God of the Scholastics is a God who has created everything in perfect order and, therefore, can be recognized from the order of the world. Christ came into the world to restore the order, which had been disturbed by the sin of the first man. At the end of time world order would finally be restored. Meanwhile the church had to be organized in a strictly hierarchical manner according to the example of the cosmos.

From these few examples it already appears how much the man of antiquity and the Middle Ages looked for support and power in his concept of the universe. The world picture accepted by everybody gave unity and internal cohesion to the medieval culture which, in fact, may be called more Greek than Christian because the Greek world picture and the philosophy derived from it formed its basis and cultural background. The spirit of the Middle Ages is basically the spirit of the geocentric world picture, which was characterized by the hierarchical concept of order.

With the disappearance of this world picture, the form of culture that owed its existence to this world picture also ends. It is indeed striking to see how, with the disappearance of the old world picture, Western cultural life fell apart. The English poet John Donne was right when he complained as follows in his poem *Anatomy of the World* (1611):

> 't Is all in pieces, all coherence gone,
> All just supply and all Relation.

Beginning with the seventeenth century, the natural sciences experienced enormous progress in every field, but there was still no question of a coherent outlook on the world and man. For that matter, every new discovery meets with heavy opposition, especially in scientific circles. Galileo Galilei was fought and rejected by the Aristotelians in almost every European university; Newton had to deal with the bitter opposition of Leibniz and of the Cartesians; opposite Lamarck, Cuvier appears with his catastrophe theory, and it took a long time before Charles Darwin received general recognition. The old world picture may have collapsed, but a new coherent outlook that could replace the former one had not yet been discovered.

Therefore it should not surpirse us that the culture of this period shows us the greatest confusion. This is especially evident in the three fields mentioned before: ethics, State organization, and religion. Suddenly all kinds of new views emerge in the field of ethics. According to some, like D'Holbach and Rousseau, we have to direct ourselves toward nature; but this is so vague that one arrives at most contradicting views when trying to outline the concept more sharply. Others, like Jeremy Bentham, make the goal of morality "the greatest happiness for the largest number." Still others, like de La Mettrie and de Sade, declare themselves supporters of Libertinism and reject even the existence of ethics. In the political field new ideologies are also put forward that will soon overthrow the old structures: power does not come from above but from below—from the people and the state, based on a silent agreement among the citizens. And finally, as far as religious thinking is concerned, the former unity is completely lost. Descartes and Leibniz will exert themselves to conceive a new theodicy, but other concepts soon emerge. With Giordano Bruno and Spinoza, Pantheism appears. With Bolingbroke, Pope, and Voltaire, Deism starts. Atheism has its defenders in Diderot and the Encyclopedists.

This period in the history of Western spiritual life is very interesting because it shows so clearly how the disappearance of the old hierarchical world picture simultaneously marks the end of the former culture and, as it were, furnishes the counterproof of the here-defended thesis. Without the disappearance of the old world picture, the breakthrough of the modern world would not have been possible. For some time, though, the old world picture kept living on as a kind of archetype in the subconsciousness of the Western world, and it still took considerable time before man realized the consequences of the turnabout that took place in his outlook on the cosmos. Then for a long time, man clung to the concept of "nature," hoping this vague concept could serve as a guideline for human activity. Soon, however, he started realizing that neither the concept of "nature" nor the old cosmos concept could offer any anchorage for the building of our culture. At the end of the eighteenth century, a new concept of freedom was born. The freedom of man does not consist in the possibility of following a pattern designed by the cosmos or by nature; freedom of man means that he has to design his own life pattern. Man is, according to the words of Johan Gottfried Herder, the first freedman from nature.

Slowly we were liberated from the old illusion, by which the cosmos formed the standard of man's behavior and conceptions in the fields of ethics, State organization, and religion. This discovery of man's freedom is an important moment in the history of Western man. Neither the cosmos nor nature can serve as a standard for man. But here a new problem arises: how can man serve as a standard for man? It is man's fate that each new conquest presents him with new difficulties and problems. For how can man understand himself, detached from but still a part of the world that surrounds him? Some philosophers from Herder to Hegel will lift man above nature to a purely spiritual realm: the realm of absolute freedom. But soon this illusion is brought to an end by two important discoveries which throw man back into the grip of nature: evolutionism and depth psychology. Charles Darwin, whose work *The Descent of Man* appeared just one hundred years ago (1871), teaches us to see how man forms a part of a larger totality and, consequently, cannot be explained without taking into consideration this larger world from which he emerged. Sigmund Freud, on the other hand, draws our attention to the somber world of subconsciousness and to the irrational instincts that influence human acting. Thus we are again made aware of the fact that man forms a part of the cosmos and that he cannot be understood without relation to it. So the old problem of the world picture returns to us in a new form. Man and world are two inseparable concepts that can only be explained together. It is not sufficient, as Teilhard de Chardin justly pointed out, to possess a science concerning the world and a separate science about man. We need a science in which man and world are considered a unity, a science in which the one by the other, man by the world and the world by man, is illuminated and explained.

II

So far we have directed our attention to the past and tried to retrace how world picture and culture have influenced each other in the history of the Western culture.[9] We have seen how the desire for order and the search for a norm for the building of society called up a picture of the cosmos that was characterized by perfect order and balance. The disappearance of this world picture opened the road to the discovery of man's freedom and to a new concept of culture.

The moment has now arrived to face our present situation. How do we see the cosmos today and how do we situate man in the totality of the world surrounding us? Is there a connection between our present view about the world and our present culture?

The first question that hereby arises is, of course, that of

[9] Another very striking example of the interaction between the world picture and culture can be found in the classical Chinese way of thinking. See, for example, Marcel Granet, *Etudes sociologiques sur la Chine* (Paris, 1933) and *La Pensée chinoise* (Paris, 1934).

the existence of a modern world picture. Does something like a coherent view of the universe exist? When answering this question the utmost caution is demanded. Natural sciences have undoubtedly supplied us with a large amount of extremely important data regarding the structure of matter; regarding the world of the stars and spiral nebula; regarding the structure and history of life. But when it comes to bring all of this together in a unified view, we enter dangerous territory. We should never lose sight of the fact that even the best-founded theory always bears a more or less hypothetical character, and by new discoveries or by a changed attitude it can be improved, or even completely rejected. The present criticism and philosophy of sciences have made us irrevocably aware of the relativity of our scientific theories and, in particular, of any theory that pursues a total-interpretation of the cosmic reality. However, for the theme that occupies us here, such a venture is of minor importance. Not the detailed analysis of such a scientific world picture, but its general characteristics and symbolic value exercise influence on culture, today as well as in the past. It is the general figure of the world picture, its general basic characteristics that put their mark on a certain culture period, notwithstanding the fact that heated discussions take place about the component elements. The question we therefore have to ask ourselves is the question about the general nature and dynamic forces that characterizes our today's view on the world.

What strikes us first of all is the lack of any concrete form or shape of our universe. Neither by means of our telescope nor through our imagination are we capable of indicating the boundaries of the universe even by approximation. Therefore our image of the universe becomes something vague and undetermined, which does not give any hold to our thinking. With the help of the cosmological principle, which assumes that the cosmos, in its totality, does not fundamentally differ from the part observed by us, we can, of course, design cosmological models. But these do not reach, no matter how ingeniously invented, much farther than to a more or less plausible hypothesis. We have the feeling of being completely thrown back on ourselves into a shoreless universe, whose boundaries, in space and time, completely escape our imagination.

Second, our outlook on the cosmos is characterized by its dynamic nature. This not only applies to the cosmos in its totality, but also to each of its parts. Everything is in a state of constant movement and change. At a certain point, namely, where it concerns living beings, this evolutive character clearly comes to light. We have the feeling that we are living in a world in which the time dimension plays a fundamental role, in a world in which new beings and situations constantly appear and then move on in the direction of an uncertain future.

Finally, the universe presents itself to us as an organic totality in which everything is connected with everything. Not a single being from without is brought into our world artificially, but each new situation is explained from former situations from which they result. Thus we notice, in spite of all changes and innovations, a fundamental unity and continuity.

Regarding these three general characteristics we all agree today, and it is difficult to imagine that it would enter anybody's mind to question them in any way. They form the spiritual background and the general framework within which the life of today's man is enacted. It is a different matter, however, when the question is to determine the place of man in the totality of the reality surrounding us. What actually is man doing in the totality of the material world? We know that at a certain moment in history he rose up from the depth of matter as a result of the evolutionary process. But this knowledge, particularly, makes it even more difficult. Far from giving a satisfactory solution, the theory of evolution made the problem still more complicated. For how can we explain that a world in which no self-consciousness and no freedom are observed, in which dead matter appears controlled only by inexorable and blind laws of nature, has created a being who is characterized by self-consciousness and freedom? In answering this difficult question, there is still much diversity of opinion.

For some among us, man is an accidental product of physical-chemical processes that can be explained by a combined action of chance and necessity. In no sense was it the intention of nature to produce man. The evolution could just as well have gone a completely different direction. Man should, therefore, be considered a kind of anomaly, an accident of nature. In the totality of the cosmos he is a border phenomenon, an accidentalness, a totally superfluous creature—one more absurdity in an absurd world. Left completely to himself and without any meaning toward the rest of the world, he can do nothing but accept his fate and, for the remainder, take his lot in his own hands.

For others, this way of representing things seems completely unacceptable because it does not give an explanation for the origin of consciousness and freedom and underestimates the meaning of these phenomena. Self-consciousness is, in fact, whatever way we look at things, an extremely remarkable and surprising phenomenon: a "redoubtable phenomenon which has revolutionized the earth and is commensurate with the world."[10] Man possesses the strange ability to absorb the whole cosmos in his consciousness. In principle, self-consciousness is coextensive with the universe. Man also possesses the power to increasingly submit nature to his will, and to make it subservient to him. Can we consider such a phenomenon the result of accidental circumstance or an anomaly? Would it not seem to be rather a central datum

10 Pierre Teilhard de Chardin, *How I Believe* (New York: Harper & Row, 1969), pp. 30–31.

forming the actual reason for evolution? Is not man actually the highest manifestation of the powers contained in nature? This problem particularly has drawn the attention of Teilhard de Chardin.[11] He thought that in order to solve this problem in a scientific way, we could work from two different hypotheses. Matter and man form, so to speak, two extreme poles of one and the same reality. One can start from matter to explain man, but one can also start from man in order to discover the true nature of matter. So far, the concept has been to take matter as a starting point to explain life and, subsequently, man. But the results thus attained do not give a satisfactory solution. Not only has no one succeeded so far in explaining how matter can produce consciousness and freedom, but, moreover, this method has resulted in declaring the most important phenomenon produced by evolution an accidental circumstance and anomaly. "Self-awareness," as C. H. Waddington wrote, "is a phenomenon of a kind for which it seems impossible to see how any explanation in terms of observable phenomena could ever be constructed."[12] And further: "Awareness can never be constructed theoretically out of our present fundamental scientific concepts, since these contain no element which has any similarity in kind with self-consciousness."[13] Teilhard, therefore, proposes that we start from another hypothesis and, instead of taking matter as a starting point, work from the other pole: human self-consciousness. In the prologue of *Le Phénomène Humain,* he writes explicitly that it is his intention to follow this second road and that his work should be read from this standpoint. He who does not keep this in

---

[11] See two books, *The Phenomenon of Man* (1938–1940) and *Man's Place in Nature* (1949–1950); several articles with the same title: *Le Phénomène humain* of 1928 (Oeuvres 9:115–28) and again *Le Phénomène humain* of 1930 (Oeuvres 3:225–43); also *La Place de l'Homme dans la Nature* of 1932 (Oeuvres 3:245–56) and again *La Place de l'Homme dans l'Univers* of 1942 (Oeuvres 3:303–26).

[12] *The Nature of Life* (London: Allen and Unwin, 1961), p. 120.

[13] *Ibid.,* p. 121.

mind must consequently arrive at a wrong judgment of this book.[14]

The problem that Teilhard puts first is a scientific problem, and the method he follows is a scientific method, whereby one starts from a hypothesis that is tested on the known facts and finally emerges as a scientific theory.

It would seem to me that the differences of opinion surrounding the work of Teilhard often find their origin in a mistaken concept of the working hypothesis from which he starts. This, however, was clearly indicated in the Preface to the *Phenomenon of Man,* as well as in other essays.[15]

He who starts from the primacy of matter will necessarily see the problem of orthogenesis differently from he who starts from the primacy of psychism. He who believes in the primacy of consciousness will inevitably be led to place man in the axis of the evolutionary process, and to consider the entire evolution as a gradual climb toward this purpose. The whole debate thus narrows down to the question: Which working hypothesis should be taken as a starting point? This question, however, can be answered only from the results that are obtained in both cases. Why would it be *a priori* more scientific to start from matter than from psychism? Both cases concern a fact of the experience. Besides, psychologically, the experience of the consciousness precedes the experience of matter. In this respect it would seem desirable to be reminded of the thinking of Sir Walter Russell Brain:

---

14 In the specific instance of the present essay, I think it important to point out that two basic assumptions go hand in hand to support and govern every development of the theme. The first is the primacy accorded to the psychic and to thought in the stuff of the universe, and the second is the "biological" value attributed to the social fact around us. As Teilhard says:

> The pre-eminent significance of man in nature, and the organic nature of mankind; these are two assumptions that one may start by trying to reject, but without accepting them, I do not see how it is possible to give a full and coherent account of the phenomenon of man [p. 30].

15 See n. 8 above.

> If the stuff of the Universe that we know directly is mind, and matter is the same thing known only by means of conceptual symbols created by mind, it would seem as reasonable to call at least that part of reality mind as to call it matter.[16]

It would therefore seem to me that the working hypothesis of Teilhard is completely scientifically defensible. Moreover, it has the great advantage of making possible a more balanced and coherent solution of the problem in question, whereas the other approach leads towards an impasse and causes the most important phenomenon appearing in the world consciousness to be declared as an accidental circumstance and an anomaly. It was the conviction of Teilhard that his stated hypothesis would sooner or later be accepted.[17] It is neither possible to discuss this theory in more detail here, nor to examine the arguments that are brought forward to support it. He who is more or less familiar with Teilhard's work knows sufficiently the impressing vision of man and the world toward which his working hypothesis has led. My intention is primarily to illuminate the meaning of this theory as it concerns the building of a world picture that might be considered as a background for our culture. As regards this aspect of his theory, Teilhard has devoted ample consideration. In his opinion, man represents a central phenomenon in the totality of the cosmos. And as such, he has to become conscious of his dignity and responsibility, which are needed if he is to fulfill his task in this world properly.

Although we have now reached agreement on many points in this new world picture, on others our joint deliberations will have to be continued. All in all, it looks as though we

---

16 Walter Russell Brain, *Mind, Perception and Science* (Oxford: Blackwell Scientific Publications, 1951).

17 "After having been regarded for many years as a scientifically subsidiary or anomalous element of the universe, mankind will in the end be recognised as a fundamental phenomenon—*the* supreme phenomenon of Nature: that in which, in a unique complexity of material and moral factors, one of the principal acts of universal evolution is not only experienced but lived by us." *Science and Christ* (New York: Harper & Row, 1968), p. 97.

are on the road to a new and universally accepted outlook on the world and on our task in that world.

To what extent this new world picture will influence the culture of tomorrow can, of course, not yet be foreseen clearly, although this influence will probably not be minor. Already we are beginning to experience some of this influence. If we try to understand what is going on in our cultural life today, it is not difficult to discover the symptoms indicating how today's man sees his world and situates himself in this world.

To the ethos of today's man belongs the conviction that he has to take his fate into his own hands and that his future depends on his own decisions. Nothing arouses our antipathy and reluctance more than a blind fatalism that lets things take their own course. We bear the responsibility for the future of mankind and for the world of tomorrow. Accordingly we shall have to design an ethic that simultaneously takes into consideration the experience of the past and ideals for the future. How this will take place cannot be determined beforehand. Through our own efforts we shall have to find the way that leads to more truthfulness, to more justice and kindness, to true freedom. Such an ethic will be characterized by its evolutive nature and will also call on our courage and initiative. Without risk, progress for mankind is not possible. Through creative imagination, through effort and risk, we ourselves shall have to set the pattern of our behavior.

Our present outlook on man and the world will also be incentive to strive for new social and international relations. A new feeling of human solidarity and co-responsibility is growing everywhere in the hearts of people, and especially in the younger generation. The former individualism and egoism fill us more and more with disgust as we make place for the insight that man is on his way to greater unity and alliance. Through the development of the communication media, we are growing more and more toward each other without losing something of our own personality and originality. In the past the main attention went toward the building of the State; from now on we have to direct our efforts toward the building of humanity on a planetary scale.

Besides ethics and politics, religion will also have to take our new feelings of reality into consideration. Any religion that keeps on clinging to an obsolete and finished interpretation will unavoidably be doomed. A commemoration of the religious dimension of our existence is carried out in the light of our new concept of man and world. Therefore, a search for a new God concept, reflective of the world picture, is evident in the scientific and theological thinking of our time.

We live in an unbounded world in which an organic growth and development is taking place. In man, evolution has reached a new stage which is characterized by self-consciousness and freedom. There is no other possibility left to man but to continue this evolution and to continue building his future if he wants to avoid compassing his own downfall.

In our scientific and philosophical activity we are now working on outlining more sharply and contemplating more thoroughly this picture of man and the world. On many points there is undoubtedly great difference of opinion, but at the same time the main lines on which we all can agree are showing themselves more clearly. It is not subject to doubt that this outlook on the world is in the process of imprinting its mark on all aspects of our culture.

The work of Teilhard de Chardin, considered in its totality, is completely in line with this venture. Despite all disputes to which they may lead, his writings have contributed to making us more aware of the historical situation in which we find ourselves, and of the possibilities that are beginning to manifest themselves for us. They also contain a stimulation to join forces and to cooperate in the advancement of humanity. The great response that his ideas have provoked in all parts of the world indicates that the problems brought forward by him are felt clearly by today's man. It is probably no exaggeration to say that already today many people unconsciously live by the picture of the world that his writings have enabled us to distinguish more clearly. In Teilhard's view of man and the world we have begun to discover the paradigm of the coming culture.

The Divine Non Sequitur

George Gaylord Simpson, Ph.B., Ph.D.

For Teilhard as a person I felt both respect and affection, but I am here as a convinced opponent of Teilhard in his roles as a scientific theorist and as a philosopher. During the many years when I was at the American Museum of Natural History in New York City, Teilhard often visited there; and in the last years of his life, which he spent in the United States with the assistance of the Wenner Gren Foundation, he was also often in my office. I heard him lecture repeatedly. We had friends in common and met socially as well as professionally. With a companion he visited my wife and me at our second home in New Mexico. I had occasion to study all his published scientific work, to hear views that he was not allowed to publish during his life, and finally to read the

Recognized by the entire world for his work in paleontology, biology, geology, and zoology, Dr. Simpson's many awards include two Elliott Medals from the National Academy of Sciences; the National Medal of Science, President of the United States; and the Darwin Medal, Royal Society of London. He is now serving as President and Trustee of the Simroe Foundation, Tucson, Arizona, where he continues to research, teach, and add to his already vast list of professional writings, which include *The Meaning of Evolution* and *Biology and Man*.

works that he left for publication after his death. One time or another, we spent many hours in discussions of science, philosophy, and religion, with frank expression of our profound differences of opinion; and we remained good friends. I make these somewhat personal remarks now because I am going to express strongly adverse views, and it must be clear, first, that this is not an attack but a discussion and, second, that I am not saying anything that I had not said directly to my friend while he was alive.

Perhaps I was invited here as the *advocatus diaboli,* but I can begin on a more favorable note. The communication between Teilhard and me became more extensive, but it began because we were both vertebrate paleontologists specializing in fossil mammals, and at first more specially in quite early mammals, long prehuman. He was my elder by twenty-one years, and when I entered the field he was already among the old masters. He was then principally known to his lay colleagues for a series of monographs on early Cenozoic mammals of France and Belgium, published from 1914 to 1928. He was, however, publishing on Chinese fossils as early as 1922, and from 1923 onward practically all of his strictly scientific research was in that field. It is well known that he became involved in the excavations at Chou Kou Tien and the discovery of "Peking man" or what was then known as *Sinanthropus pekinensis* (now referred to as *Homo erectus*). I find that nonpaleontologists generally do not know that he did none of the technical scientific work on that group of fossil men, but he did play a useful role as advisor and publicist. His own research continued to be on nonhuman and for the most part prehuman fossils in China. His last original scientific work consisted of collaboration with Father Pierre Leroy on two memoirs on Chinese fossil carnivores, published in 1945.

As far as I have learned, Teilhard's first strictly religious publication was a rather long article on Lourdes, which appeared in 1909 when he was about 28. Thereafter his theological publications became increasingly numerous, and writings denied publication in his lifetime became even more voluminous. During his last few years he devoted all of his still astonishing energy to elaboration and repetition of the body of philosophy and theology that is now so widely hailed as his essential legacy.

Teilhard's thought and life work thus lay between and touched two poles: one was basic research in systematic paleontology and the other an idiosyncratic mystic theology. With the latter, as a distinct subject, I am neither willing nor competent to deal. I can and must deal with the former, and on that basis, with what really is the most important thing: the connection between the two, especially the question of a presumed nexus or sequitur between Teilhard's science and his theology.

Teilhard's work in paleontology is extensive and important. The science would be poorer without it. He was not much interested in the legalistic aspects of classification and nomenclature, and his occasional cavalier treatment of them has caused some distress to those who feel obliged to treat them more respectfully. However, even though they are essential, these more legalistic parts of systematics are not the real meat of the science. No one will ever be able to study the early Cenozoic of Europe or the late Cenozoic of China without a real debt to Teilhard.

From this base, not perfect (Teilhard was human, too) but both solid and admirable, we must try to follow to the "Omega" that was the end point of Teilhard's thought, as he says it is of all else. The first step is Teilhard's early recognition and lifelong conviction that evolution is indeed a fact, as testified by the fossil record among many other observations. "It is," as expressed in the English version of *Le Phénomène Humain,* "a general condition to which all theories, all hypotheses, all systems must bow and which they must satisfy henceforward if they are to be thinkable and true." That sweeping statement purposely makes no essential distinction between the transmutation of elements and the origin of man, both subsumed by Teilhard in the same overall process and under the same term. That point of view led him to a panpsychism that ascribed a primitive form of psyche even to an isolated atom.

Already at this point a non sequitur has appeared in the sequence of Teilhard's argument. There is absolutely nothing in the fossil record, Teilhard's firsthand material basis for his views, or elsewhere in the known material data for organic evolution that logically supports the view that, among other things, the transmutation of elements or the histories of stars and the evolution of organisms are parts of the same process. Confidence that some sort of connection exists reflects only the facts that the universe has a time dimension and that organic and inorganic configurations interact through time. To conclude that because man is made of matter and man thinks, therefore a psyche is inherent in all matter, is mere nonsense, not to mince words. However, this is not the essential point on which I must focus attention, and to pursue it here would take time from still more important matters. It would also lead into such relatively barren semantic questions as the shifting French distinction between *evolution* and *transformation,* which to the non-French sometimes seems confusing and over-subtle.

Let us then grant that if *evolution* means only "change through time," it is true that evolution is indeed "a general condition," although we cannot logically deduce that forms of change all involve identical or even analogous processes or are all parts of a single sequence. For now and just here, the important point is that Teilhard, above all a devout Christian and one deeply versed in theology, insisted on the fact of organic evolution, and specifically of the origin of man by evolution. In itself that mere statement has no particular bearing on the scientific study of evolution, but it has had considerable effect on the acceptance of the fact and of man's involvement in nature, hence on recognition of his own true nature. The fact that a Roman Catholic priest, also versed in some aspects of science, was an ardent evolutionist does not affect bigots who insist that Christianity is incompatible with evolution. It has, however, comforted many who were troubled by just those claims of incompatibility, and it has helped them to accept both the scientific fact and the theological creed.

We now move on to the next point on the road from fossils to Omega. Once it is established that organic evolution occurs and that man is among its products, it is necessary to consider its causes, or, because "causes" might involve us in further semantic and philosophical problems, perhaps we had better speak of the processes involved. This is a crucial step, perhaps the most crucial of all to a scientific student of evolution. Here, speaking strictly as such a student, I must say that I find Teilhard's discussions unsatisfactory, generally vague and overly metaphorical, sometimes to the point of incomprehensibility. However, a careful sifting of his many texts brings out fairly clear opinions on Darwinism or Neo-Darwinism, Lamarckism or Neo-Lamarckism, and orthogenesis.

Teilhard spoke of Darwinism or Neo-Darwinism as evolution by chance. He did not deny that a process so labeled occurs, but he considered it unimportant. He betrayed a complete failure to grasp the theory that he called "Neo-Darwinism," now often called "the synthetic theory," although its debt to Neo-Darwinism, strictly speaking, is acknowledged. Far from envisioning evolution by chance alone, this is the only theory of evolution that gives a guiding role to a nonchance, directional process, the reality of which has been factually established both in the laboratory and in nature. That process, the basic Darwinian factor, is natural selection. I have searched in vain for any clear statement on that subject by Teilhard. For example, the words *natural selection* do not occur in the index of *The Phenomenon of Man,* where there are ten page references to orthogenesis. It is strange indeed for a purportedly scientific study to reject out of hand a widely accepted theory without even mentioning its main point. (In that same work there are six index references to Darwin, but the text nowhere indicates what Darwin's theory was.)

Teilhard shared the general but not completely accurate conception of Lamarckism and Neo-Lamarckism as the inheritance of acquired characters, and he sometimes gave it the interesting characterization of evolution by "invention." He seems to have been somewhat ambivalent toward this doctrine, but on the whole he was favorable to it and considered it as an anti-chance factor more important than Darwinism, which, as noted, he wrongly considered a chance factor. In fact, there is hardly any modern evolutionist who considers the so-called Lamarckian factor as real, let alone as dominant in evolution. Teilhard was well aware of this consensus, and at least once he called Lamarckism *vieux jeu*. Nevertheless, he accepted it, and as usual he gave no reasons for opposing the almost unanimous view of his colleagues and said nothing about their evidence.

In speaking of evolution as a directional process, which it evidently is, predominantly but not exclusively, Teilhard, having not merely opposed but totally ignored the directional process of natural selection, most often used the word *orthogenesis. Orthogenesis* is a term that has been used in so many different senses that it is practically meaningless unless each user gives his own careful definition, and a clear and consistent definition was never given by Teilhard. If *orthogenesis* is taken to mean merely directional change, it has no explanatory content and indeed no sense as scientific terminology, because all change is directional and once we accept evolution we necessarily imply change.

Teilhard defined orthogenesis in different places as the "law of controlled complication . . . in a predetermined direction"; as "the manifest property of living matter to form a system (in which) terms *succeed each other exponen-*

tially, following the constantly increasing values of centro-complexity"; as "directed transformation (to whatever degree and under whatever influence the direction may be manifested) "; as "a vast . . . movement of involution on an ever-greater complexity and consciousness"; as "directed morphological transformation, of *balasted* (*lestée*) evolution"; and in various other ways. (The quotations are translated from Teilhard's French; italics are his.) I submit that those definitions are indeed neither consistent nor clear. The last definition quoted is of particular interest. It is the conclusion of an example crucial to the present enquiry and hence warrants special notice. Although, as previously stated, Teilhard gave many useful descriptions of fossils, his views on the processes of evolution were usually highly abstract and separate from any observable evidence bearing on them. The present case is an almost unique exception. In 1942 Teilhard described a number of fossil forms of the genus that he incorrectly called *Siphneus.* (Under the International Code of Zoological Nomenclature the correct name was then already established as *Myosplax.*) These are curious, mainly Chinese rodents often given the artificial vernacular name *mole rats.* Teilhard then remarked (publication in English) that these animals "taken as a whole . . . become just as useful and illuminating in the line of "group-differentiation and group-orthogenesis" as for instance the *Drosophila* fly does in the line of Heredity." After that statement, it seems fair to take this example as a test case for Teilhard's theoretical views on differentiation and orthogenesis.

At a colloquium in Paris in 1947 (published in 1950) Teilhard spoke at length on this group of rodents, which he characterized (in French) as "truly exceptional, marvelously prepared to permit us to study the phenomena of evolution in an *isolated and pure group,* with the least possible chances of error." (Italics his, as in other quotations from Teilhard.) He announced that the sequences of fossils in three lineages of this group clearly demonstrated "two interesting categories of phenomena." First they were said to have begun by rapid morphological divergence. Second, thereafter a series of three parallel modifications was said to have occurred simultaneously in all three lines.

It may not be entirely crucial, but it has some importance that the latter statement is not supported by Teilhard's own published observational data. In his 1942 paper (he had made no later study) he distinctly stated that one of the three characters in question, the evolution from rooted to rootless molar teeth, did *not* proceed simultaneously in the three lines. Data on another character, fusion of cervical vertebrae, are too scanty to warrant a generalization. These bones were unfused in a Pontian (early Pliocene) species (*Prosiphneus licenti*) and are fused in recent species, but the intermediate stages are largely unknown. This is part of a progressive adaptation to burrowing. Its absence in at least one of the oldest known species contradicts Teilhard's statement (1942) that the mole rats were already "completely adapted to their underground life" at the dawn of the Pontian. As for the third character, increase in size, this seems to have been a common trend, as it is in many phyletic sequences, but the available figures in Teilhard's own publications do not show it as regular and universal. For example, a late Pliocene species (*"Siphneus" omegodon*) was no larger than its somewhat earlier presumed ancestor (*Presiphneus praetinqi*) or than a much earlier Pontian species (described but not named by Teilhard).

The changes really observed thus were not so regular, or linear, or, if you like, so "orthogenetic" as was claimed. Nevertheless they did occur. They were all quite plainly adaptive, each representing a distinct increase in fitness, in the Darwinian sense, to the way of life that these animals have, in fact, followed, as shown by their survivors. This is in complete accord with the principle of natural selection, and it is excellent evidence for the reality of that process and its effectiveness over long spans of past time. I must again state the conclusion that I reached after discussion of Teilhard's presentation at the 1947 colloquium (in remarks made in English but published in 1950 in French):

> It would thus seem that the directional factor, the effect not due to chance that is seen in this example of evolution, cannot be anything but natural selection, and I see no reason to look for any other explanation when that one is sufficient.

Indeed Teilhard's test case does not provide clear support for orthogenesis under *any* of his definitions of that word or for *any* of his views on the processes or causes of evolution. I see no objective way in which these animals were becoming more complicated. Are rootless teeth more complex than rooted ones? The coronal pattern of the molars did not change significantly, and in some instances, at least, may even have become somewhat simpler. It could also be argued that the structure and mechanism of fused vertebrae are simpler than those of separate vertebrae. Certainly they are not more complex. Nor can mere increase in size, in itself, be considered to involve "increasing values of centro-complexity." These animals were all simply becoming increasingly adapted to a highly specialized and peculiar way of life, in similar but not identical ways and at different rates.

Teilhard himself noted that the mole rats seem to have originated by a rapid process of divergent evolution. But from such examples Teilhard concluded that orthogenesis and, through it, evolution as a whole constitute a vast movement of involution. "Involution" may mean merely "complication," and we have seen that this is not true of his example. It is also not a *general* feature of evolution, although it does of course occur among the many phenomena of evolution.

"Involution" may also mean an infolding or a drawing together, and this is inherent in Teilhard's philosophical message and his philosophical interpretation. But this test case shows precisely the opposite, and it is rather surprising to find that Teilhard himself so stated, without noticing the contradiction. The example shows a divergence, a more or less radical separation, a drawing apart. That is also true of evolution as a whole, as is demonstrated not only by the entire fossil record but also by all the organisms living today.

Perhaps I have dwelt too long on this single although crucial example. It is my duty to tell you that Teilhard's views as to the processes and causes of evolution were not logically derived from his own—or from any—objective evidence and scientific observation. To justify that statement I have necessarily considered that evidence and I have had to exemplify, at least, the fact that Teilhard's inferences do not really follow from it.

The life work of such men as Sir Julian Huxley and Professor Theodosius Dobzhansky has involved thousands of observations from which they have logically drawn conclusions about evolutionary processes and causes that were largely ignored by Teilhard but are flatly contrary to Teilhard's views. If Teilhard was right on these points, the work of Huxley, Dobzhansky, and hundreds of others was not only wrong but meaningless. I do not believe that. Objections have been made to citation only of authorities who are not French and not paleontologists. I therefore add an eminent, devout French paleontologist, who was certainly Teilhard's peer as a scientific student of human evolution and of evolution in general: the late Professor Camille Arambourg. In 1965 he said of Teilhard's views that they seemed to him far removed from the probabilities that knowledge of the origins and past of mankind as well as the general laws of transformist evolution allow us to consider. It is also a French scientist, Georges Pasteur, who has recently (1971) declared that the French mentality in general is incapable of understanding natural selection and who maintains that rejection of Darwinian explanations of evolution in France is explicable only by "Anglophobic chauvinism." (Let me add, however, that there are French biologists who understand natural selection and who accept Neo-Darwinian factors in evolution, although Teilhard was not among them.)

It was noted even before Darwin and has seldom been

doubted by capable students of evolution that there is a directional element in evolution; that is, that evolution has not occurred entirely at random. To that extent Teilhard was on firm, well-trodden ground, even though he was demonstrably mistaken as to the nature, uniformity, and universality of such directional factors. However, merely recognizing that some directionality exists, or giving it a name such as *orthogenesis,* is not an explanation. It only points out something that needs to be explained. Teilhard recognized this. The last sentences of his crucial colloquium paper on the mole rats were (in French) : "The phenomenon [of what Teilhard called 'orthogenesis'] can no longer be denied. But the correct explanation [*bonne explication*] of the phenomenon is still to be found." That was a cautious, perhaps even a sly statement, because, in fact, he was then sure that he had found it.

Up to this point I have been examining strictly scientific aspects of Teilhard's work, considering them by strictly scientific criteria, and finding them in certain respects unacceptable by those criteria. Now the next step in Teilhard's enquiry introduces elements no longer strictly scientific, and an anomaly occurs in what is building up to a complex *non sequitur.* Again Teilhard himself noted the presence of a contradiction, but it cannot be that he fully appreciated its significance, for in that case he would have been guilty of conscious deceit. The contradiction is inherent in his whole train of thought, and it is explicit in *Le Phénomène Humain.* He insisted from the start (in the Preface) that that book is "purely and simply . . . scientific treatise." But in the last chapter he stated that his conclusion, which was not only the reason for writing the book but also the essence of Teilhard's philosophy, is "strictly undemonstrable to science." So we have a book presented as pure science when its own author states that its purpose, theme, and conclusion are not scientifically demonstrable.

Something has gone badly wrong here. What? Here we

encounter the master paradox, the gaping non sequitur not only of Teilhard's works but of his ruling philosophy and of his own life. I am not here impugning his sincerity. I also endorse certain important principles or concepts that he presented sometimes as premises and sometimes as conclusions. Among these, four stand out especially.

First is a very old concept, which we may have acquired from the Greeks but which early appeared as necessary to almost every pragmatically viable form of philosophy and religion: that there is an orderliness in the universe, that it makes some sort of sense.

Next is the concept that the orderliness of the organic world, at least, is the outcome of a historical process of development and change that we call evolution. It cannot be separated from that general concept that man in particular is involved in that process and is one of its untold millions of products.

Third, and here entering a different category of thought and belief, is the concept that life is valuable, that we ourselves are valuable, and that it is worthwhile for us to be alive.

Finally is the conviction that acceptance of the scientific views here involved, especially those on organic evolution, is compatible with a philosophy of value and a sense of religion.

I have long had to struggle, as I am still doing here, with the fact that a few men whom I consider great scientists and for whom I have almost unbounded respect and admiration have declared themselves to be Teilhardians in some sense of that word, even though it is inconceivable to me that they are blind to blatant descrepancies between his theories and theirs or that they accept his non sequiturs. I can only conclude that they agree with the four important points just listed, with which I also agree; and that for them, Teilhard's support of those points and his making them palatable to an audience not hitherto so receptive, outweigh his faults of theory and logic. With that I do not agree.

It is perhaps not overly important that none of these points is specifically and particularly Teilhardian. They all had been made over and over again, both separately and in conjunction, before Teilhard; and all are supported by many who, like me, are nevertheless firmly opposed to Teilhardism.

The truly important point is that Teilhard's interpretations of each of them, his attempts to find what he called the *bonne explication,* are untenable. If we take the Teilhardian arguments as the support for each of these grand generalizations, we are logically obliged to conclude that they are more likely to be false than to be true. Thus I cannot accept that recommendation of Teilhardism on these grounds is justified in the cause of a rational attitude toward the universe, evolution, man, and religion.

I have already briefly but sufficiently demonstrated that Teilhard's concept of an orderly universe, inextricably connected with his ideas on orthogenesis, does not follow from his ostensible evidence. On the second point, as regards the actual processes of evolution, I have also indicated that Teilhard simply ignored the consensus on this subject, did not understand theories current in his own lifetime, overlooked or brushed aside practically all the evidence for them, and ostensibly based his own views on evidence that does not, in fact, logically support them.

The concept of the value of life is perhaps just where the rift in Teilhard's sequence becomes most widely apparent. He did not here give even an ostensible connection with the supposed biological evidence for orderliness and orthogenesis. In fact there is a logical connection with evolution, but only through evolutionary factors that Teilhard either ignored or rejected. Sufficient discussion of this point would extend to book length, and would merit such treatment, but here I must be as brief as possible.

The value of life is one of the inherent and finally inevitable consequences of the evolutionary process. The vast majority of all the species that ever existed have become extinct without issue. The organisms that now exist are just those whose ancestral populations always maintained the ability to survive as such; that is, as populations and not necessarily in any particular way or to any particular degree as individuals. Natural selection, a material process, can be viewed as a winnow that acts precisely for this: the elimination of most populations and the survival of some. In the vast majority of organisms this rather clearly has no emotional or psychological concomitant. It is really nonsense to speak of "a will to survive" as general among living organisms. However, in some animals (inchoately in some but more and more definitely in others) there is a will to survive, which is selected for as long as this promotes survival in the population, and not, or not only, in the individual. Man happens to be the culmination of that sort of natural selection as far as it has yet gone. This is the most fully self-conscious animal; and the will to survive, favored by natural selection as a characteristic of populations, here has become a part of the value system of individuals as well.

In the Teilhardian canon no value judgment follows logically from the evolutionary premise. Indeed it is quite clear throughout Teilhard's theoretical, philosophical, and theological work that premises and conclusions are not only confused but also quite reversed. I pointed this out in a review of *The Phenomenon of Man* in 1960 and again in a chapter on Evolutionary Theology in *This View of Life,* a book published in 1964. I can now only state again what I think must become clear to anyone who really studies the Teilhardian testament closely. It has been claimed, and he himself seems to have believed at times, that he was reasoning from scientific premises to theological conclusions. In plain fact, he did exactly the opposite. His premises were all in a variety of mystical Christianity; and his ostensible science, apart from straight observation, was a body of theory deduced from those nonscientific premises. I was interested and, I must confess, somewhat surprised to find that the circular announcing the present symposium virtually accepts that view when it admits that Teilhard's "scientific disciplines are tugged, shaped, and fitted into a vision." Of course, a discipline so treated ceases to be scientific.

I am not competent to judge the Teilhardian mystic theology, and I have nothing to say about its validity in itself. I do say that it does not follow from any of Teilhard's scientific work or any other premises acceptable as science. When so presented it is indeed a divine non sequitur. We must rewrite the first sentence of *The Phenomenon of Man.* It should say:

"If this book is to be properly understood, it must be read not as a work on science, but purely and simply as a metaphysical treatise on a variety of mystic theology."

REFERENCES

Arambourg, C. "L'Evolution transformiste des hominiens." Rev. Fac. *Letras* Lisboa. 3rd ser. no. 9 (1965), pp. 3–15.

Pasteur, G. "Evolution in France." *Science* 171 (1971): 751.

Simpson, G. G. *Discussion of Teilhard, 1950.* Colloques Internat. Cent. Nat. Rech. Sci. 21, *Paleontologie* (1950): 178–79.

———. "On the remarkable testament of the Jesuit paleontologist Pierre Teilhard de Chardin." *Scientific American* 202 (1960): 201–7.

———. *This View of Life.* New York. Harcourt, Brace & World, 1964.

Teilhard de Chardin, P. "New rodents of the Pliocene and lower Pleistocene of North China." *Pub. Inst. Géobiol. Pekin* no. 9 (1942). pp. v–xiii, 1–101.

———. *Sur un cas remarquable d'orthogenèse de groupe: l'évolution des siphnéidés de Chine.* Colloques Internat. Cent. Nat. Rech, Sci. 21, Paleontologie (1950), pp. 169–73.

———. *Le Phénomène Humain.* Paris: Editions du Seuil, 1955.

———. *The Phenomenon of Man.* New York: Harper and Row, 1959. (Translation of the above, with a different introduction.)

Biology and the Human Condition

Theodosius Dobzhansky, D.Sc.

How can the two realms of our experience, those of the outer and inner world, be brought to a unity within the framework of an evolutionary universe? Teilhard de Chardin devoted his life to search for an answer to this question. It is implicit in all of his writings. An answer that can be felt to be reasonably valid is a necessity for every thinking person. It is even more necessary for a society. If this were not so, the present Symposium would be superfluous.

To be at all acceptable, an answer must be no less than a coherent world view, a *Weltanschauung*. This is what Teilhard attempted to develop, without ever pretending that he had arrived at a world view that was finished, complete, and

---

Internationally famed geneticist, Dr. Dobzhansky was born and educated in Russia, where he was a colleague of Philipchenko before immigrating to the United States in 1927. Among his many professional publications, *The Meaning of Evolution* and *Mankind Evolving* deal with man's spiritual as well as biological nature. Among other honors, he has received the Elliott Medal from the National Academy of Sciences; the National Medal of Science from the President of the United States; and eighteen honorary D.Sc. degrees from universities all over the world. He is currently Professor of Genetics at Rockefeller University, and serves as President of the American Teilhard de Chardin Association.

acceptable to everybody. As a scientist, he knew that (in order to be admissible in our age) a world view must be "within the framework of an evolutionary universe." But he was wise to recognize also that, while a world view must include what science has brought to light, it needs to encompass a great deal more. Man does not live by bread alone or by science alone. He yearns for love, beauty, reconciliation with his finitude, adoration of what he conceives as the ultimate and the holy. In addition to being a scientist, Teilhard was a poet, mystic, philosopher, and before all else a deeply religious man. He was uniquely qualified to attempt a synthesis.

This synthesis has so many and so disparate constituents that it is equally exposed to hostile criticisms by scientists and nonscientists. I neither can nor need appraise these criticisms, except one. Did Teilhard seek either to derive his religious views from, or to bolster them up, by his biology? Not only was he sagacious enough to know that this cannot be done, but secure enough in his faith not to need anything of the kind. Since, however, his synthesis did include his science, *and* his philosophy, *and* his religion, his highly distinctive manner of writing failed to conform to customary style in any one of these fields. Those who overlook the nature of the task he set himself find easy grounds for censure. Poetic imagery, suggestive and sometimes emotionally charged symbolisms, putting unusual meanings in some words, all this not only makes formidable difficulties in translation but disenchants some people habituated to more sedate scientific writings. But before you reject Teilhard, consider that he never claimed finality for his synthesis, that he would have been the first to admit the need for revisions in the light of growing scientific knowledge and changing existential experience of our times, and finally that many of his ideas can be communicated in ways different from his.

As early as medieval times, theologians, notably St. Thomas Aquinas, sought to discover a rational basis of ethics and values. His premises were that man is created in God's image, that all humans have the same "nature," and that this "nature" is the source of the same moral law. The problem presents itself in a new light since Darwin's discovery of the evolutionary ascent of man. Man has evolved from ancestors who were not human. Human nature and moral law must also have evolved. Moreover, there are valid reasons to think that there is no single human nature; there are as many variant human natures as there are men. These findings lead to many new questions. Since the creation of God's image in man is not an event but a process, the moral law is not a sudden imposition but a product of evolutionary development.

What causes brought about this development? There is a feedback relationship between biological and cultural developments in human evolution. Biological evolution formed the foundation for the growth of culture, including ethics and morals. The development of culture led, in turn, to further strengthening of the biological basis of the moral law. The Teilhardian view clearly indicates that the ethical principles that have been regarded as an appendage, superimposed more or less by our own free will upon the laws of biology, are now showing themselves—not metaphorically but literally—to be a condition of survival of the human race. In other words, Teilhard saw that evolution, in rebounding reflectively upon itself, acquires morality for the purpose of continued advancement.

In what sense can it be claimed that evolution acquires morality? Here we must check carefully the cardinal points of our discussion. Has the biological evolutionary development that made the ascent of man possible endowed mankind with some particular ethics? Or has it merely made all non-pathological members of the human species capable of being taught various kinds of ethics and morality and of being trained for various kinds of behavior? These are very different propositions, and yet in many discussions of the alleged biological basis of ethics they are hopelessly confused. An analogy with human symbolic language will make the difference plain.

Some congenitally malformed infants excepted, any human baby is born with a genetically guaranteed capacity to learn a language. By contrast, nonhuman primates, even so close a relative of man as the chimpanzee, do not have this capacity. Though their voice organs seem to be capable of uttering most sounds of which human language is composed, the impediment to learning resides in the structure of the brain. On the other hand, there are no genetic predispositions to learn a particular kind of language. All humans can, at least during childhood, learn any language of the hundreds or even thousands of existing language groups. An African Bushman child learns the Bushman language with its peculiar "clicks" just as easily as it could learn some European language, or a European child could learn Bushman language. Human genes evidently enable us to speak, but they have nothing to do with what particular language we utilize in speaking. Even less do they determine just what any one of us can or will say in any language.

Biological evolution is, by and large, utilitarian. It is not programmed inside the organism; neither mankind nor any other species was foreordained to arise. Evolution is a creative response of living matter to its environments; it maintains or improves the adaptedness of living species to their surroundings. However, evolutionary changes are not imposed on the organism by the environment. The environment presents challenges to the species living in it. A species may or may not respond by adaptive genetic modification. Successful responses allow the species to survive and to expand. But it is possible to become adapted to the same environment by different means. For example, some desert plants cope with dryness by various devices that reduce evaporation, while others grow, flower, and mature seed very rapidly when moisture is available.

Our ape-like ancestors were not bound to respond to the

challenges of their environments by becoming human; they might just as well have become another species of ape. In reality, they did respond by evolving the genetic basis of culture, language, and ethics. The environments that are "natural" for mankind, in the sense that the human species is biologically committed to live in them, are environments contrived by man's cultures. Mankind could not survive long in the environments of its ancestors of ten thousand years ago, not to speak of a million years ago. It is egregious nonsense to call these environments "natural," and yet this is a cliché frequently used.

Almost a century ago, Darwin concluded that "moral sense or conscience" developed in human evolution as an outgrowth of what he called "social instincts." Considered purely biologically, mankind has become by far the most successful form of life that evolution ever produced. It has inherited the earth; it has no serious competitors, and other species exist on its sufferance; unlike most other biological species, it is unlikely to become extinct, except through some kind of suicidal madness. Mankind is a zoological species, but it is not true that it is "nothing but an animal." According to Hallowell, for example, man, unlike his animal kin, acts in a universe that he has discovered and made intelligible to himself as an organism capable of consciousness, self-consciousness, and reflective thought. But this has been possible because the use of speech and other extrinsic symbolic means have led to the articulation, communication, and transmission of culturally constituted meanings and values. An organized social life in man, because it transcends purely biological and geographical determinants, cannot function apart from communally recognized meanings and values.

Meanings and values are "culturally constituted." They are communicated and transmitted from generation to generation by instruction and learning from parents, teachers, playmates, books, and what are nowadays called "media." There are no genes for meanings and values, yet it is the human genetic endowment that makes their articulation and transmission possible. Human infants are born with a capacity to become, in Waddington's words, "ethicizing beings," that is, with a capacity to acquire ethics and values, but without any specific innate ethics and values. Furthermore, "It is only man who becomes an ethicizing being and goes in for ethics."

Do animals other than man lack capacity for ethics? Students of animal behavior as eminent as Rensch and Thorpe believe that the rudiments of something like moral sense may be present. For example, dogs may behave as though they have guilt feelings and bad conscience. Yet I agree with Dr. Simpson when he says that it is nonsensical to speak of ethics in connection with any animal other than man. And Dr. Simpson adds that there is really no point in discussing ethics, and indeed the concept of ethics is meaningless, unless certain conditions exist, namely that there be alternative modes of action, that man be capable of judging the alternatives in ethical terms, and that he be free to choose what he judges to be ethically good.

The Book of Genesis gives an unexcelled poetical account of the decisive evolutionary step from animal to man: "And the Lord God said, behold, the man is become as one of us, to know good and evil." The capacity to know and to foresee the consequences of one's own and of other people's actions is, indeed, the fundamental biological precondition for becoming an ethicizing being. Both individually and as a species, man acquires ethics when he gains knowledge about the world and his place therein—and when this knowledge gives him foresight. He is held responsible for his actions if he knows their consequences. It is futile to look for special genes for ethics or for values. It is the genetic endowment as a whole that makes us human. Not special genes but the total genetic system of our species makes us capable of symbolic thought, of acquisition and transmission of knowledge by means of language, of self-awareness and death-awareness, and hence makes us ethicizing beings.

It is not my contention that all men are genetically uniform in their temperaments and inclinations. Though the evidence is not so complete and detailed as we may wish it to be, it is safe to say that there are genetic variations in intelligence, temperament, special abilities, inclinations, and consequently in behavior. A tall, muscular, athletic boy with features conforming to the popular ideas of good looks may be expected to behave differently from a not-so-well-formed or physically weak individual. An individual with an obvious musical talent, or mathematical ability, or aptitude for painting or versifying may well choose a different life work or career from individuals not so endowed.

However, it cannot be insisted too strongly that all these variations condition your behavior and bias your choices, but they do not amount to rigid determination. Moreover, and this is crucial, the manifestation of a genetic endowment depends on the social, economic, and educational environment in which its carrier is placed. We all know edifying stories of poor but talented boys working their way toward achievement; no stories are written about the equally talented ones who did not succeed. The basic fact is still that most humans can be brought up and trained for most of the professions and occupations that the society needs. But this statement is not contradictory to the recognition that some people are more easily trainable than others for some occupations, and that there are some callings, such as conductor of a symphony orchestra, for which only a small minority of individuals are qualified by their genetic endowments.

An appalling amount of printed paper, time, and energy are wasted on disputes of whether aggression and violence, or amity and kindness, are biologically given. Ethologists (students of animal behavior) have described a remarkable variety of aggressive behaviors, threat displays, and territorial defenses in many animals, including primates, the nearest relatives of man. It is no wonder that even so outstanding a scientist as Konrad Lorenz succumbs to the temptation of ascribing to man all these things as innate instincts. Of the ways the findings of ethology have been twisted by some sensationalist popular writers on alleged territorial imperatives, the less said the better.

Lorenz's argument is briefly as follows: Aggression in animals is usually ritualized; a threat of violence from a stronger dominant animal is answered by a weaker subordinate one by an innately fixed gesture of submission. This gesture of submission acts as a kind of biological lightning rod—the threat is not followed by an attack. The trouble with man, says Lorenz, is that he has invented powerful means of aggression, from stones to knives to bullets to hydrogen bombs, and no corresponding ritualized behavior to appease the aggressor. The really astonishing thing to me is that Lorenz, while he is of course fully aware of the psychological restructuralization that conferred on mankind mental abilities that none of its ancestors had, failed to see that these can function to defuse aggression.

The theory of innate goodness or gentleness of man is just as far off the mark. Ashley Montagu assures us that "Babies are born good, and desirous of continuing to be good." It is an evil society that frustrates their desire to be good and makes them grow into varying degrees of badness. I really do not know how to elicit an inborn moral philosophy from a baby; in my very limited experience I find babies usually desirous of much simpler and matter-of-fact benefits. Anyway, if it is true that a good society makes babies become good men, and a bad one makes them bad, then I conclude that babies are born neither good nor bad. They are born with the potentialities of developing into good or into bad men according to the circumstances that they encounter. This is, of course, just what the evolutionary view of human nature lends support to. One can be brought up to be gentle or violent, peaceful or aggressive. Anthropologists have ample evidence to show that cultures of different people demand different modes of behavior in their members, and that these demands are usually complied with.

Some authors claim that evolution has done more than implant in the human species an impartial capacity to learn various kinds of ethics and modes of behavior. Julian Huxley, for example, is convinced that traditional religions are noxious superstitions, and wishes to replace them by what he calls the religion of Evolutionary Humanism (with capital letters). He realizes that a religion must provide ethics, and must tell by what authority these ethics are sanctioned. He is careful to avoid proposing any new ethics, and accepts by implication the ethical system evolved by Judeo-Christian religious thought, which he has just denounced as a delusion. However, he puts forward what he thinks is a criterion by which one can evaluate rules of behavior and judge them to be good and desirable or bad and undesirable. This is what he calls the criterion of "evolutionary direction," and he adds that anything that permits or promotes open development is right, but that anything that restricts or frustrates this development is wrong.

This, I fear, is altogether too easy. As Dr. Simpson has quite rightly pointed out, no directions or trends in evolution are really general or universal. Trends vary from group to group and from time to time. Although every biologist intuitively feels that evolution has been on the whole progressive—that's what Teilhard insisted on—nobody has succeeded in defining what constitutes evolutionary progress or advancement. But this is actually not the most serious objection to Huxley's evolutionary ethics. Suppose that we do find that biological evolution in general, or human evolution in particular, has been going in a certain direction. Why must we necessarily consider this direction good? Why must wisdom be (and that by definition) helping the evolutionary process to go on as it went on in the past? Dr. Simpson has said that it is reasonable to consider capacities for feeling, knowing, willing, and understanding as improvements, and if that highly restricted definition is agreed upon, the matter can be discussed clearly in those terms. The wisdom of considering just these capacities as improvements is not, however, deducible from our knowledge of biological evolution; it comes from the general body of human wisdom, much of which had evolved before biology as a science started to exist. To be sure, one biological species, man, which developed this capacity to the greatest extent, is biologically the most successful existing species. However, is this pragmatic test an irrefutable validation of ethics? Is success always right?

Mankind has discovered that it is a product of evolution, and that evolution is a process. By this discovery, man has gained the right to judge the merits of evolution. The past cannot be changed regardless of our judgment, but man is no longer obliged to accept future evolution caused by blind and impersonal forces of nature. Evolution may eventually be managed and directed. Must it go on in the same direction in which it went in the past? Possibly so, yet only provided that this direction appears, in the light of human wisdom, good and desirable.

No, evolution is not by itself a criterion for deciding what ought or ought not to be. Ethics are products of the evolution of human culture: in turn, cultural evolution is made possible by the evolution of mankind's genetic endowment, but it is not imposed by or rigidly determined thereby. The teachings of Christ and Buddha have been accepted as guiding lights by billions of human beings because of their beauty, not because they were scientifically proven. In point of fact, life rigidly determined by rational constraints evokes passionate protests and rebellion in some people.

Dostoevsky described a rebellion with unsurpassed force in one of his early writings, *Letters from the Underground.* The Underground Man declared that he quite naturally wanted to live in order to satisfy his entire capacity to live and not just to satisfy his rationality, which might only account for one-twentieth of his capacity to live. Worse still, if it were proven to the Underground Man that inexorable laws of nature make it sensible and advantageous for him always to act in a certain way, the Underground Man would choose to be a madman, merely to insist that he is free to live according to his "stupid will."

Isn't this revolt perverse and destructive? It certainly is, in my opinion. However, we had better be aware of the fact that this perversity is no longer hidden in undergrounds. It has become worldwide, especially among the young, and is spreading. It has opened a gulf between generations, a gulf much wider than the father-son dissension generally is. The fathers are blamed for bequeathing to their children a society so depraved that the children reject it out of hand and embark on a futile search for delusory substitutes, often with aid of drugs.

I for one believe that the world that we fathers are leaving to our sons and daughters is really not worse, and in some ways is better, than that we received from those who were before us. We are blamed for the indecency of the Vietnam war, but we faced the vastly greater peril of Hitler's war. The danger of overpopulation has, to be sure, grown more imminent in recent times; and there appeared a quite new peril, that of worldwide suicide by means of nuclear war. However, the spread of education, from simple literacy to university training, might make more people conscious of these perils. And finally, here is the affluent society—to be sure, including only a fraction of mankind. It is derided by many who nevertheless take its facilities for granted.

Anyway, the answer to the revolt against the alleged tyranny of rationality is not irrationality. It is rather a demonstration that rationality is not incompatible with human freedom. An Age of Science need not lack endeavors of the human spirit other than science. It is debatable whether the extravagances of some modern artists represent novel achievements or degradation; but what is undeniable is that art masterpieces can now be enjoyed by vast numbers of people, whereas they used to be within reach of only the privileged few. Beethoven's music is now heard by numbers of listeners thousands of times greater than during his whole lifetime. Notwithstanding the inanities of some of the mass media, cultural values become accessible to ever greater numbers of people, first in technologically advanced countries but gradually all over the world.

I conclude that the criteria by which the validity of ethics must be tested must come from religion. Religion in an Age of Science is not a popular-science digest, however. My personal opinion is that at present it should have as its core one of the traditional religions. At some future time, this core may be a synthesis of several or of all traditional religions. However, religion should not only be aware of, but also receptive to all the achievements of human thought, and this surely includes science.

Teilhard de Chardin made an attempt to achieve one possible variant of religion in an age of science. His is not a new religion; it is a theology of nature rather than a natural theology. Teilhard was a Christian and a scientist. He has not tried to invent scientific proofs for his religious beliefs. This is sheer misunderstanding. But in his views evolutionary development has a religious meaning. He felt that the universe is no longer a State but a Process, and that the cosmos has become a Cosmogenesis. All the intellectual crises through which civilization has passed in the last four centuries arise out of the successive stages whereby a static *Weltanschauung* has been and is being transformed, in our minds and hearts, into a *Weltanschauung* of movement. What does this have to do with the biological basis of ethics and values? According to Teilhard, the man who sees nothing at the end of the world, nothing higher than himself, will find daily life filled only with pettiness and boredom. He calls upon mankind as a whole, collective humanity, to perform the definitive act whereby the total force of terrestrial evolution will be released and flourish; an act in which the full consciousness of each individual man will be sustained by that of every other man, not only living but the dead.

Time and the Growth of Complexity

Bernard Towers, M.B., Ch.B.

In this last third of the twentieth century we seem to be living through a period of revolution in thought comparable to, but even more significant than, those other two scientific revolutions of the last three hundred years. These were: 1) the seventeenth-century realization of the sheer magnitude of three-dimensional space and of the eccentric place of the planet earth in it; 2) the nineteenth-century insight into the sheer magnitude, again, of the fourth dimension, time. Now it seems that in the twentieth century we are just gradually beginning to realize some of the real implications of those discoveries. What meaning, if any, is to be discovered in the "space-time continuum" when we look at it, as we now know we must, not as a series of *states* but rather as a *process?*

Educated in the medical sciences, Dr. Towers taught and did research at universities in England and Wales before coming to the University of California, Los Angeles, where he is now Professor of Pediatrics and Anatomy. He was the first chairman of The Teilhard Association in Great Britain and Ireland, and is co-editor of The Teilhard Study Library. His publications encompass anatomy, embryology, and the relationship between science and religion.

My theme today is that of "Time and the Growth of Complexity." Basing my ideas on some of the insights of Teilhard, I want to suggest to you that mankind today, after having learned how to handle *magnitude* in linear space and linear time, is now on the verge of realizing something new, a new *dimension,* the dimension of complexity. We are beginning to realize that when matter is extended in both space *and* time, it always tends to produce increasingly sophisticated levels of complexity-in-organization. It will go on doing so unless we ourselves choose, either through ignorance or obstinacy, through stupidity or greed, to end it—at least on our own planet. So I want to discuss complexity as a dimension that develops as a function of time.

The seventeenth-century realization that the earth is not the center of the universe, but that it is a very small planet in a rather small solar system on the edge of a rather insignificant galaxy, forms the basis (or rather the first of a number of bases) for modern man's existential fear and anxiety. It is the foundation-stone for the *angst* that lies behind so much modern art and philosophy: the very real fear that man is no more than a minuscule puppet, a sport of nature, a meaningless, insignificant speck in a cold, cruel, uncaring universe, whose infinite spaces and deathly silence so terrified Pascal. This unease was much increased when it was realized in the nineteenth century that the earth is not nearly so *young* as had been thought, certainly not just a few thousand years old. Just how much older was a matter of serious and heated scientific controversy about a hundred years ago. The contemporary geologists and physicists, such as Lord Kelvin, were not prepared to allow that the earth could be anything like as old as Darwin and his followers were demanding in support of their theory of the very slow, gradual evolution of biological forms by a process of natural selection of the small variations that occur as between offspring and their parents. But even on the physical scientists' reckoning (and we should never forget that it was the scientific rather than the theological community that was initially most opposed to Charles Darwin[1]), it became clear that the history of the world could no longer be counted in thousands of years. This figure had to be multiplied by hundreds, and thousands, and indeed eventually by hundreds of thousands of *times.* This was "big-time time," as before man had had to teach himself to think of "big-time space." The result was to make him feel even more insecure than before—no longer merely a minute, insignificant speck in space, but also, like a mayfly, a being with the briefest of life-spans on earth; infinitesimal not only in terms of his individual life, but infinitesimal, too, in terms of the human race as a whole. Even Dr. Leakey's current estimate of 20 million years for the *Hominidae* is infinitesimal compared to four thousand million years for the history of life on the planet Earth.

Of course, where time is concerned one can always, as with space, be content with the here and now of one's own experience. We naturally tend to use the dimensions of our own bodies as a yardstick for judging distances, and our own experiences in time for judging time-spans. Our personal perceptions of time alter at different periods in our lives, and under the stress of different emotional states. What seems a long time to a child, for the most part seems very much shorter to an adult. We generally experience at a personal level a kind of acceleration or contraction of time as we grow older. In this, as is well recognized to be the case with regard to physical aspects of growth and development, it seems to me we recapitulate in some curious way the evolutionary history of the world out of which we have been formed.[2] As we ourselves grow, as embryos and children, in physical complexity, and then as we grow in the complexity of our memor-

1 Bernard Towers, "The Impact of Darwin's 'Origin of Species' on Medicine and Biology," *Medicine and Science in the 1860s,* ed. F. N. L. Poynter (London: Royal Historical Medical Library, 1968).

2 Bernard Towers, "Human Embryology and the Law of Complexity-consciousness." *Evolution, Marxism and Christianity,* ed. Anthony Dyson and Bernard Towers (New York: Humanities Press, 1967).

ies and other psychological experiences, we seem eventually (if circumstances do not impede the natural process) to begin to "zero in" on what is really significant in life. It is rather like the "ultimate trip" that Stanley Kubrick tried to portray in his film *2001: A Space Odyssey*. Our own experience of the passage of time and our reflections on it can be, or can become, the beginning of wisdom; and it may be that wisdom is always the ultimate goal. I want to put it to you that our understanding today of the nature of evolution is tending more and more toward this kind of appreciation. This "revolutionary thinking" is another manifestation of the causal relationship between Time and the Growth of Complexity. Though bound to appear strange to traditional, linear thinkers, it was continually hinted at in that remarkable book published in 1966: *The Voices of Time: A Co-operative Survey of Man's View of Time as Expressed by the Sciences and by the Humanities*.[3]

Let us return to our outline history of the development of evolutionary theories and their effect on man's appreciation of his own worth and significance. The early decades after the mid-nineteenth century—and by early decades I mean decades stretching right up to the 1970s—led to even further distress to the human psyche. Man was seen in his biological setting as *nothing but* an animal (1860s version), as *nothing but a* "Naked Ape" (1960s version).[4] The scientific method, as either practiced or pretended,[5] has nearly always adopted the *nothing but* argument of reductionist philosophy. This philosophy has had a good run, and now at the end of it[6] (despite its survival among some molecular biologists[7]) we

---

[3] Ed. J. T. Frazer (New York: Braziller, 1966).

[4] Desmond Morris, *The Naked Ape* (London: Cape, 1967); John Lewis and Bernard Towers, *Naked Ape or Homo Sapiens?* (New York: Humanities Press, 1969).

[5] Peter Medawar, "Is The Scientific Paper a Fraud?" A *Series of Scientific Case Histories*, ed. D. Edge (London: B.B.C. Publications, 1964).

[6] Arthur Koestler and J. R. Smythies, eds., *Beyond Reductionism: New Perspectives in the Life Sciences* (London, 1969).

[7] Francis Crick, *Of Molecules and Men* (Seattle: University of Washington Press, 1966); Jacques Monod, *Le Hazard et la Nécessité* (Paris, 1971).

find its exponents saying things that are literally absurd; absurd not merely because they *seem* crazy, but because on their own grounds they have to say of themselves that they *are* crazy. For instance, a serious article in the distinguished newspaper *The London Times* (March 17, 1971) was devoted to the newly published book by Jacques Monod, which seems to have taken Paris by storm and which, its author claims, will "sweep the slate clean of virtually all previous philosophies of life." Let me quote from *The Times:*

> Recent discoveries about basic organic matter demonstrate, Professor Monod holds, that all forms of life are the product of pure chance—through unpredictable mutation—and of necessity, or Darwinian selection. . . . "Armed with all the powers, enjoying all the wealth they owe to science," Professor Monod writes, "our societies are still trying to practice and to teach systems of values already destroyed at the roots by that very science. Man knows at last that he is alone in the indifferent immensity of the universe, whence he has emerged by chance. His duty, like his fate, is written nowhere. It is for him to choose between the kingdom and the darkness. . . . What I have tried to show is that the scientific attitude implies what I call the postulate of objectivity—that is to say the fundamental postulate that there is no plan, that there is no intention in the universe."

Writing in French in this nineteenth-century vein, it is not surprising that he attacks Teilhard for giving "an evolutionist interpretation of the universe in which man is a sort of achievement which had been predicted from the beginning. It is again an interpretation which denies the principle of objectivity," he says. That represents, in my view, a serious misinterpretation of Teilhard. His theory says nothing about man as we know him having been "predicted from the beginning." Rather it is Teilhard who is *thoroughly* objective in his analysis of the facts.

We now know that throughout evolutionary time there has been a tendency for matter, in its totality, to become organized into states of increasing complexity at the physicochemical level. Once the complexity became great enough to warrant the description "living," then each subsequent rise in complexity in organization has resulted in increased levels of information-exchange, or information-flow, between the organism and its environment, including members of its own and other species. That means increase in awareness or consciousness. The chance nature of the underlying energy-patterns is never questioned by Teilhard. What he is concerned to do is to give an objective and complete account of what in fact has happened in evolution and what kind of results have been achieved. It is, of course, as a result of the evolutionary process that we are meeting here this week-end to see whether or not we can make any sense out of it. For Monod, with his philosophy of "chance and necessity," there can be no sense or meaning in our deliberations, no more than there can be in his own—which is where the ultimate absurdity comes in.

The reductionist fallacy concerning man came about because of reciprocal confusions over two nineteenth-century scientific insights. One of them is true, but was not appreciated on its universal scale in the nineteenth century. The other of them is true within its own restricted area, but in the nineteenth century it was put on, and has remained on, a universal scale to which it does not apply. The first of these two insights is that *everything,* including man is the result and both part and product of a universal evolutionary process. The other is the famous Second Law of Thermodynamics, which correctly states that in any closed thermodynamic system all differences in energy levels are bound eventually to disperse, and that a general state of "mixing up," loss of differentiation, and increase in disorder of "entropy" is bound to ensue. That is true enough. But why the universe should have been thought of for so long as a "closed system" is something of a mystery.[8] We now know

[8] Evry Schatzman, *The Origin and Evolution of the Universe* (London: Hutchinson, 1966).

much more about the universe than they did in the nineteenth century, and it has often been pointed out by modern astronomers[9] that there really is no justification for the notion (or for the fear it engenders) that the universe is moving irrevocably toward a heat-death. The combination of Darwinism and Increasing Entropy, seen as the end result of the evolutionary process, formed a strong argument a hundred years ago for denial of meaning or purpose in nature. Thus Emil du Bois Reymond said in 1876,[10] in words very reminiscent of Monod's a century later: "The possibility, even so distant, of banishing from nature its seeming purpose, and putting a blind necessity everywhere in the place of final causes, appears therefore, as one of the greatest advances in the world of thought, from which a new era will be dated in the treatment of these problems."[11] This is a prediction that Monod is now claiming has come true by virtue of his "postulate of objectivity."

Now, nineteenth-century scientists tended still to think of themselves as eighteenth-century deists thought of God: as standing outside the phenomena on a kind of privileged platform from which they could examine things wholly objectively. I doubt if Reymond has really grasped the fact that he himself was also a part of nature and that he himself would share with the rest of nature that banishment of "seeming purpose" which he so welcomed. In modern physics (and physics was traditionally the most objective of the sciences) it is now recognized that complete objectivity is sometimes impossible of attainment. We ourselves are part of our own observations, and in some areas of physics it is impossible to make an observation without altering the phenomena themselves. The brave and stoical attitude of a nine-

9 William Saslaw, "*Entropy and the Universe*," *The Teilhard Review* 3 (1969) :76–79.

10 Emil du Bois Reymond, *Darwin versus Galiani* (Berlin, 1876) .

11 For an analysis of "final causes," see Bernard Towers, "Teleology and the Anatomist," *Concerning Teilhard: and Other Writings on Science and Religion* (London: Collins, 1969) .

teenth-century scientific positivist such as Thomas Henry Huxley and his academic heirs such as Monod, provides little comfort for the despair of modern man. If the process of evolution, of which we know ourselves to be the product, *is* fundamentally meaningless, being based on nothing but "chance and necessity" as both Monod and Reymond have held, then this implies that we ourselves are meaningless, absurd creatures at a most fundamental level. And then, it seems to me, an existential *angst* is inescapable by anyone who is prepared to take the proposition seriously. This has been the basis for that "cold clutch of emptiness" that seems to have motivated so many of our creative artists to write for the theater of the absurd, or to paint or sculpt or write poetry in the moods of cynicism and despair that our age knows so well. Man cannot live with total absurdity. He will go on strike, as Teilhard used to say. How many of our contemporaries have done just that, whether by becoming social dropouts, or by escaping into the fantasy world of drugs, or by suicide, or by that total cynicism which allows a man to exploit the very society that he despises and mocks? Such promulgation of meaninglessness, whether in the name of science or of art, will destroy, or may destroy, all the astonishing things that the evolutionary process managed to produce during the countless millions of years before man ever developed the notion that there was such a process, let alone that he himself was part of it.

I want now to put forward another point of view, and will try to speak as a "modern man" in the sense in which Teilhard defined that term. I refer to a passage in which he says:

> What makes and classifies a "modern" man (and a whole host of our contemporaries is not yet "modern" in this sense) is having become capable of seeing in terms not of space and time alone, but also of *duration,* or—and it comes to the same thing—of biological space-time; and above all having become

incapable of seeing anything otherwise—anything—*not even himself.*[12]

Teilhard regarded the history of science as constituted of three main phases. The first was that of which I spoke above, namely the sheer magnitude of space and of time. This Teilhard called the "Science of the Infinitely Large," and he analyzed, as I tried to do above, the kind of human disquiet to which it led. Man became somehow diminished in his own eyes because of the sheer magnitude of everything outside himself. In more recent decades there followed, as the second phase, what Teilhard called the "Science of the Infinitely Small," which is the science of atomic and subatomic physics, where uncertainty and randomness are such dominant features that again man feels his insecurity. It is as though one's very reality, the actual structure of one's physical body, is shown to be a lie. You may remember how this was expressed by Eddington[13] in terms of a table. The layman sees it as solid and as real as anything could be. To the atomic scientist its "solidity" disappears during the analysis of what is "really there" into empty space for the most part, with particles and energies flying through the nothingness in an apparently aimless and chaotic manner. Now a vital element is seen to be missing from both these accounts, but it is the very element that will resolve the conflict and allow the table to be what it is. Both the layman's and the scientist's accounts deal with the table only on the basis of the here and now, and only in terms of linear, or spatial, dimensions. *The missing element is time.* Older scientists (and surely Professor Monod, also) would say that they *are* aware of the time-dimension, and of the fact that the table, too, is in some sense a product of evolution. But then one has to ask, what does this mean or imply? One can look at the fourth dimension,

12 Pierre Teilhard de Chardin, *The Phenomenon of Man* (New York: Harper and Row, 1959), p. 219.

13 Sir Arthur Eddington, Introduction to *The Nature of the Physical World*, Gifford Lectures, Edinburgh, 1927.

you see, in just the same linear way as the other three. This is what the ancients did.[14] It is what anybody does when he interprets time as no more than a measure of the *sequence* or *succession* of events. Evolution *can* be, and often is, regarded as no more than "one damn thing after another."

But if one looks at time and matter together in a truly evolutionary setting, something very different from this linear breakup emerges. Teilhard looked at nature in the above-defined "modern man's" way, that is, in terms of the real space-time continuum, or what he called, you remember, biological space-time. By doing so he was able to define the present phase of scientific enquiry as the "Science of the Infinitely Complex," following on his "Science of the Infinitely Large" and "Science of the Infinitely Small." We are only, as yet, at the very beginning of analyzing its features. But one can be sure that the time factor (time seen as a molding or sculpting agent) will henceforth always be an integral part of the system in much the same way that, in a modern mobile sculpture, motion is incorporated into the sculpture itself. In *The Future of Man* Teilhard writes as follows:

> Hitherto, in the eyes of a Science too much accustomed to reconstruct the world on one spatial axis extending in a line from the infinitely small to the infinitely great, the larger molecules of organic chemistry, and still more the living cellular composites, have existed without any defined position, like wandering stars, in the general scheme of cosmic elements. Now however, simply by the introduction of another dimension, a new order and definition become apparent. Traversing the rising axis from the infinitesimal to the immense another branch appears, rising through Time from the infinitely simple to the supremely complicated. It is on this branch that the conscious-phenomenon has its place and eventually shows itself. There is first a long, obscure stretch which seems dead but is in fact "imperceptibly alive." Then, at the stage of cor-

---

[14] Cornelius A. Benjamin, "Ideas of Time in the History of Philosophy," *The Voices of Time*, ed. J. T. Frazer (New York: Braziller, 1966).

> puscles reaching a million atoms in their complexity (viruses), we come to the first flush heralding the dawn of Life. Later, after the cell, there is a definite radiation growing richer and more intense with the formation and gradual concentration of nervous systems. And finally, at the extreme end of the known spectrum, comes the thinking incandescence of the human brain.[15]

Now it is, of course, by the exercise of this "human brain," this product of matter seen in biological space-time, that we ourselves come to be engaging ourselves with these problems at this conference. If it is the case, as the reductionists insist, that our brains and the thoughts they produce are "nothing but" the result of the operation of "chance and blind necessity," then we are wasting meaningless time even in reaching that bleak conclusion. On the other hand, if honest and full analysis of what has actually occurred in the world's history is a worthwhile exercise, then we have an intriguing problem before us. It won't be solved by appeal to extra-phenomenal or supernatural agencies, by ghostly magicians pulling rabbits out of hats or creating men and women out of nothing. The problem is a human one and can only be solved through human resources. We must use all the resources we have and not behave like Procrustes, lopping off any part of the human phenomenon that does not seem to fit our Procrustean bed, our narrowly mechanistic and reductionist scientific paradigm.

One can be fairly sure, I think, that major progress toward a solution of the problem (that is, toward discovering what if anything our lives might signify) will be made only by those who have become "modern" in Teilhard's sense. That is, one has to make the quantum jump from merely giving *notional assent* to the theory of evolution to giving *real assent* to it. Then one must be prepared to follow out the consequences wherever they may lead. When one begins to

15 Pierre Teilhard de Chardin, *The Future of Man* (New York: Harper and Row, 1964), p. 131. Quoted by permission of Harper & Row, Publishers, Inc.

give real assent to the fact that everything that one sees, feels, tastes, and smells in the world around one, including oneself, is a direct product of the world-in-evolution, then one's appreciation of, and concern for, every feature of the physical, biological, social, and cultural environment undergoes a profound change. It gives one a respect for the environment and a feeling for the ecosystem. Many young people are experiencing this today. One develops a kind of awe and humility before the facts, which is a feeling that used to be said to be the hallmark of the natural scientist. This, then begins to affect one's actions at a primary gut level. All that man is and all that society achieves is an expression of the potential of the selfsame matter that we study in the chemistry laboratory, in our experimental animals, in outer space, and in our hospital patients. We are matter become conscious of itself. We not only know, but we know that we know, as Julian Huxley puts it. That is, "consciousness is raised to the power of two," as Teilhard says—"consciousness squared." Its implications are shattering in their extent and profundity. This world has taken some four thousand million years to get to where it is, and that in a universe that has a history, in its present phase of expansion, of more than twice that period of time. It is given to us, toward the end of the twentieth century, to begin dimly to comprehend the nature of the process at work. Time is the sculpting agent, and *time is contracting*. The process of evolution still continues at the psychosocial level. In *The Appearance of Man,* Teilhard refers to life as "the privileged exaggeration of a fundamental cosmic tendency (as fundamental as entropy or gravitation) which may be called the "Law of Complexity-Consciousness." He further states:

> Left long enough to itself, under the prolonged and universal play of chance, matter manifests the property of arranging itself in more and more complex groupings, and at the same time in ever-deepening layers of consciousness; this double and combined movement of physical unfolding and

> psychic interiorisation (or centration) once started, continues, accelerating and growing to its utmost extent.
>
> This tendency towards complexity-consciousness (leading to the formation of more and more astronomically complicated corpuscles) is easily recognisable on the atomic plane, and it is confirmed on the molecular. But it is patently on the plane of life that it is revealed in all its clarity—and all its additiveness; and here it can, at the same time, be translated into a convenient and simplified formula: *the tendency to cerebration.*[16]

Teilhard is absolutely right to pick out the nervous system as manifesting the most complex and most potentially conscious form of living matter. But we must not forget that tendencies are tendencies. They are not perfect blueprints designed in advance. Moreover, it is the system *as a whole* that is producing increasingly complex forms. Those forms can neither develop nor survive unless and until other forms are available to provide them with the "means of subsistence." So we are dealing with an open-ended and cooperative system, in which some areas are privileged, rather like some organs of the body, to manifest the full potential of the system more readily than others. With privilege goes responsibility. We ourselves carry the biggest responsibilities of all in the evolutionary process.

Teilhard's law of complexity-consciousness is like the laws of classical physics in that it is an expression of a statistical variation, in this case with a built-in bias in time toward increasing complexity. Always there will be individual elements that go in the opposite direction. And since at the roots there lie the uncertainties of which we spoke above, one must always expect to find reversals on the local and temporary scale. That is why Teilhard spoke of evolution as essentially a process of "groping." Groping implies the possibility—indeed the inevitability—of taking wrong turnings and ending up in blind alleys. Nothing guarantees success in any individual endeavor. But the point is that this

16 Pierre Teilhard de Chardin, *The Appearance of Man* (New York: Harper and Row, 1965), p. 139.

groping process is nothing if not dynamic. Like Waddington's "chreod,"[17] it implies that finally a path will emerge that was somehow inherent in the ceaseless dynamics of the system though incapable of specific prediction in advance.

If complexity and consciousness go on increasing with time at the biological level, then there is every reason to suppose that the speed of change (which is the only proper way to measure time) is continually increasing at the sociocultural stage of evolution in which we are now engaged. And this is what we see. We ourselves are involved in this game of both chance and skill. With every advance in complexity-consciousness it is as though the stakes are raised ever higher for those who are prepared to stay in the game. The stakes have never been so high in the history of our planet. It is nothing less than the choice (as one places one's bets, and then uses one's skill to effect a favorable outcome) between pursuit of the perfection of man in hope and faith and love, or alternatively of giving up the unequal struggle and dropping out, dropping back into the chaos out of which the process itself has so far led us with reasonable success. We are now participants at a conscious level. We can certainly wreck the process if we wish. That is the measure of our responsibility as human beings.

---

17 C. H. Waddington, "The Basic Ideas of Biology," *Towards a Theoretical Biology,* ed. C. H. Waddington (Edinburgh: Edinburgh University Press, 1968).

From Savannah to City and Beyond

L. S. B. Leakey, Ph.D., D.Sc.

Discoveries concerning the origin of man and the evolution of his culture, as well as the development of his spiritual awareness, have been made at such an ever-increasing rate that if Teilhard de Chardin could be back with us here today, he would rejoice at the incredible extension of our knowledge during the past twelve years or so.

We now know that man has only come to his present position of being fully *Homo sapiens,* with enormous spiritual, mental, and reasoning potential, after a very lengthy apprenticeship in terms of evolutionary processes. We now have evidence of his prehuman stages in the Lower and Upper Miocene, side by side with fossil apes of various kinds.

Distinguished archaeologist, paleontologist, and prehistorian, Dr. Leakey's excavations in Kenya's Olduvai Gorge have dramatically extended our knowledge of Man's earliest origins on earth. He is the recipient of many academic distinctions, including Fellowship in the British Academy, the Royal Medals from both the British Geographic and Swedish Anthropologic Societies, and The Haile Selassie Award and Medal. Among the many scientific works he has authored is the now-famous *Adam's Ancestors* and the more recently co-authored book titled *Unveiling Man's Origins.* He is presently the Honorary Director of the Centre for Prehistory and Paleontology, Kenya, East Africa.

Also, we now have much information about his development prior to arriving at the *Homo sapiens* stage when he was "man the thinker."

As far back as the Lower Miocene period in East Africa, which can be dated by Potassium Argon dating techniques as between 20 and 25 million years ago, the Superfamily of the Hominoidea had already begun to subdivide and there were already present representatives of the following families: Hominidae; Hylobatidae, or gibbons; Pongidas, or Great Apes; the Proconsulidae, an extinct family of the Superfamily; and the Oreopithecidae, another extinct branch. In other words, the Superfamily of the Hominoidea had already broken up by Lower Miocene times, much as most other mammalian Superfamilies; and man's evolution from his prehuman direct ancestor to *Homo sapiens* was a long and slow process with the development of sapient powers coming relatively recently.

It is now practically certain that the separation of man, both from his immediate ancestors and from his nearest relations, must have taken place in the Oligocene. In this connection, it is very interesting to note that those who were teaching physical anthropology when Teilhard de Chardin was training in France, as well as those who taught me this subject in Britain, had already arrived at this conclusion on theoretical evidence. The writings of Sir Arthur Keith are an illustration of this point.

It was only much more recently that scientists began to doubt the early separation of the Family of man from the Families of the apes. Now it can be factually shown, on fossil evidence from East Africa, that the separation was over 20 million years ago; and that those who taught Teilhard de Chardin and myself were correct, and that the modern theoreticians are not to be taken seriously—especially those who place the separation of the great apes (Pongidae) from man (Hominidae) at only 5 million years ago.

Let us look at some of the evidence very briefly: In 1951

Le Gros Clark and I described some fragmentary fossil remains from the Lower Miocene of Kenya as "*Sivapithecus*" *africanus*. This was done tentatively and we indicated that on the one hand they resembled some, but not all, of the Asiatic fossils classified as *Sivapithecus*, and we also hinted at the presence of resemblances to *Ramapithecus brevirostris*.

Since that time, it has become evident that these specimens, as well as a number of others found at our Lower Miocene sites, represent an earlier stage of the Upper Miocene hominid, which we named *Kenyapithecus wickeri* in 1962. This evidence has been published and is based on a number of characteristics (not just one or two), all of which point in the same direction and distinguish these early hominids from the pongids. Amongst other characteristics are the shortening of the face, which is linked with a marked backward divergence of the molar and premolar series, resulting in a basic mandibular rectangle approaching that of man himself; the virtual absence of a diastema between the relatively large canines and the third premolars; the fact that the incisors do not protrude at the alveolar margin markedly in front of the canine sockets; the relatively simple structure of the molar crowns in marked contrast to the forms seen in the contemporary *Proconsuls* and pongids, which exhibit much more complex cinguli and cusp pattern; and the nature and structure of the symphasis, as well as the structure of the upper incisors. All of these features and a number of others taken together rather than singly, indicate strong hominid affinity and a marked divergence from the other higher primates that were present at this remote date of some 20 million years ago.

In 1962 we found the first example of a species of *Kenyapithecus* more advanced than the one mentioned above and this was named *wickeri*. The site was at Fort Ternan, Kenya, in deposits some 600 feet below the present surface and in association with very extensive fossil fauna. At first *Kenyapithecus wickeri* was attributed to the earliest Pliocene, but recent Potassium argon and then faunal evidence suggests that an Upper Miocene date somewhere between 12 and 14 million years ago is more probable. In *Kenyapithecus wickeri* the upper central incisors are even more like Man himself than in *Kenyapithecus africanus,* while the canines have become much reduced in size and are similar in size to some species of *Homo* today. In morphology they are not wholly manlike. They have, however, strongly compressed lateral roots of relatively small size. The third premolars are still basically monocuspid with a slight suggestion of development of a second cusp, but the fourth upper premolars and molars are extremely hominid in structure.

Associated with this material representing a definitely hominid morphology rather than any other higher primals, we got evidence in 1967/68 of animal bones that had been clearly smashed by heavy blows with a blunt instrument. Both Elwyn Simons and I had reached the conclusion, on the evidence of dentition, that *Kenyapithecus* and his close relation, *Ramapithecus* in Asia, had already developed an omnivorous diet that probably included flesh. The broken bones that we discovered indicated that the diet also included bone marrow and brains.

Then in 1969 we found a stone of about 4 inches diameter at its greatest measurement, which had originally consisted of an angular lump of lava that had weathered from the external surface inwards to a depth of about 1 centimeter, while the internal part remained wholly hard and unweathered. This lump of lava was found on a palaesol at Fort Ternan and its associations with the broken bones and skulls were particularly interesting. A part of its original weathered angular surface was missing, having been broken away to expose the gray-black hard laval core. Even the broken-off fragments were not near the place where the specimen was found. The remaining part of the angular surface exhibited two right-angle damaged edges—this damage being in both directions and closely paralleling what can be produced by the author by knocking a similar stone on a hard surface.

Lying as it was on a palaesol some 600 feet below the present surface and in association with the broken bones and skulls, as well as the fossil remains of *Kenyapithecus wickeri,* there could be little doubt that it represented one of the stones used by this hominid to break open the animal bones.

It must be emphasized that this specimen was not, strictly speaking, a tool, but nevertheless most certainly represents a stone that was utilized by a hominid some 12–14 million years ago to obtain protein foods.

In 1931 my expedition to the site of Kanam, on the shores of the Kavirondo Gulf in Kenya, discovered a fragment of a human mandible. It was exceedingly heavily mineralized and there was evidence of a fracture through the jaw during life which had healed, and during the healing process an ossified sarcoma had developed on the internal aspect of the symphysis. This fossil mandible was dug out from *in situ* deposits by one of my African staff, Juma Gitau, while excavating for a *Deinotherum* molar, and it was unquestionably found *in situ* in deposits of Lower Pleistocene age. In spite of its fragmentary condition and the fact that many of its teeth were damaged, I consider that it undoubtedly represented a member of genius *Homo,* but one that was distinct from *Homo sapiens* in some characteristics and I named it *Homo kanamensis.*

At the time of publication of this material the vast majority of anthropologists still accepted the evidence of the "Piltdown fossils" as representing the morphological characters of man during the Pliopleistocene. Since the Kanam mandible differed so markedly from the mandible allegedly found at Piltdown, most of my colleagues decided to place my specimen in what they called a "suspense account," to await further evidence of its validity.

After the exposure of the "Piltdown fossils" as forgeries in 1953, the situation was altered completely and now an increasing number of my colleagues accept the fact that *Homo kanamensis* represents a Lower Pleistocene man.

In 1970, when my son Richard Leakey and his wife were

working in the fossil deposits in North East Rudolf, which were dated by Potassium argon methods as more than 2.6 million years old, they discovered numerous fossils representing the Family Hominidae. Some of these are clearly Australopithicine and are related to *Australopithecus robustus,* as well as to the group that includes *Australopithecus* (*Zinjanthropus*) *bosei*. On the other hand, there are also specimens that are clearly much more closely related to man himself. One mandible in particular, found by Maeve Leakey, exhibits characteristics with remarkable similarity to the Kanam mandible. As it is of approximately the same geological age, I am strongly inclined to regard it as another specimen of *Homo kanamensis* from the Lower Pleistocene.

This new specimen is much more complete than that of 1931 and has the lower margin of the mandible intact as well as more teeth present. On a preliminary examination, I have no doubt that it represents an early form of the genus *Homo* and I would classify it as such. In all probability it represents *Homo kanamensis* and there is thus new evidence, which almost certainly supports that of 1931—that the genus *Homo* was present at the time of Pliopleistocene boundary, 2.6 million years ago.

In the same geological period in the North East Rudolf deposits, my son and his team have located several sites with stone tools of an early stage of the Oldowan Culture dating back to 2.6 million years.

Next comes the evidence from Olduvai Gorge. In Bed 1 at Olduvai, in deposits that range from 1.8 million years upwards to less than a million (these are Potassium argon dates), there is now clear evidence that the genus *Homo* as represented by a number of specimens, including a recently discovered nearly complete skull from D.K. 1, was present at this remote time. The material is still claimed by a few who have not seen it as representing an advanced australopithecine, but the new skull from D.K. 1 completely confirms our original diagnosis of the less complete material and shows that the overall morphology of the brain case, the face, the teeth, the temporal fossa, and the like, are entirely hominid and not australopithecine.

Olduvai Gorge has also produced evidence in the form of both skull and limb bones of an African variant of *Homo erectus* living side by side both with the later stages of *Homo habilis* as well as the end stages of the *Australopithecus* group.

The deposits of Olduvai Bed 1 have large numbers of sites yielding stone tool-kits, first of the Oldowan culture and later of the Developed Oldowan. This evidence, together with that from N. E. Rudolf, indicates that from 2.6 million years until about 1 million years, or even later, there were hominids making progressively more complete tool kits of stone. While it is not possible to state categorically, at this stage, which of the hominids was responsible for these stone tools, or even whether more than one type of hominid was responsible for them, it seems generally more likely that *Homo habilis* and, presumably, his direct ancestor (whom I consider was probably Homo kanemensis) were principally responsible for this activity. There is, however, some reason to believe that the African variant of *Homo erectus,* in Bed 2 times, was responsible for at least one branch of the Handaxe Culture, which is typified by numerous rather crudely made handaxes and cleavers; while the end stages of the developed Oldowan, which was contemporary, had a tool kit with many different types of tools, and only a few handaxes and cleavers, which are, however, much more beautifully made than the ones that were associated with the *Homo erectus* branch of man.

In 1931 and 1932 we discovered numerous fossils in deposits of Middle Pleistocene age at Kanjera, on the south shores of the Kavirondo Gulf. On the eroded slopes of this deposit we picked up fossilized skull bones of four individuals in exactly the same state of fossilization as the extinct animals. Excavation into the deposits at the site where the human skull bones lay on the surface resulted in the discovery *in situ* of two further fragments that fitted into parts of one of the skulls found on the surface. The geological evidence, the faunal evidence, and the presence of handaxes in the deposit all suggested an age comparable with Bed 4 at Olduvai Gorge.

As in the case of the Kanam evidence, the veil of false data derived from the Piltdown forgeries caused most of my colleagues to place the Kanjera skulls from the Middle Pleistocine in the "suspense account," since they clearly represented a primitive form of *Homo sapiens.*

Subsequent discoveries in Europe as, for example, the parts of the skull from the Swanscombe Gravels near London, the Steinheim skull from Germany and the *Font e Chavade* skull parts from France (all of which were found also in Middle Pleistocene deposits) were similarly either rejected or declared not to represent *Homo sapiens.* It was only in 1969, at an International conference under the auspices of UNESCO, that these specimens and the Kanjera one finally took their rightful place and were accepted unanimously as representing the presence of *Homo sapiens* in Africa and Europe during the Middle Pleistocene.

In the short space of time available to me this morning I cannot hope to present the full story of man's subsequent development from the variants of *Homo sapiens* represented by the above-mentioned skulls to his final appearance as the subspecies *Homo sapiens sapiens,* who was beginning to develop religious beliefs, magic, art, music, conceptual thought, and a language much more fully articulate than it could have been in the earlier stages. While we do not know the exact date (or rather period of time) in which this final development was achieved, we do know that somewhere round about 40,000 years ago there is evidence of religious thought, as indicated by the development of ritual burial of a deceased, accompanied by offerings for the spirit world. The other various manifestations of an advanced *Homo sapiens sapiens* are also widespread. It is assumed that conceptual thought must have been developed by this time to enable these things to be achieved.

We, therefore, have to ask ourselves what special new discovery, if any, made it possible for man to cease to be "Man the mere animal" and to become "Man the thinker," with all the attributes listed above. After many years of giving this problem careful thought, I reached the conclusion a few years ago that the solution lay in man's discovery of how to make fire *at will,* as distinct from how to use it and temporarily keep it alive when he occasionally captured wild fire and took it to his home and tended it carefully until, by accident, he lost it.

I would interpolate here that, in my view, the first major milestone in human evolution was achieved at the time when our ancestors, *Kenyapithecus wickeri,* learned to utilize animal products and, in particular, learned to use a stone to break up bones and skulls to obtain marrow and brains to augment an otherwise vegetarian diet. For me, the second milestone was achieved when man began to make definite "tool kits" that included bone tools and a number of different distinct stone-tool types made regularly. By this time he must also have been using a wide range of perishable materials, such as bark and hide, for his various needs. As I have noted above, we can now carry the date of this milestone, thanks to the work of my son Richard and his colleagues at N. E. Rudolf, back to 2.6 million years; and I have not the least doubt that we shall carry this event still further back beyond the 3 million mark.

After this milestone had been reached, the making of bone and stone tools went on developing for an immense period of time, and eventually a very high degree of skill was achieved. Occasionally, during the last two or three thousand years of this stage, fire was captured, used, and lost, but still not made *at will.*

So far as my researches indicate at the moment, the presence of continuous humanly induced fire *made at will* appears on the scene at almost exactly the same time as the beginning of drilling holes through various objects, some of them hard, in order to suspend them around the neck as amulets.

I can easily imagine two early *Homo sapiens,* on the threshold of becoming *sapiens sapiens,* sitting down to drill a hole through the root of the tooth of a hyena or cave bear . . . one man holds the drill, a long thin wooden sapling such as is used today by primitive tribes for fire-making, while the other man holds the object being drilled firmly down on a piece of dry wood or bark. Suddenly, as the final twirl of the drill is given to penetrate the last millimetre of the root of the tooth, the hot drill-point bursts through into the dry wood or bark below.

I have done this experimentally and since by this time the point of the wooden drill was already very hot, the immediate result is a thin curl of smoke. I can imagine one of the two men saying to the other in these circumstances: "The spirit of fire must exist inside that piece of wood (or bark)," and so saying, abandoning all further thought for the time being of making amulets and proceeding to drive his drill further into the bark or wood. I, too, have done this experimentally, and within a few seconds a glowing spark appeared on the pile of wood-dust that I was drilling out; and as I watched, this spark grew and then, when I applied it to some dry leaves and blew gently, I got a flame.

Fire made at will—man's third milestone.

Before this time, except on those rare occasions when he had captured and temporarily tried to domesticate wild fire, man could not avail himself of the wonderful safety that is provided by smoke and, above all, the smell of burning.

By day both the men and the women of hunting and food-gathering tribes (until the discovery of fire) would have had little opportunity to develop complex speech forms and conceptual thought, and with those things religion, art, and so on. The daylight hours of both the men and the women of a hunting and food-gathering community (as I have found, myself, by accompanying them) are very fully occupied with their activities—the men and boys hunting, and the women, girls, and younger children gathering nuts and berries, edible roots and insects, and the like.

Even on a very successful day, when the hunters have made a kill early, they do not relax. Luck was with them, therefore they must go on in the hope of a further kill while the luck held, since they knew well there might be many days to come when they would make no kill at all. Besides, the surplus meat could always be dried to biltong. Similarly, the women, even if they had filled their fruit bags early, would not let up, because there was always a chance that the men would return without meat, and always an equal chance that, suddenly rounding a bush, the women would come across a juvenile animal crouching in the grass and be able to kill it. Before the advent of fire-at-will, both the men and the women could not have spoken very much during the day (their successors today do not do so either). In the evening, without fire, they would have to return to their sleeping place. And when darkness fell, after they had eaten their uncooked meal, they would have had to take turns at sleeping while others remained awake on the alert for danger.

Once it was possible to make fire *at will,* all this changed. In the first place, fire made it possible to use caves and rock shelters as homes; food could be cooked and smoked; and a little fire could be set to burn at the entrance, and this in itself provided a defense against wild beasts and reptiles. (I know of no dangerous animal or poisinous reptile in the wild state that will approach the smell of burning.) But much more than this was achieved. The hours of darkness after the evening meal could be spent in developing complex words and language forms; in sharpening the powers of reason; and in talking about such abstract things as a spirit world, what happens after death, and other abstract ideas such as love and hate. It was also possible to use the light provided by fire to seek out deep recesses of the caves and rock shelters and, by the light of the fire, work on paintings and engravings expressing magic and religion.

Let me repeat the principal results of firemaking. Once he had achieved this skill, early man could *use* some of the hours of darkness and especially have time and safety to develop thought and speech. He could move into the shelter of caves and rock shelters away from rainstorms and cold winds. He could take his growing knowledge of art processes into the deep dark recesses of caves and, by the light of the flame, paint or engrave for the purposes of expressing magic and religion. In fact, once man had achieved this third milestone of fire-at-will, he was now *Homo sapiens sapiens*—developing all the attendant attributes of religion, magic, art, music, and eventually writing and literature, as well as science.

For me, the fourth milestone came when man began to develop the complex arts and sciences of agriculture, of domesticating wild animals, of building houses, of the potter's wheel, and all the things that we call the dawn of civilization. This event took place around 8,000 years ago. It has culminated in man as we know him today. Men like the Masai and the Bushmen still prefer the life of the countryside. Man whom we call "civilized" tends to flock to the towns and cities to enjoy what he considers to be the luxuries of "civilized life," although they often bring him little satisfaction.

On the whole, man is becoming more and more a city-dweller and has developed extraordinary and complex achievements, not all of which are necessarily praiseworthy. There are atom bombs and biological warfare as well, of course, as the ability to land on the moon.

But I am not going to dwell on whether or not these achievements do contribute to greater happiness or to the development of greater powers of abstract reasoning. I want instead to conclude by asking whither we go? And what may, or may not, be the next milestone in man's 20-million-year journey? Today, some believe that man is about to witness his own destruction—and certainly the portents are ominous. Poverty and pollution, hunger and violence, and all the other evils that result from man's abilities and his weaknesses, stalk the land. These things are becoming more and more noticeable, more and more dangerous as man's population increases, and yet very little is being done by man himself to combat these evils. When we compare what he has done and is doing with the scarcely used power of his brain-potential and of his fabulous material resources, the picture is frightening.

Were I a pessimist, I would join ranks with those who believe that 30 years from now man will have disappeared from this earth. But I am not a pessimist. I do not believe that this is the inevitable end of man's long journey through time. I do believe, however, that unless we—and especially the younger generation of all races and nations—decide here and now to take urgent steps to eradicate the terrible evils brought about by human complacency, eradicate the real threats posed by atom and germ warfare, by atmospheric and water pollution, by the uncontrolled use of pesticides and, above all, by our failure to utilize our powers of *reason,* then our future is very limited.

My message is not to you here in this hall. The very fact of your presence shows that you are among those who believe that the world must change its course. You here are, rather, my sounding board for a message to the youth of the world, as well as those not so young. Let us here and now put aside the man-made dogmas and doctrines of formalized religion which only serve to hide the truth and which, in many cases, lead to the rejection of scientific truth. Instead (as Teilhard believed we can do and as I most strongly believe it, too) let us go forward and persuade men that a synthesis between scientific truth and spiritual thinking is the only thing that can preserve our wonderful heritage: true religious belief of glorious art, wonderful music, and inspiring literature, of conceptual thought and sound reason. We stand today at a very important crossroads. Either man will, in a very short time, face inevitable self-destruction and, instead of another milestone in progress, we shall erect a tombstone to humanity; or, if we take the right turning now, if we insist on the things that reason tells us we must insist upon, we can erect another milestone—a milestone that will lead us and our children, and our grandchildren, and many generations to come, in the direction of another 20 million years of progress.

Christianity and the Change in Human Consciousness

Christopher F. Mooney, S.J.

As early as 1936 Pierre Teilhard de Chardin had concluded that something quite extraordinary was taking place in the human species. He wrote:

> We now have to accept it as proven that mankind has just entered into what is probably the most extensive period of transformation it has known since its birth. . . . Today something is happening to the whole structure of human consciousness: a fresh kind of life is beginning to appear.[1]

The Reverend Mr. Mooney, educated in the United States, England, and France, was chairman of the Theology Department at Fordham University prior to becoming President of Woodstock College. His Teilhardian writings were honored by the Catholic Press Association, and his *Teilhard de Chardin and the Mystery of Christ* won the National Catholic Book Award. He is a member of various theological and educational organizations, including The Society for the Scientific Study of Religion.

1 Pierre Teilhard de Chardin, *Science and Christ* (New York: Harper & Row, 1968), pp. 128–29.

Just recently Nobel Prize physicist Sir George Thompson, in his book *The Foreseeable Future,* said that to understand man's present experience we have to think in terms of an event such as the invention of agriculture in the neolithic age. One clear symptom of what is going on is that mass neurosis which Alvin Toffler has christened "future shock": an acute sense of stress and disorientation induced by the experience of too much change in too short a time. Man is being asked to adapt psychically to phenomena he does not yet understand, and his ability to do so is being taxed beyond healthy limits. Above all he experiences the fear that he is not going to adapt at all: the premature arrival of the future frightens him precisely because it is premature and he himself unprepared. Accustomed for centuries to measure change in terms of institutional development and economic growth, man is now being forced for the first time to evaluate his history in terms of what is going on inside him. For it is his consciousness, that most inclusive of interior realities, that is undergoing major displacement, and he is not at all sure whether this change is for the better or for the worse.

Now the main thrust in the work of Teilhard de Chardin, as is well known, is that this change is for the better. Far from being the result of a naïve optimism, this conviction of Teilhard arose from a very keen sense of the harsh realities of life and the risks of human freedom. The forces of counter culture moving toward fragmentation and dispersal were vivid realities for him. On the occasion of a friend's death he once exclaimed:

> What an absurd thing life is, looked at superficially. It is so absurd that you feel yourself thrown back upon a stubborn, desperate faith in the reality of spirit and its survival. Otherwise (if there were no such thing as spirit, I mean) we should have to be idiots not to call off the whole human effort.[2]

[2] Pierre Teilhard de Chardin, *Letters from a Traveller* (New York: Harper & Row, 1962) , p. 202.

His explanation of man's present experience, then, is a highly complex and nuanced one, intimately linked to the Christian message of universal love and the community of all men with the person of Jesus. Teilhard says quite explicitly that the ultimate grounds for man's hope in the future must be religious, since such grounds alone can provide the strong ethical drive to *act* in the present crisis, along with that assurance that one is being helped to transcend one's own frailty and limitation. For ethical conduct can no longer be concerned with merely keeping rules. It must involve a sense of responsibility for the whole material world, just as religion now directs itself not toward observances but toward that which makes any observance at all worthwhile, namely, man's ability to live in the world and before God in a fully human way. Hence the theme of this present paper is that in Teilhard's evolutionary system of thought the significance of Christianity for the present shift in human consciousness is that it offers hope to man that such change is in fact good, in both its inception and its outcome; and that it will indeed, if followed to its completion, succeed in making man more fully man.

I

Before we see what Teilhard has to contribute to the current sense of crisis, let us take a closer look at the crisis itself. Erik Erikson, characterizing it quite simply as one of identity, has written:

> The traditional sources of identity strength—economic, racial, national, religious, occupational—are all in the process of allying themselves with a new world-image in which the vision of an anticipated future and, in fact, of a future in a permanent state of planning will take over much of the power of tradition.[3]

[3] Erik H. Erikson, "Memorandum on Youth," in "Toward the Year 2000," *Daedalus* 96 (1967) : 864.

Erikson sees two principal ideological orientations basic to the formation of future identities, the technological and the humanist, and even the great politico-economic alternatives will, he believes, be subordinated to these. The cultural conditioning along technological and scientific lines has already been taking place for some time, according to Erikson, but is being opposed more and more by a humanist orientation, which insists that beyond the technological there is a much wider range of human values and possibilities now in danger of being lost. The technologists and the humanists seem to live in separate ecologies and almost to belong to different species: they oppose and repel each other; the acceptance of even part of one could result in an ideological slide in the other's whole cluster of images, aspirations, hopes, fears, and hates. Erikson sees this polarity to be most important in fostering a dynamic interplay between the technological and humanist identity, leading, he is convinced, to radically new modes of thought and daring innovations in both culture and society. But he makes a point of adding to this judgment an ominous condition: "provided we survive."[4]

This question of survival hovers in the background of most discussions of the present crisis, whether it be described as one of identity or otherwise. By and large what is behind the present student unrest is the growing fear that, in spite of what their elders say about progress, mankind has no future to look forward to at all. Psychiatrists have argued that there is serious psychoanalytic evidence for saying that people today are suffering from an unconscious despair lurking just under the surface of their lives; a despair arising on the one hand from fear of becoming an appendage to the machine, and on the other from the sense of having less and less to say about their own destiny.[5] Beneath the unrest of students,

---

[4] *Ibid.*, pp. 864–68.

[5] For example, Erich Fromm, *The Revolution of Hope* (New York: Harper & Row, 1968).

wrote Lewis Mumford only a few months ago, "is a deep and well-justified fear: that the next step in technological progress may bring about the annihilation of man. With good reason the young regard the atrocious methods of conducting American military operations in Vietnam not only as a threat against their own existence, but as an ominous prelude to the whole human future. . . . In their unconscious, the young are living in a post-catastrophic world, and their conduct is rational in terms of that world.[6] They see survival as problematic precisely because we do not seem able to control the technology we have created, and because the technological society we *thought* we were making is not being made at all.

Just now in France this despair of survival is being greatly fostered by a best seller entitled *Chance and Necessity,* written by Jacques Monod, winner of the 1965 Nobel Prize in medicine for his studies in genetics. His avowed task in the book is to sweep the slate clean of virtually all previous philosophies of life. He locates our present crisis in the fact that we are using the wealth of modern science to practice and teach systems of values which that very science has already destroyed at the roots. He wants to show, he says, that there is no harmony whatsoever between man and his world, and that man himself is a product of pure chance, a quite accidental mutation in the evolution of the universe. Like Albert Camus, who he admits influenced him greatly, Dr. Monod sees man faced with the utterly meaningless task of Sisyphus endlessly pushing his stone up the mountain only to have it roll back down again into the valley. Yet even though he believes with Camus that "the struggle towards the summit is itself enough to fill the heart of man," he wonders nonetheless whether man will actually continue this struggle in the future. "There is absolutely no doubt," he concludes, "that the risk of the race committing suicide is very great. In my opinion the future of mankind is going to be decided within the next two

---

6 Lewis Mumford, "The Megamachine," Part IV, *The New Yorker* (October 31, 1970), p. 81.

generations."[7] Completely alone in a fundamentally unreliable and hostile world-process, man must now choose whether to move forward or to stop.

While this analysis of Jacques Monod is admittedly a pessimistic extreme it nonetheless highlights the crossroads at which modern man finds himself, as well as the paradox of estrangement and participation that we encounter everywhere in society. Gibson Winter puts his finger on the nerve center of this divided consciousness when he remarks that it "arises from a sense of belonging together and yet thinking of ourselves as isolated individuals called upon to make our way by private initiative."[8] The tight web of interdependence created by technology thus tends to produce greater alienation and estrangement, since the desire to participate is not yet strong enough to accept the new social reality before us. "We are witnessing," continues Winter, "a communal movement of national and even global scope. The participating consciousness is accompanied by a profound search for a new sensibility," of which drugs and rock festivals are only symptoms.[9] The all-important question, however, is whether this humanizing tendency will triumph, whether participation will indeed emerge as the creative principle in converting the oppressive society into a liberated humanity. Charles Reich has underlined the same basic problem in his *Greening of America.* What he describes as "Consciousness III" is a vivid awareness on the part of youth that the human values of love, community, and interpersonal creativity are being smothered by a tendency to sacrifice the individual to collectivity, which is a characteristic of "Consciousness II." Totally absent from Reich, however, is any sense of that all-important third factor in our present crisis, namely, despair of survival.

It is interesting to compare the diagnosis we have been discussing with that made by Teilhard de Chardin over thirty years ago.

---

7 Cf. the interview published in the *New York Times,* March 15, 1971.
8 Gibson Winter, *Being Free* (New York: MacMillan, 1970), p. 22.
9 *Ibid.,* p. 94.

> O man of the twentieth century, how does it happen that you are waking up to horizons and are susceptible to fears that your forefathers never knew? . . . Here at this turning point where the future substitutes itself for the present . . . do our perplexities inevitably begin. Tomorrow? But who can guarantee us a tomorrow anyway? And without this assurance that tomorrow exists, can we really go on living, we to whom has been given the terrible gift of foresight? Sickness of the dead end. . . . This time we have at last put our finger on the tender spot.[10]

It is this tender spot, namely, the growing suspicion that he has nowhere to go in the universe, which is causing modern man to ask whether or not he has been duped by life. An animal may rush headlong down a blind alley or toward a precipice, but man, precisely because he can *reflect* upon his condition, will no longer continue to take steps in a direction he knows to be blocked. In spite of his control of material energy, in spite of the pressures of immediate needs and desires, without a taste for life mankind will simply stop inventing and constructing. The human species, in other words, is quite capable of going on strike. Indeed, if will surely do so unless, as Teilhard says, "we should be assured the space and the chances to fulfill ourselves, that is to say, to progress till we arrive (directly or indirectly, individually or collectively) at the utmost limits of ourselves."[11]

It is here, however, that we face the crucial question. Where is such an assurance to come from? How shall we be liberated from the fear that the struggle between individual and collectivity, between personal and technological, is a hopeless one that will destroy us? Teilhard's answer is that assurance must come first of all from man himself, from his own experience of being part of an evolutionary movement that has come from pre-life to life, and then to man himself.

---

10 Pierre Teilhard de Chardin, *The Phenomenon of Man,* (New York: Harper & Row, 1965), pp. 228–29. Quoted by permission of Harper & Row, Publishers, Inc.

11 *Ibid.,* p. 231.

> To bring us into existence it has from the beginning juggled with too many improbabilities for there to be any risk whatever in committing ourselves further and following it right to the end. Life, by its very structure, having once been lifted to its stage of thought, cannot go on at all without ascending higher.[12]

But Teilhard always believed that man needed and indeed sought assurance on a much deeper level than his experience of the world around him. This is the level of his religious experience, his awareness of a divine presence and initiative in this world. For Teilhard, this divine presence was concretized in the Person of Jesus Christ to such an extent that he could say: "Christ comes to modern man . . . not only to save him from legitimate revolt against a life with the least threat or suspicion of total death, but also to bring him the greatest possible stimulus, without which living thought on our planet could surely never reach its destiny.[13] With this background, let us examine in turn the two assurances of Teilhard: the one from man, the other from Christ.

II

Teilhard's whole system of thought can be characterized, I think, as an effort to explain to contemporary man that what is happening to him in the twentieth century is first of all intelligible, and second, capable of success. The intelligibility that Teilhard proposes depends, of course, upon his understanding of evolution, which he saw to be not simply change but directional change; not simply development, but development with a purpose. Hence his description of the process as "genesis," from the French word *genèse,* which can be applied to any form of production involving successive stages and oriented toward some goal. In the case of evolution, or "cosmogenesis," this goal is man. Far from being an exception

12 *Ibid.,* p. 233.
13 Pierre Teilhard de Chardin, *Le Christique* (unpublished essay), 1955.

to biological evolution, man is in reality the key to the entire process, since the phenomenon of thought, or reflective consciousness, comes at the end of a progressive interiorization of matter over millions of years and represents "a mutation from zero to everything."[14] From now on the evolutionary process continues its development not so much in the sphere of life, as in the sphere of mind and spirit, the "noosphere." This particular type of genesis is best described not as "cosmogenesis" but as "noogenesis." Thus, "the social phenomenon is the culmination and not the attenuation of the biological phenomenon."[15]

It is at this point, however, that Teilhard makes a most unusual analysis of that directional change in human history called noogenesis. Let us imagine, he says (using the geometrical image of meridians on a globe), that a pulsation enters a sphere at its south pole and spreads out inside the sphere in the direction of the north pole. The movement of this wave is a converging movement from the start, since it is on a curved surface, but it has two very different phases: one of expansion from the south pole to the equator, the other of contraction from the equator to the north pole. Now, no better image illustrates the crisis of growth through which mankind is passing at this very moment. In the first millions of years of its existence it has been expanding more or less freely, slowly covering more and more of the uninhabited earth. The result of this lack of pressure was that, century after century, the socializing process was extremely slow. There was a gradual branching out into the various races; civilizations were able to grow and rub shoulders on a sparsely inhabited planet without encountering any major difficulty. Teilhard writes:

> But now, following the dramatic growth of industry, communications and populations in the course of a single century,

[14] Pierre Teilhard de Chardin, *The Phenomenon of Man,* p. 171.
[15] *Ibid.,* p. 223.

we can discern the outline of a formidable event. The hitherto scattered fragments of humanity being at length brought into close contact, are beginning to interpenetrate to the point of reacting economically and psychically upon each other.[16]

Given the fundamental relationship between geographic compression and the heightening of consciousness, the result is an irresistible rise within us and around us of the level of reflection.

In other words, what we have been experiencing for some time now, without being aware of it, is in reality the beginning of the second phase of noogenesis, the phase of contraction. In our own time mankind has crossed the equatorial point and entered into a new stage in the development of the species. In 1950 Teilhard wrote:

> From the first beginnings of history this principle of the compressive generation of consciousness has been ceaselessly at work in the human mass. But from the moment—we have just reached it!—when the compression of populations in the teeming continents gains a decided ascendency over their movement of expansion upon the earth's surface, the process is speeded up to a staggering extent. We are today witnessing a truly explosive growth of technology and research, bringing an increasing mastery, both theoretical and practical, of the secrets and sources of cosmic energy at every level and in every form; and, correlative with this, the rapid heightening of what I have called the psychic temperature of the earth. A single glance at the overall picture of surface chaos is enough to assure us that this is so.[17]

Teilhard, however, was not only concerned to explain modern man's anxiety and so make it intelligible; he also wanted to assuage it, by showing man that what was taking place in and through his developing consciousness was in-

---

16 Pierre Teilhard de Chardin, *The Future of Man* (New York: Harper & Row, 1964), p. 294. Quoted by permission of Harper & Row, Publishers, Inc.

17 *Ibid.*, pp. 275–76.

deed capable of success. This he does, first of all, by locating today's existential fear in man's sudden realization that he is now in control of the evolutionary process. Through him evolution has not only become conscious of itself but free to dispose itself. Until the mid-twentieth century the vast majority of men were like passengers closed up in the hold of a ship, distracting themselves like the men in Plato's Cave. As more and more of them climbed up to the bridge, however, they gradually became aware not only of the drift of the universe, but also of the risks and dangers in guiding the ship. To use Teilhard's phrase, the task before them now is "to seize the tiller of the world," to take hold of the energies by which man has reached his present position and use them to move ahead.[18] This is a fearful task, however, and to counteract his awesome power to refuse it, man must cultivate his moral sense of obligation to life. If he does not, then he faces both ecological disaster and nuclear destruction. Thus the fundamental law of morality for Teilhard is to liberate that conscious energy which seeks to further unify the world. This energy is what he calls "the zest for life," that disposition of mind and heart that savors the experience of life, and manifests itself particularly in the relish a man has for creative tasks undertaken from a sense of duty.

> Such a man would see the greatness of his responsibilities increasing almost to infinity before him. Hitherto he could think of himself in nature as a bird of passage, local, accidental, free to waste the spark of life that is given him, with no loss to anyone but himself. Suddenly he finds in his heart the fearful task of conserving, increasing and transmitting the fortunes of a whole world. His life, in a true sense, has ceased to be private to him. Body and soul, he is the product of a huge creative work with which the totality of things has collaborated from the beginning; if he refuses the task assigned to him, some part of that effort will be lost forever and lacking throughout the whole future. . . . For the briefest moment the success of the

[18] Pierre Teilhard de Chardin, *The Activation of Energy* (New York: Harcourt Brace Jovanovitch, 1971), pp. 73–74.

whole affair, of this huge universal childbirth actually rests in the hands of the least among us.[19]

This effort of Teilhard to show that what is taking place in man is indeed capable of success, had to deal eventually with a fear much stronger than the fear of freedom: the fear of collectivity. For nothing is more terrifying today than the spectre of the mechanized, impersonal world of George Orwell's *1984,* spawned by a vast technological complex that is blind to the needs and values of individual men. Yet, when man looks into the future what he sees is precisely this social destiny, a destiny quite capable of stifling his personality rather than developing it. In Teilhard's mind this is the reason for the world's present discouragement with the whole human aspiration toward unity. Up to now every gigantic effort to unify men seems to have ended by stifling the human person. What men forget, however, says Teilhard, is that, monstrous though it is, modern totalitarianism is really a distortion of something magnificent, namely, a unifying energy based not upon coercion or fear but upon love. Love is the only energy in the world that is capable of personalizing by totalizing, of promoting synthesis without destroying personality. It alone unites human beings in such a way as to complete and fulfill them. And the reason is that "in any domain—whether it be the cells of a body, the members of a society or the elements of a spiritual synthesis—*union differentiates.* In every organized whole the parts perfect themselves and fulfill themselves."[20] This familiar evolutionary pattern of differentiating union is thus applied by Teilhard to the personalizing union of beings who relate to each other as persons. In this way "the grains of consciousness do not tend

[19] Pierre Teilhard de Chardin, *The Vision of the Past* (New York: Harper & Row, 1967), p. 137. I am indebted here to the work of Francis X. Winters, whose doctoral dissertation, *Teilhard de Chardin's Morality of Movement,* was recently defended at Fordham University.

[20] Pierre Teilhard de Chardin, *The Phenomenon of Man,* p. 262. Cf. the more thorough development of this idea in Christopher F. Mooney, *Teilhard de Chardin and the Mystery of Christ* (New York: Harper & Row, 1966), pp. 46–55.

to lose their outlines and blend, but, and the contrary, to accentuate the depth and incommunicability of their *egos.* The more 'other' they become in conjunction, the more they find themselves as 'self.' "[21]

Hence the importance of the concept of "amorization" in Teilhard's work, which is the gradual release of the power of love, the response of truly free men to increased social pressure. It is only love that can turn increasing socialization from a threat to a promise. Men need not fear the contemporary drift toward unity as long as they can freely relate to each other through what is most intimate to themselves. This fostering of freedom through love is what will counteract necessity in technological expansion, so that man will not be forced to actualize a technological achievement simply because he *can* do so. The question of whether he *should* do so must be asked, and it must be asked in the context of the primacy of the person and the need for mechanisms to manage change in ways more humane than those so far in use. Consequently, through amorization, or the growth of love, man copes with his tendency to turn in upon himself in isolation and to allow his world to become more and more mechanized and impersonal. As Teilhard said:

> Considered in its full biological reality love—that is to say the affinity of being with being—is not peculiar to man. . . . If there were no internal propensity to unite, even at a prodigiously elementary level—indeed in the molecule itself—it would be physically impossible for love to appear higher up, with us, in "hominized" form. . . . Love in all its subtleties is nothing more, and nothing less, than the more or less direct trace marked on the heart of the element by the psychical convergence of the universe upon itself.[22]

III

The question I have been asking in this paper is how modern man can be liberated from the fear that the present

[21] *Ibid.,* p. 262.
[22] *Ibid.,* pp. 264–65.

struggle between individual and collectivity is a hopeless one that will eventually destroy him. I have so far discussed the answer that Teilhard de Chardin found in man himself, namely, that the present crisis of consciousness is a turning point in the whole evolutionary process, whose movement toward greater socialization can be successfully personalized by the free and conscious release of love energy. Teilhard was the first to admit that this analysis of man's chances of success was based upon an act of faith. Neither on the side of pessimism nor on the side of optimism, he wrote, "is there any tangible evidence to produce. Only, in support of hope, there are rational invitations to an act of faith."[23] Teilhard was well aware, moreover, that these rational invitations, however strong, were not enough either for him or for his fellow man. For such a faith would always remain fragile and insecure, and what Teilhard sought above all was an assurance that would be grounded upon some absolute. Hence his eagerness to give to the contemporary change in consciousness a religious dimension. In particular he points to the meaning that Christianity, and Christianity alone, gives to the two phenomena most involved in the change, namely, that of death and that of love.

"The radical defect of all forms of belief in progress," he once wrote, "is that they do not definitely eliminate death. What is the use of detecting a focus of any sort in the van of evolution if that focus can and must one day disintegrate?"[24] It is psychologically impossible, Teilhard believed, for man to take part very long in the struggle of life unless the best of his achievements is preserved from total destruction. For a primary attribute of human consciousness today is precisely the will to survive. Applied to the individual, the idea of total extinction may not at first sight appall us; but extended to humanity as a whole it revolts and sickens us. The fact is that the more humanity becomes aware of its duration and

[23] *Ibid.,* p. 233.
[24] *Ibid.,* p. 270.

the enormous burden it must bear in order to survive, the more does it realize that if all this labor is to end in nothing, then we have been cheated and can only rebel. The new consciousness must therefore face the need of assurance in regard to some ultimate conquest of death. Can it really accept a total death, an unscalable wall, on which it would crash and then forever disappear? And can this really be reconciled with the mechanism of reflection without that mechanism breaking its mainspring? It is here, Teilhard concludes, "in its proper place in terms of science, that we come to the problem of God."[25]

More specifically, we come to the Christian phenomenon and to the message it proclaims to the world that the true meaning of death is the passage to new life in and through Christ.

> We shall find the Christian faith absolutely explicit in what it affirms and practices. Christ has conquered death not only by suppressing its evil effects but by reversing its sting. Through the power of the resurrection nothing any longer kills inevitably. . . . The great victory of the Creator and Redeemer, in the Christian vision, is to have transformed what is itself a universal power of diminishment and extinction into an essentially life-giving factor.[26]

This transformation, moreover, takes place precisely in and through matter. This is what Teilhard means when he speaks of the "hominization of death." Just as a current causes a ship to deviate from its course, so the cosmic influence of Christ is responsible for the general "drift" of matter toward spirit. The positive meaning of the Christian doctrine of redemption is, according to Teilhard, the support given by Christ's suffering, death, and resurrection to the upward movement of man in the noosphere. Christ gives this support because, through his Incarnation, he has achieved in his own Body-

---

25 Teilhard de Chardin, *The Future of Man,* pp. 180–81.

26 Pierre Teilhard de Chardin, *The Divine Milieu* (New York: Harper & Row, 1960), pp. 54 and 61.

Person the purpose of the whole evolutionary process: the union of humanity with God in and through a purification of matter. The world is therefore above all a work of creation continued in Christ. And Christ saves the world in the sense that, without him, man's effort would be without ultimate hope of success, and this would mean that man would inevitably lose his taste for life and abandon altogether his task on earth.[27]

The significance for modern consciousness of Christian hope in the victory of life over death naturally leads Teilhard to underline the relationship of faith in the risen Christ to the phenomenon of human love. It is of capital importance, he writes:

> on an appreciable region of the earth there has appeared and grown a zone of thought in which a genuine universal love has not only been conceived and preached, but has also been shown to be psychologically possible and operative in practice. It is all the more capital in as much as, far from decreasing, the movement seems to wish to gain still greater speed and intensity.[28]

The historian of religion who measures the movement of Christianity not by quantitative expansion but by the qualitative evolution of an act of love, immediately finds himself tracing the curve of a true progress. For since the time of Christ, the theory and practice of total love have never ceased to become more precise and to be transmitted in ever-wider circles. "The result is that, after a spiritual experience of two thousand years, our capacity for union with the personal Center of the universe has grown as much in the richness of its power to express itself as has our capacity for union with the natural spheres of the world after two thousand years

[27] This last statement is the conclusion of a very lengthy theological analysis of the Incarnation within an evolutionary system of thought. Teilhard's position is given in Mooney, pp. 67–86.

[28] Teilhard de Chardin, *The Phenomenon of Man,* p. 296.

of science."[29] What modern man needs, according to Teilhard, is to find the source of a truly universal love, for only this will conquer his "dread of that frightful cosmic machinery in which he finds himself entangled." The enthusiasm engendered by naturalistic humanisms eventually becomes cold, joyless, and hard. Christianity alone can teach man "not only how to serve (which is not enough) but how to love deeply, in all its manifestations, . . . a universe whose very evolution has been impregnated with love."[30]

It should be noted at this point, however, that although Teilhard believed strongly in the power of Christ to activate the love energy of the world, he in no way minimized either the risk of human freedom or the frailty of human love. Indeed, it is because the risk is great and this frailty perennial that ambiguity will always characterize human progress. Essentially, says Teilhard, "progress is a force and the most dangerous of forces. . . . Progress is directed toward fostering in the human will reflective action and fully human choice."[31] Noogenesis is thus a movement endangered from within. For the collective growth it fosters in man's capacity for reflection, love, and global unity is precisely a growth in *capacity,* not in love itself. And with growth in the power to love comes also growth in the power to refuse love. The prospect must be faced that the universal love of Christ may ultimately give life and fulfillment to a fraction only of the noosphere. There may well be what Teilhard calls "an internal schism of consciousness," divided on two opposite ideals of evolution, and in this case the positive attraction of Christ would be exerted only upon the hearts of those who turn toward him. In any case, Teilhard says:

> There is not to be indefinite progress, which is an hypothesis contrary to the converging nature of noogenesis, but an ecstasy

29 Pierre Teilhard de Chardin, *Human Energy* (New York: Harcourt Brace Jovanovitch, 1971), pp. 157–58.
30 Pierre Teilhard de Chardin, *Réflexions sur le Bonheur* (Paris: Seuil, 1960), pp. 67–70.
31 Teilhard de Chardin, *The Future of Man,* pp. 19 and 21.

transcending the dimensions and framework of the visible universe. Ecstasy in concord or discord; but in either case by excess of interior tension: the only biological outcome proper to or conceivable for the phenomenon of man.[32]

IV

What I have attempted to do in this paper is to sketch in briefest outline the significance of Pierre Teilhard de Chardin for the change taking place today in the consciousness of man. Long before recent diagnoses, Teilhard located the crisis of change in a loss of nerve. For large numbers, the arrival of the future has been accelerated to an alarming degree; and growing technological control appears to be either an invitation to self-destruction or a headlong return to the regimentation of the anthill. Does man really have nowhere to go as man? Is life really so absurd that the values of the individual person, his desire for community, interpersonal creativity, and the preservation of the world of nature around him can no longer be fostered after so many centuries of growth? Teilhard insists that all this fear of survival is at its root a fear of total death for the species, and that if there is no assurance of life to be had, then the human enterprise is surely pointless and what happens to us totally irrelevant. But an assurance of life *does* exist, and it resides in the enormous capacity of human love to bring individuals, and indeed the whole species, closer and closer together in more complex social structures without injuring what is most personal and intimate. For love fosters freedom and expansion, not repression or diminishment. Human love, however, in spite of its capacity to unite without depersonalizing, cannot motivate mankind without a further assurance; for each man is aware of the frailty of his own love. Some divine power must strengthen human love and support human freedom or the ultimate success of noogenesis will forever remain doubtful and insecure. As a Christian, Teilhard saw this ultimate

---

[32] Teilhard de Chardin, *The Phenomenon of Man,* pp. 288–89.

source of love in the Person of Christ, who, by his Incarnation, death, and resurrection, has conquered man's native tendency toward repulsion and isolation. Ultimately what God has done in Christ brings assurance to man that his creativity is a participation in God's creativity and that the outcome will therefore be on the side of life and not of death.

Nevertheless, we must recognize that this hope of Teilhard was not vision. In Christianity he saw rational invitations to an act of faith in the future. His whole life was an affirmation of that faith in spite of the discouragement he felt at the obvious failures and stupidity of man. "It is a terrifying thing to have been born," he wrote once. "I mean to find oneself, without having willed it, swept irrevocably along a torrent of fearful energy which seems as though it wished to destroy everything it carries with it."[33] The terror experienced by men today as they take responsibility for the future was a terror experienced by Teilhard himself. Through Christ, however, he saw that a new impulse of hope was possible and was now beginning to take shape in human consciousness. This hope was that the time-space totality of evolution would be immortalized and personalized in Christ to the extent that it would become lovable. Hence he could say in prayer: "What I want, my God, is that by a reversal of forces which you alone can bring about, my terror in the face of nameless changes of renewal may be turned into an overflowing joy at being transformed into you."[34] Like all men whose hope is strong, Teilhard cherished every sign of new life and was ready at any moment to help the birth of that which is ready to be born. Yet he was a man who hoped in the midst of doubt, doubt which, like the sufferings of men, he recognized as the price and condition for the perfection of the universe. And under these conditions, he was content to walk right to the end along a road of which he was more and more certain, toward a horizon more and more shrouded in mist.

---

33 Pierre Teilhard de Chardin, *Hymn of the Universe* (New York: Harper & Row, 1965), p. 29.

34 *Ibid.*, p. 29.

Panel Discussion

Moderator:

Mrs. Allan E. Charles — Vice President, Board of Trustees, Stanford University

Panel Members:

Conor Cruise O'Brien
Joseph L. Alioto
N. Max Wildiers
George Gaylord Simpson
Theodosius Dobzhansky
Bernard Towers
L. S. B. Leakey
Christopher F. Mooney

MRS. CHARLES: I would like to say before I begin to moderate this gentlemanly, I hope, panel, that I am as astonished to be here as some of you may be to see me in this scholarly company. The only excuse I can give is that perhaps I may represent something of what others feel in contemplating this great man, Pierre Teilhard de Chardin. That is, simply, that I feel he is a personal friend of mine. I discovered him for myself many years ago in the library and have had the great joy of having him speak to me from the pages of his books. In the best of the translations there are a warmth and a humanity that come to you when you read him that do make you feel that he is your friend; that he is helping you to resolve in a positive way some of the confusions that we face in this modern world; that his conception of the convergence of men's minds can make us believe that there is a way that this can all be resolved. I only hope that our panelists today haven't succeeded in making it so much more complex that we are not going to be able to understand it again.

I am going to have to give some ground rules to these gentlemen. And before I do, I thought I might tell a story about a friend of mine, a little girl, who was recounting having raced her brother to a fence. She said, "He got there ahead of me, but I pulled him back and I kicked him in the stomach and I said, 'Ladies first, damn it.' "

I have been told that we are going to give each speaker here two minutes for himself and then we are going to start on our questions.

As Dr. Conor Cruise O'Brien was the dinner speaker last night, which occasion not all of you were able to attend, he will be given the rare privilege of having three minutes in order to make a statement to us.

DR. O'BRIEN: It's unnerving to be conceded such a privilege in such company. And it makes me lean to the hypothesis that the universe is governed by blind chance.

I want in the few minutes I have just to say something about that debate, because it has been underlying most of the very intellectually exciting discussion we have been having here. That is: the collision between the idea that the universe is governed by chance and the idea that it is governed by purpose, to each of which terms we attach epithets—*blind* chance, *divine* purpose—which make it even more Manichean than it would otherwise be.

Frankly, I think this is to some extent a false debate in

that it's more a clash of temperaments than of actual evidence. I don't see how any of us can have the degree of certitude that some of us proclaim, either that the universe is governed by chance or by purpose. We have only been around for, at the very most, as Dr. Leakey has said, twenty million years, and a lot of that in a pretty poor shape.

Now chance and purpose are human words in our human vocabulary, and I don't see that we can stamp the seal of these words on the universe with quite so much authority as we seem to do. In fact I think the wisest thing for us to do in this matter would be to wait another five million years or so until we are in a position to make up our minds on the basis of more evidence and the better development of our minds. But, of course, we are not going to do that—obviously. We are not the kind of animal that does wait around in that way. We are going to make affirmations in the meantime.

And I think the affirmations do to a great extent depend on temperament. There is the temperament, there is the kind of person, who cannot live without hope, without a sense of there being a purpose in the universe, and who must cleave to that hypothesis, who must live with that. There is the kind of man to whom that idea of hope and purpose, unverified at present, seems to be mere quackery, something that he feels he must have the stoicism to resist as part of his intellectual integrity. And I think those two families of spirits must be allowed to coexist and to coexist with a third family of spirits, which will keep the two hypotheses in suspense in its head.

Now Teilhard obviously chose one hypothesis, and we know what it was. But I think that his great merit has been in cooling the old rather bullying clash between the men of science and the churchmen. Men of science are supposed to be humble before the facts. Churchmen are supposed to be humble before God. But neither class seems to be humble before anything else—with certain great exceptions, of whom, of course, Teilhard was one. And I think it is the humility of the spirit and the compassion that comes through his work that are perhaps more effective than any single thing he wrote.

And we have been reminded here by many who knew him that his work as we have it shouldn't be taken as in its final state. It's rather his spirit that is working here among us.

I hope I haven't overrun the three minutes. Thank you.

MRS. CHARLES: Perfect. Thank you very much.

Ladies and gentlemen, I am now going to call on each of the speakers of today for a brief comment. And I will take them in the order in which they have spoken to us, which means that I will next call on our Mayor, Joseph Alioto.

I want to say just a word, Mayor Alioto, of my appreciation as a citizen of San Francisco (and I am sure many others) that you have been very instrumental in bringing to us this tremendous intellectual and spiritual exercise. Thank you.

MAYOR ALIOTO: Thank you very much. I would like to say that I hope it will not all end after this two-day intellectual feast, but rather that it will be the beginning of three things. First of all, I hope that this can be the beginning of a wider distribution of the ideas of the eminent French Jesuit; second, that it will be the focal point around which we might organize a Teilhard Society in Northern California; and finally, that that society might be the instrument by which we might start a continuing dialogue, or a forum for a continuing dialogue, between those who believe that they are in total and continuous opposition. Syntheses can be worked out to accommodate the views of those of us who think we are in serious contention. This does not mean that anybody would have to give up his serious convictions. That should not be required of anyone. But I do suggest that things we thought were totally contentious twenty-five years ago, for example, have somehow smoothed out and we can see now that there is a way of accommodating several viewpoints within a framework of integrity. I would hope that this symposium would be the beginning of dialogue to seek the synthesis of many such conflicting viewpoints.

MRS. CHARLES: Thank you.

Now, Dr. Wildiers, would you say a word to us?

DR. WILDIERS: Well, I would only stress an idea expressed already at the beginning of Dr. Leakey's speech when he said that we should always remember that Teilhard never ever proposed a closed and finished system, but that he always changed his ideas, in the sense that he tried to progress beyond the viewpoints he once discovered, and that he was absolutely opposed to any kind of systematization of his teaching. So I think we must always keep in mind that we have before us a living spirit who is always going ahead, knowing that he still had a very long way to go. Several times he specifically expressed the hope that the hypothesis he proposed on the meaning of man in the evolutionary process would become the subject of further research and study.

MRS. CHARLES: Thank you. Dr. Simpson?

DR. SIMPSON: Yes. In a meeting like this the other speakers always raise questions that one wants to discuss or to object to, and in two minutes one has to take some at random.

One point is that there's been a great deal of either/or sort of talk. And I think that one can raise objections to that. Dr. O'Brien did raise objections to the chance-purpose either/or. I would also raise objections to the either/or question about man as an exception to evolution or the key to evolution. Of course, he's neither one. He's an *example* of evolution.

In addition to that I would simply say that we also have been told, or it's been suggested, that we should not attempt to discuss or criticize on the basis of what Teilhard did or said while he was alive, but of what he would believe and say if he were alive now. So my final word would be: If he were alive now, he would agree completely with me.

MRS. CHARLES: Thank you, Dr. Simpson.

Dr. Dobzhansky, I trust you are not going to agree with Dr. Simpson?

DR. DOBZHANSKY: I want to comment about the dichotomy of chance and purpose. I believe this is a false dichotomy. Purpose in evolution would mean that somebody has predetermined how evolution will take place. If this were so, evolution would be a rather uninteresting process; nothing really new could arise in the world. Everything would be predetermined. You would just have to wait five million, or whatever number of millions of years until it appears. Chance is also not a good word; to say that man appeared by chance, or that any other organism happened by chance, is to say precisely nothing.

Here is a real problem, a problem I believe we need the help of philosophers who would work out, if you please, a synthesis of "chance" and "purpose." Evolution is a creative process. And this creative process is not all cut and dried. It really produces novelties, and one such novelty is man.

MRS. CHARLES: Thank you very much, Dr. Dobzhansky.

Dr. Leakey?

DR. LEAKEY: I only want to add one thing to what I said earlier and that is that I most sincerely believe that the so-called conflict between science and religion is not a real thing. On the one hand, religion or religions have added many things that are not essential to them—not true faith and not true belief. On the other hand, many scientists have added to and augmented what is fundamentally true science and proclaimed these additions to be truths, also.

But I don't believe that there is any real conflict between truth and truth; and I believe that we could and we must begin much more definitively to try to get at the *basic* truths of science and religion and cut away all the verbiage and all the things that disturb us and create such conflicts in the minds of believers in each group.

MRS. CHARLES: Thank you, Dr. Leakey.

Dr. Towers?

DR. TOWERS: Thank you, Madam Chairman.

I would just like to say how very interesting I find it that this conference, like others that have been organized over the last five years by the Teilhard Association in London, is proving to be an example of the way in which Teilhard believed that man, at the psychosocial stage of evolution, *should* be conducting his affairs. That is, by discussion of sharply divergent points of view.

A principal hypothesis of Teilhard's was that "union differentiates." It's only when you get a sharp differentiation of opinion that you finally see your way through to any kind of true synthesis. The collective movement is not one that will obliterate differences, but one that heightens and sharpens them, so that we can hope for a really good ongoing debate. This is what seems to be emerging in this discussion today.

At our conferences in London, we have dealt with topics like Marxism and Christianity and China and the West: Mankind Evolving. It turned out that there would often be members of the audience who would say, "but what has this got to do with Teilhard? We came here to learn about Teilhard." On one occasion when I was chairman and this objection was raised from the floor, my reply was that in organizing conferences of this sort, we are not at all concerned with promulgating "messages" from Teilhard. What we are really trying to do is to stimulate the kind of conversation, discussion, or debate in which Teilhard himself would have enjoyed taking part.

This, it seems to me, is what is happening at this conference. I am very glad to see it.

MRS. CHARLES: Thank you. And Dr. Mooney.

DR. MOONEY: In the context of our discussions so far degarding whether or not life has a purpose and whether or not we can know whether life has a purpose, I would agree with the remarks of Dr. O'Brien: that temperament plays a very large place in how a person feels in this regard. But what I would like to underline is that the problem is not with those who are convinced that life has a purpose or with those who are convinced that life has no purpose, because neither group ends up being afraid. It's the people who don't know, the people who really don't know, whether life has a purpose or not, or whether they can get up tomorrow morning to face life; it is with these people who experience fear that the problem lies.

I would say that if there is a single influence that Teilhard has had, or single key to the influence that he exerts on men's lives today, it is his affirmation in the fact of all the evidence of science and all the evidence of human progress, as well as the type of dangers that human progress faces, that life does have a purpose. All of us, to some extent at least, are looking for assurance in some form or other, and to the extent that Teilhard touches the nerve center of our own desire for assurances, he exerts a magnetism upon us that is manifested in our conference these days.

MRS. CHARLES: Thank you.

Now we are going to proceed to the questions. I am going to address this first question to Dr. O'Brien. It is: "With regard to the classic type of individual and the romantic, each opposing the other in their way of viewing the world, I would like to know how there can be a convergence to Point Omega and a world without conflict as long as these two polarities exist?"

DR. O'BRIEN: In the Teilhardian idea of progress, as far as I understand it, there isn't an idea of ironing out these differences of temperament, outlook, manner, which are precious to us as human beings—in the classic and romantic difference, for example, which is rather hard to analyze. Whatever else it has done, these are two poles of the enrichment of our literature, these express bunches of tendencies in literature and in man's mind. And there shouldn't be any need to try to move toward their elimination in whatever kind of progress we may have. I would be inclined to regard the tendencies of that kind, or clumps of that kind, as part of the system of antennae that we have as human beings for understanding ourselves and understanding and expressing the world around us—and for playing, too.

MRS. CHARLES: Thank you.

Dr. Simpson, there were several questions in this same vein, all asking what was Teilhard's reaction to your criticisms. What *were* his answers to your pointing out such non sequiturs as you mentioned to us today?

DR. SIMPSON: This is, of course, a rather difficult question. The conversations went on over years and on many occasions each conversation went on over hours. On the whole, he would be slightly dismayed that I didn't immediately agree with him. He would, however, feel that this was rather irrelevant and also he would shift the conversation up to a different level. I won't say he would be evasive, but, rather, forgetful of the level at which it started: the level of observation of fossils, for example. He would almost immediately shift the conversation so that we were talking about the soul and about God and so forth, things that he knows or that he knew a great deal about and that I never knew anything about, so that he thus succeeded in putting me at a disadvantage. If I am making him sound a bit Machiavellian, I should add that he wasn't. He didn't do this to put me at a disadvantage. He did it simply because that was the way his mind worked.

He was a very loving sort of person and he reciprocated a feeling that he aroused in everyone who knew him, a very friendly, pleasant sort of person. He was a bit arrogant about just one thing, and that was the idea of Omega and his personal theological point of view.

MRS. CHARLES: Thank you. I sometimes think that the most innocent people are the most Machiavellian, don't you?

DR. SIMPSON: Yes, I think in effect it turns out that way.

DR. O'BRIEN: You don't just think that. You know it, ma'am.

MRS. CHARLES: Thank you. Yes, that's right. That's my opinion.

Now I have a question that is addressed to both Dr. Leakey and Dr. Towers. It seems to me that it might come from some of the young people in our audience. There were several questions along these lines, too.

"You speak of the need for change and relate it to problems

such as atomic and biological and chemical warfare and pollution. And you call on young people to make the change. How?"

DR. LEAKEY: First and foremost, I believe that the change can only be made by building a proper overall world opinion against these evil forces. At the moment we have far too much laissez-faire. Far too many people say, "Well, it's not for me to do. Let somebody else do it."

If every single person who has heard this discussion today believed and convinced others to believe, then public opinion could be snowballed to a point where no politician would dare to go on with that atomic warfare or the germ warfare or anything else along these lines. It is the building up of public opinion of a very, very high order and as a very strong force that I believe must be done and done immediately.

DR. TOWERS: Yes, it seems to me that, through the advances in scientific technology in the last twenty or thirty years, we really have the possibility now of a participating democracy, as it were, on a worldwide scale. It was put in a way that I found very striking by Robert Jungk, the futurologist; he said that in his discussions with students in countries all over the world he had come to realize that for young people today there is no such thing as "foreign policy" as distinct from "domestic policy." Such a concept is meaningless to them. You can no longer think of domestic policy in terms of your own country and foreign policy as your relationship with other countries because we are all living together on this small "spaceship earth" (as Bucky Fuller puts it) with limited living room. We simply have to learn to get along with one another.

When you have been through the experience (as youngsters today go through the experience) of watching television and seeing things happen all over the globe—in a way that people of my age never did as children; when you actually *see* global things happening here and now; or when you have actually seen the earth encircled within the camera lens of the astronauts and you know that here are people who have been on the moon talking now about coming "home," not home to Houston, Texas, but home to *earth,* then suddenly your concept changes. I think this is happening to young people today. I think all one can say to you is to have confidence in yourselves; have confidence in the future. If you will only *engáge* and articulate your feelings! I say your "feelings" almost more than your intellectual analyses, because it's what happens at the feeling level that finally gets done. It's what happens at the feeling level that politicians finally take notice of. If only you will express what you *feel* about these things, then I think there will be some hope for the future.

The one thought that dismays me about the future is the possibility that many young people will opt out. It is the opting out which I am afraid of. If they will only opt in, then I am happy.

MRS. CHARLES: Thank you.

MAYOR ALIOTO: Mrs. Charles, I would just like to express the viewpoint of one who's been on the firing line. I find it a little strange that the young should ask any of us on this panel how they might get attention for their ideas. I think their own devices have been quite inventive.

MRS. CHARLES: Is there any other comment of the panel to this question?

DR. O'BRIEN: I would like to say something quickly here. I think a turning point, an axis, in all this is the Vietnam war. That is to say that the American withdrawal from the Vietnam war, if it is obtained, will be a major turning point in history. (applause)

I am very glad that you feel that. I think this is tremendously important because this could be a tidemark in the use of the wealth of the advanced world. If the young people of this country say, as they have said—and many of the middle-aged say, too—"No," to this war; "No, this use of our resources must end here," then if the war is ended, there can be the beginning of the use of these resources in a more positive way. This could be one of the great turning points of history.

DR. SIMPSON: Just ten seconds. I would say that if this does not happen, there will be another turning point that will be absolutely fatal.

DR. O'BRIEN: Yes.

MRS. CHARLES: Dr. Dobzhansky, this question is addressed to you.

"If you say that man was an accidental, not a necessary, product of evolution, how do you determine that evolution is directed toward an Omega and that the Omega is Christ?"

DR. DOBZHANSKY: In the first place, I said nothing of the kind. In the second place, in my two minutes at the beginning of this panel, I tried to point out that the categories of necessity versus accident, and predetermination versus creation are false dichotomies. We need a concept, possibly a new concept, whereby evolution will be recognized as a creative process, as a creative process producing real novelties. Teilhard developed his concept of Omega by extrapolation of the course of evolution observed to date: by extrapolation in the light of his faith rather than of his scientific knowledge. Omega is an extrapolation from his faith, not an extrapolation from his biology.

MRS. CHARLES: Thank you.

Dr. Wildiers, "If Teilhard is only valid philosophically or religiously, does it therefore follow that man can only evolve through philosophy or religion?"

DR. WILDIERS: I can agree neither with the assumption made in this question, nor with the suggested conclusion. I think, first of all, that Teilhard's views are valid scientifically in many questions, and especially in the question of man's place in nature. The validity of his scientific work has been acknowledged by many outstanding scientists: Sir Julian Huxley, Jean Piveteau, von Koenigswald, de Terra, George G. Barbour, and many others.

As far as the further evolution of man is concerned, this

will, of course, involve many aspects, biological as well as cultural. The whole of human activity in *all* fields—science, technology, politics, arts, as well as philosophy and religion—is a part of the spiritual evolution of mankind.

MRS. CHARLES: Thank you.

Here's a question for our Mayor. "The Mayor has applied Teilhard's evolutionary concepts to politics by suggesting that each subculture within the city must reach fruition on its own before there can be a true community in the larger sense. Yet as a politician he must be aware that each subculture expects to develop fully only at the expense of some other subculture of the establishment. Does the Mayor consider small revolutionary actions to be part of a larger progression of evolutionary processes?"

MAYOR ALIOTO: Well, I guess what we are really talking about is a definition of revolution, and definitions do change in different generations, depending on changing social conditions. The American Constitution is one of the great documentations of this evolution of ideas. Exactly the same words have been interpreted differently as the philosophical and social atmosphere has changed in succeeding generations. In this context, consider the First and Fourteenth Amendments to the Constitution, which give us the right of dissent. I think we have demonstrated over a long period of time that we can bring about substantial change in our constitutional principles and in our society by reason of dissent. I think dissent in American life is the raw material of progress. And I don't think it is necessary to resort to violence.

Now the blunt fact of the matter is that we have always had violence in American life. It is not a new phenomenon. Some of you who would read, for example, the history of women's suffrage will see that the very prim Victorian-looking ladies were not above bombing and setting fires in downtown London and downtown New York. Take the most conservative elements in our society right now, who are supposed to be the farmers. It was only in this generation that there were sheriffs on the one side and farmers on the other side, and they both had guns and they both used them. And there was a good deal of violence in the history of the struggle of our labor unions to achieve the rights of collective bargaining, or to achieve certain recognitions and constitutional protection for those recognitions. But I think we have learned from that violence.

I believe in strong dissent with full opportunity for dissent, and everybody ought to encourage it. We ought to encourage the expression of ideas that we regard as despicable, because in another generation, in another time, in a different social setting, they might not be quite that despicable.

If the question is: "Do I believe in violent revolution by subcultures in order to get a unification?", the answer is that I don't really think it's necessary. We have examples in our own life. I happen to use the example of the Chinese in San Francisco life where there was none of the violence that you are talking about and yet full rights have been accorded and they are now in the mainstream of San Francisco society. I think we can accomplish this in connection with other racial tensions. The right of dissent can bring about a great deal of change, necessary change, within the subcultures, as they are called, without necessarily impinging upon the rights of others.

MRS. CHARLES: Thank you.

I have one last question. Father Mooney, perhaps you would direct your attention to this, particularly.

"Since Teilhard was open to change in thought patterns, might he find that the current revolt against reason among the young and angry segments of the world population is not purely mystique? In other words, would his concept of evolution include the possibility of reaching Omega by renouncing reason?"

DR. MOONEY: Well I think what he would say, first of all, is that the present tensions in the reactions of youth to their culture, their environment, their whole world, is a manifestation of a heightening tension in human consciousness, which has come as a result of the particular threshold that we have reached at the present time. Teilhard saw only hope in this tension. The reason is that what he called the psychic temperature of the noosphere is undergoing radical change, and it is this change which is causing the upheavals now taking place in society. These upheavals are therefore symptoms of growth and not symptoms of diminishment. Now, the extent to which he could justify that conclusion depends upon the extent to which one subscribes to his particular evolutionary system, his particular explanation of the growth in consciousness in function of growth in complexity.

DR. WILDIERS: This question reminds me of the theory of the German psychologist Ludwig Klages, who defended the idea that reason is the enemy of life. I think this theory is wrong; the highest realization in man is his reason. We have to develop our reason, increase our creativity in all fields, as I said. I believe that this is the only way to move in the direction of completion of which Teilhard speaks and which he calls the Point Omega.

MRS. CHARLES: Thank you, Dr. Wildiers. Does anyone else want to say a last word? Dr. O'Brien?

DR. O'BRIEN: I would like to go off briefly on a tangent to that question. Dr. Leakey, speaking earlier today, focused our attention on the importance of fire made at will in the development of human speech and discussion. I think it may be that the leisure explosion of today is analogous to that moment of the fire, and that is what is happening among the young. And if we think that what is happening among the young may not be always altogether reasonable, we may consider that perhaps some queer things also went on around that primeval fire.

DR. LEAKEY: May I have a word?

MRS. CHARLES: Please, Dr. Leakey.

DR. LEAKEY: My reaction to that one is that unfortunately leisure today is so often centered around "the box," which would seem to me to be a passive rather than a creative use of time.

Comments on Scientific Methodology

Robert A. Thornton, Ph.D.

Some remarks in appraisal of Teilhard's thought and his use of the scientific method need to be examined. These remarks very strongly indicate that scientific methodology is only concerned with a mechanistic approach to an assessment whose ingredients are only facts and inferences from these facts—the validity and truth of which can be established by some operational or observational procedure.

The scientific method includes much more than this. It actually has a dual nature. The early stages of scientific method—science in the making—do not manifest themselves in the final product, but they make it possible. If scientific methodology is defined only by its end results—the institutionalized science of textbooks, research papers, and conclusions—then it is limiting and restricting. Any definition

---

Professor Thornton has taught at various academic institutions, including the University of Chicago and Brandeis. He has published articles on education and is also co-author of three texts on physics. Early in his career he collaborated on a private scientific study with Professor Albert Einstein. A former Dean of the School of Natural Sciences at San Francisco State College, Dr. Thornton is currently Professor of Physics at the University of San Francisco.

must take into account the beginnings of scientific methodology, which are characterized by what might be called the free license of creativity.

The nuclear physicist Smythe summed this up very beautifully. He said: "We have a paradox in the method of science; the research man often thinks and works like an artist, but he has to talk like a bookkeeper in terms of facts and figures and logical sequences of thought."

The prevalent idea of scientific creativity is that it is a rigid, orthodox procedure whose chief trait is accuracy and explicit identification. This is not true. Many of the greatest theoretical scientists testify that during the early stages of their work they do not know what they are talking about. They use nonconventional symbols and concepts. At this stage, the motivation and even the enchantment of the scientist may be largely nonrational and noncommunicable. He cannot refuse to accept provisional ideas and concepts simply because they do not meet the rigorous tests demanded by a rigid and limited conception of the scientific method. When scientists are creating and struggling with a problem, there can be little conscious limitations on their free, and at times audacious, constructions. They must speculate, and someone has said that to set limits on speculation is treason to the future.

The very fact that the scientist speculates and is preoccupied with a certain set of ideas indicates a bias. At this creative stage, the personal and intangible characteristics of the innovator are dominant. A. N. Whitehead said that "science can find no individual enjoyment in Nature; science can find no aim in Nature; science can find no creativity in Nature." But the scientist himself, in making science, is highly motivated and very creative–motivated by a personal purpose; by creative nonrational, nondemonstrable, noncommunicable preoccupations; and, as John Dewey says; "an enjoyment of the doubtful." For example, Galileo was looking for a proof of the Deity in the laws of nature, and out of this came $s = \frac{1}{2} at^2$.

Teilhard, like all other scientists, was looking for unity and order. Order does not display itself. One cannot point a finger at or take a picture of order. In a deep sense, it must be created. This requires the search for similarities, the use of metaphor, tentative definitions, idealizations, and other types of creative mental activity. And the scientist uses these nonexistent concepts in order to deal with reality. A good example is *perfect gas,* which is fantasy, but a necessary one to enable the physical scientist to deal with real gases.

When Teilhard uses some concepts or expressions that do not have a clear referent, cannot be seen, measured, or mechanically manipulated, why be critical and reject his right to that personal and creative act which is a legitimate part of his methodology? Critics of Teilhard who take issue with him in these terms would do well to give more scholarly attention to the fuller meaning of scientific methodology in *all* its aspects.

The Personal Meaning of Perfection

Ralph R. Greenson, M.D.

INTRODUCTION

I assume that I was invited to participate in this symposium on "Teilhard de Chardin: In Quest of the Perfection of Man" and to speak specifically on the subject, "The Personal Meaning of Perfection," because of my professional experience as a psychoanalyst. I want you to be aware that I spend most of my working life as a clinician, attempting to help patients, and others, who struggle against different forms of imperfection like anxiety, depression, and guilt. I have no competence in philosophy, paleontology, geology, genetics, evolution, and theology, and I am honored to represent psychiatry and psychoanalysis in a multidisciplinary symposium with such distinguished participants. My

A clinical Professor of Psychiatry at the University of California, Los Angeles, Dr. Greenson is a widely known lecturer on the practical individual meaning of psychiatry and its relationship to greater social issues. His professional associations include past presidency of the Los Angeles Psychoanalytic Society, and current chairmanship of the Scientific Advisory Board, Foundation for Research in Psychoanalysis. Dr. Greenson is author of numerous general and technical publications on psychiatry.

own contribution shall be limited to what I have learned about *some* of the sources and the antecedents of the quest for perfection from patients and nonpatients, in whom the striving for perfection was a central issue. Such people offer valuable insights into the beginnings of the sense of, and the quest for, perfection.

I hope the audience is familiar with the historical development of psychoanalysis insofar as it began by studying abnormalities and failures which then shed important light on the achievement of normalcy and success. Analogously, the analysis of people who suffer from a heightened sense of *imperfection* may illuminate certain aspects of the meaning of perfection.

I would like the audience to be cognizant of the psychoanalytic point of view that man is not born with any innate drive for virtue, but with drives that are self-seeking and not altruistic. Whatever virtue man achieves is the result of an uphill battle between his drives on the one hand and society and its internal representatives on the other. Society tempts and confuses man with contradictory and unreliable promises of rewards and punishments. I mention these points to introduce my approach to "The Personal Meaning of Perfection." I want to stress that Teilhard's theories about the perfection of man dealt primarily with man in a distant future, man as a species, not the ordinary man of today. I shall now turn to my clinical material, studies of people who were unusually concerned with perfection, because I believe that people's thoughts, fantasies, and behavior are more illuminating than our theories.

CLINICAL MATERIAL: WHAT PERFECTION MEANS TO DIFFERENT KINDS OF PEOPLE

1. A 29-year-old artist, outstandingly successful in his career, ostensibly happily unmarried and sexually satisfied, is, for some "indefinable reason," driven to taking drugs. He

begins with taking marijuana for a few years, then goes on to heroin and finally to LSD. His first three LSD "trips" are good ones, but the fourth leads to a period of psychosis with terrifying visual and auditory hallucinations. After they subside he becomes a phobic about drugs, finds himself unable to work, and finally seeks psychiatric help.

The analysis of the "indefinable reason" that drove him to take drugs is central to my presentation. Despite his professional success, the young painter was disappointed in his work and was dimly aware of a mild but constant discontent. He felt his paintings were too heavy, did not get off the ground, and had reached a monotonous plateau. Subjectively he felt bogged down and locked up within himself. The young man had the recurring fantasy that if he could become weightless, if he could let his mind soar, "flip out," he would have a limitless palette and then, and only then, would he reach the acme of his talent and skill. He was determined to reach the absolute heights in his art; anything less was mediocre and meaningless. Drugs seemed to offer the key to his untapped resources. He realized that drugs were dangerous, particularly the LSD, but he was not afraid of dying and he was not afraid of going crazy, which he knew could happen with LSD. Analysis revealed that actually his fearlessness was not entirely factual. The young man was able to recall that he had been terrified of fighting as a boy. Any bodily harm he reacted to as irreparable damage, and it stirred up fantasies of body destruction and death. It also turned out that during puberty he wondered from time to time whether he was going mad. There were occasions when he felt an uncanny emptiness inside himself, times when he was uncertain if he were really himself. He recalled on occasion when the sound of his breathing sounded like his father's and he wondered if he *were* his father. Yet he dared to take LSD—partly in search of perfection in his art through the sensation of limitless perceptions, and partly to prove to himself he was not afraid to die or go mad.

During treatment the young painter described his unhappy childhood, stressing, in particular, the fact that he had had an invalided mother who could provide little loving bodily contact, and he was cared for primarily by a succession of practical nurses, whose major task was to take care of the mother. In one session he unexpectedly recalled some happy memories of early childhood, of being lifted up and tossed in the air by his gigantic father. His original fright was transformed into delicious ecstasy when he became certain that his father would always catch him. His father was not usually an emotionally or verbally expressive man and this occasional game of being tossed in the air and caught was especially gratifying to the boy. He painted the experience verbally for me as follows: "I felt little and helpless and at the mercy of this big man whom I needed and loved. He had the power to toss me away or to rescue me and cradle me snugly in his arms."

To this man, taking LSD, in addition to all its other meanings, was a re-living of the tossing game with his father. He was willing to face the terrible fears of madness and death in order to reach the scary heights and then be rescued. He then could enjoy the special pleasure of returning to the snugness of sanity and reality. To this man, perfection meant to brave the dangers of achieving the pinnacle, to be admired above all others and yet also to be safe.

2. A middle-aged, genial business tycoon was tyrannized by the compulsion to be exact, precise, and accurate about details his better judgment told him were trivial. Despite his enormous financial success, he felt forced to personally supervise the minutiae of his various business enterprises, which were scattered all over the world. A minor physical illness forced him to stay put for several months and for the first time in his life he developed conscious anxiety and depression. He was startled. He had always considered himself a robust person emotionally.

Our brief analytic work revealed the following relevant

material: His mother adored him and obviously preferred him to his father, but she was obsessed with cleanliness. This meant to the boy that she loved cleanliness more than she loved him, and he was right. To her, cleanliness was truly next to Godliness. He was free to play with the other boys as long as he returned spotless and stainless. As you can imagine, he did not do much playing with the boys but substituted for this by playing with numbers. He became a mathematical wizard and soon outshone his father. The family was poor and the young boy vowed to become rich someday so that he could give his mother the luxuries and jewels he felt she deserved and did not receive from his father. The patient, the son of an inept businessman, specialized in taking over run-down businesses, which he rehabilitated by mastering the financial intricacies and by demanding flawless execution from himself and all his subordinates. Each business triumph brought him a glowing feeling, a feeling that reminded him of his mother's loving embrace when he was her "angelic (translated: clean) little boy." It was in her arms that he first rememberd the feeling that they were an unbeatable combination–he and his mother. This was in marked contrast to his feeling of abject despair, a sense of being utterly abandoned and unlovable, whenever his mother discovered he had done something dirty. The image of his mother's face turning away from him in disgust and scorn always accompanied any activity he performed with less than his customary flawlessness. In his adult life his exactness and precision had become internal demands, residuals of his mother, which he now carried around inside himself. They tyrannized his life unconsciously, but they also made him feel consciously omnipotent.

The tycoon's ruthlessness toward all errant employees was an expression of loathing for his own natural urge to enjoy dirtiness and sloppiness, which he had managed to repress. It was as well his symbolic revenge against his father, an incompetent (translated: sloppy) businessman. The quiet but frantic compulsiveness of this man's life was a quest for perfection. He toiled all his life to earn the love of his mother. It was a never-ending task, as any fall from perfection would call up the face of his mother distorted by disgust. Therapy eventually helped him become a little less concerned with his dead mother and more involved with his living wife and children. He also became less obsessed with the quest for perfection.

3. There are many people, patients among them, who carry within themselves a feeling of being deficient, defective, and incomplete. They try to overcome this state of affairs by attaching themselves to a lover or spouse, a leader, a cause or a faith, thus becoming both whole and perfect. Their difficulties come to the surface when the beloved person or belief that confers the sense of wholeness is lost through death or disillusionment. The lowly members of such partnerships are apt to become slaves rather than equals, and are quite willing to endure great hardship and suffering to ensure the love and protection of their idealized and mighty beloved. When the partnership is dissolved, through separation or disappointment, these people go through a severe depression, characterized by bitterness and hostility toward the external world, accompanied by severe self-reproach and a return to their old feelings of worthlessness. I shall try to illustrate this with a clinical example:

A woman in her early forties came for help because she had lost all desire to live and alternated between spells of feeling murderous rage and periods of suicidal despair and emptiness. This state of affairs began suddenly. She had been blissfully and happily married for over twenty years to a man she considered perfection incarnate. Her "perfect" marriage abruptly disintegrated when her husband broke off all relations with their eldest son when he married a foreign girl and went to live abroad. The blissfully happy married woman suddenly saw the image of her perfect husband crumble before her very eyes. The man who had been her ideal, "Mr. Wonderful personified," a man who could do no wrong, who was above reproach, became transformed into a petty, jealous, nasty, selfish, and mean human being. She, who melted at his very touch, was repelled by his animal lust. His brilliant mind turned into an instrument for torture, his lofty imagination became vapid, his ethereal gentleness became disgustingly effeminate.

As her feelings toward her husband changed, the patient became increasingly more miserable. She had not only lost an ideal husband, she had also lost her self-esteem. She, who for over twenty years had basked in the sunshine of feeling constantly warmed by a superior creature, felt cold, empty, and worthless. This was a return of an old feeling state she had experienced in her growing-up years. Being the product of a miserably married mother and father had made her feel deficient and defective. Her mother had admonished her for years not to marry a man beneath her as she had done. The mother blamed all her own ills on the inadequacies of the father and promised her daughter a life of bliss if she only would find the "right" man. The patient realized that she was serving as an extension of her mother and was not truly loved in her own right. As it turned out, the mother found this "right" man—a young doctor who was treating the mother. In six weeks she had persuaded her daughter and the young doctor to marry. To consolidate the marriage, the mother had donated all her life savings to them as a wedding gift. It was not a bribe, she claimed, but a token of her admiration for her daughter's husband.

For twenty-three years the perfect husband made this woman, who had felt defective and inadequate, behave and react as though she were whole, complete, and a partner in a perfect marriage. She had been oblivious to all her husband's shortcomings, or considered them trivial. He could do no wrong. His weaknesses were lovable and made him more human, his frailties were quaint and made him more endearing, his tyrannies were strengths and made him more admirable. She felt privileged to live with him. He had blanketed her deep sense of inadequacy and deficiency and she was now participating in a higher level of existence.

Her husband's rupture of the relationship to her beloved son tore the veil from her eyes. She fell from bliss back into the black hole of her childhood, from which hole she had believed she had evolved. The patient now hated and despised her husband. She found him selfish and pretentious. She felt she had been mistreated and misled and that she deserved it—she was nothing but a defective fool; besides, who else would have married her? The magic aura of the perfect man had evaporated and her childhood identity was reinstated.

4. An even more extreme example of the blissful partnership I have just described is that special emotional state of perfection in which people feel a joyous sense of losing their self-boundaries and flowing into, or merging and becoming one with another person or being—like God, Fate, or Nature —and thus attaining perfection. This is thought to occur when infants are transported from painful hunger to blissful satiation when they are lovingly fed by their mothers. It is also seen when people fall in love or experience a sense of religious or philosophical ecstasy. It may also occur at the peak of sexual orgasm. It is characteristic for these so-called oceanic-feeling states that a person feels relatively small and becomes fused with someone grand and powerful. To many this is experienced as a state of ecstasy and the acme of perfection. I would like to highlight some of the elements that lead to this sense of merging and fusing with a beloved in the following pathological example:

A young physician undressed himself completely and lay down in a bathtub. He then cut both his wrists and his neck with his surgical scalpel. He was discovered by accident and rushed to a hospital, unconscious and very close to death. Sometime later, when he had physically recovered, I had the opportunity to work with him analytically. I was impressed by his clear description of the meaning and purpose of the suicide. The young doctor told me that he had been severely depressed since his mother's suicide a year earlier. She had been found in her bathtub drowned as a result of having lost consciousness after she had taken an overdose of sleeping pills. Since then he had been full of torturesome self-reproach for having neglected his mother. Although he realized the notion of neglect was not realistic or logical, he was unable to stop his self-torture.

His mother had been a quiet and undemonstrative woman. Their greatest joy together had been in playing piano duets as a boy. She had hoped he would go on to become a musician but he had chosen to study medicine, which meant giving up the piano and leaving home. The young doctor felt guilty for his decision and tried to be particularly considerate and thoughtful of his mother. The father of the family had died many years earlier and my patient was accustomed to looking after his mother. Her suicide was sudden and inexplicable to him.

The young physician yearned for his lost mother and his self-reproaches became intolerable. He finally decided his only recourse was to die. In that way, he would cease to suffer and he would join his beloved mother. He described to me that as he watched the blood draining from his body, his self-reproaches ceased, he felt a growing sense of peace, and he visualized himself being taken into the arms of his mother, who had been waiting for him. Just before he became completely unconscious, he felt his blood mingling with hers, a feeling that was utter bliss. In fact, when he awakened in the hospital he was terribly disappointed and wept bitterly. He had lost that state of bliss for which he had striven.

THE DYNAMICS

I have chosen these four clinical vignettes in order to demonstrate how the quest for perfection looks to a psychoanalyst.

In all four cases the patients carried inside themselves, from childhood on, the feelings of not having been loved sufficiently, which eventually led them to feel that they were bad or deficient. Children who feel unloved first rage against the unloving parent and the outside world. Eventually they turn their rage inward and develop a sense of internal badness. They yearn for a constant loving mother they never had and create an *idealized* mother who is unattainable because of their sense of internal badness. They continue to hope for some special form of approval, acceptance or union with this perfect mother who never existed in real life. The young painter tried LSD to reach her, the young doctor attempted suicide to join his mother. The business tycoon built a financial empire to please his idealized mother, and the housewife tried to achieve this approval by becoming an extension of her mother. All these attempts fail, not only for the reasons I have just described, but for additional reasons I shall now try to explain.

In each instance the wish to be loved and to be found lovable is opposed by *unconscious* harsh and unrealistic self-criticism. The artist was driven to face death and madness, the physician was tormented by sadistic impulses directed against the self, the business tycoon is haunted by the dread of being found unlovable and repulsive if he is anything but flawless, the housewife has to renounce her own defective identity to live as an extension of her "perfect" husband.

In order to better understand these problems, psychoanalysis has focused on certain basic factors in man's struggle to mature, to become civilized. Man is born helpless and dependent on the external world and remains so longer than any other animal. He is also born with two opposing sets of drives, one loving, Eros, and one aggressive (Freud, 1920). The concept of man's innate aggressiveness has never been popular, but disliking it will not make the evidence of man's destructiveness and hatred disappear. Man seeks satisfaction for his drives, which is first limited and then opposed by the external world. In order to adapt to the world around him, man has to renounce some of his libidinal strivings, but above all, he has to curtail his tendency to react to frustration by outward destructiveness and rage. To do so, the child eventually creates an internal agency, a super-ego, which is modeled after the mighty parents and which punishes him for every transgression. The super-ego, or conscience, is only partly conscious and reasonable. It is essentially unconscious and irrational. It is not merely a replica of the parent but has in it the child's hatred for the frustrating parent. Furthermore, the super-ego punishes the self not only for acts but even for thoughts and fantasies that it considers bad. The more aggression is deflected from outward expression, the more it is turned onto the self. The result is feelings of guilt, which can only be absolved by punishment of the self. Every renunciation of instinctual gratification will lead to an increased severity of the super-ego, to greater self-criticism and self-destructiveness (Freud, 1930) . The more virtuous the person, the more harsh the super-ego.

The result of this conflict between the search for happiness and the wish to be approved of by the super-ego or its external representatives is essentially a struggle between the urge to express love and agression on the one hand, and to escape guilt, mainly unconscious guilt, on the other. Absolution, in the extreme examples I have described, is only possible by first neutralizing or killing off the cruel super-ego. I have illustrated these attempts in each of the four patients. The artist used LSD, the businessman offered one success after another, the housewife submerged her own identity, and the doctor cut his wrists and throat. All were efforts to appease the sadistic super-ego each patient possessed. In all these people we find the attempt to escape helplessness, the helplessness of aloneness and unlovableness—all terrible dangers. These are the fears that drive such people to seek perfection. Perfection to them means: I am not helpless, I am not alone,

I am lovable and protected by a loving and powerful internal or external force.

DISCUSSION OF TEILHARD DE CHARDIN'S IDEAS

If I now turn to the writings of Teilhard de Chardin, I am impressed, most of all, by Teilhard's excessive optimism. I agree that one needs some optimism in order to have hope. With no hope there is only gloom and despair, which serve no useful purpose. I feel, however, that Teilhard goes too far. He seems to believe that universal evolutionary processes and the convergence of the different elements of the universe will make for greater knowledge and love and eventuate in a superior type of human being. I am not qualified to discuss his scientific findings, or his philosophical speculations, but I would like to make a few comments as an observer of the world scene. Man may well be part of an evolutionary process, but I see little evidence that man's scientific and technological progress has brought him more peace or happiness. The atom bomb, Viet Nam, My Lai, the hero worship of Lieutenant Calley, the situation in Pakistan and in the Near East, the race riots, the violence between police and anti-war protesters —and I could go on—point to man's greater propensity for hatred and destructiveness. I agree with Professor Leakey that unless we change, we are on the road to the extinction of man—not to his perfection.

My main disagreement with Teilhard's views is his almost total disregard for man's aggressiveness and its consequences. In his major work, *The Phenomenon of Man,* there are only three pages in an appendix devoted to "On the Part of Evil in the World in Evolution." Teilhard, himself, is aware of this omission and I would like to quote him:

> Throughout the long discussions we have been through, one point may perhaps have intrigued or even shocked the reader. Nowhere, if I am not mistaken, have pain or wrong been spoken of. . . .

> True, evil has not hitherto been mentioned, at least explicitly. But on the other hand surely it inevitably seeps out through every nook and cranny, through every joint and sinew of the system in which I have taken my stand.[1]

Teilhard ends the three pages of discussion with a remarkably frank admission: "On this question, in all loyalty, I do not feel I am in a position to take a stand: in any case, would this be the place to do so?"[2]

My answer is yes. I believe that evil, which "inevitably seeps out through every nook and cranny, through every joint and sinew of the system," is too important to be disregarded. I do not believe that man can attain perfection by merely evolving, by merely waiting. I further believe that the very conception of the quest for perfection is too awe-inspiring and tends to make man either too frantic or too passive and submissive. It seems to me more effective to struggle for improvement rather than perfection, for ideals rather than utopia. I do not believe it is helpful to ask man to aspire to unattainable ideals, which are so far beyond his capabilities that they only result in his feeling unworthy and guilty. Man has enough difficulty with his guilt and aggression and should not be burdened with such lofty injunctions as "Love thy neighbor as thyself," which run counter to his original nature. It seems to me it would already be a tremendous advance if man would be able to stop killing his neighbor.

Teilhard de Chardin's writing and thinking has an unusual personal and intimate quality. As a psychoanalyst I cannot resist noting a few items in his personal history because they seem to shed some light on his later interests. Pierre Teilhard was one of eleven children, *seven* of whom died while he was a child. His mother considered the dead

---

1 Pierre Teilhard de Chardin, *The Phenomenon of Man,* trans. Bernard Wall, (New York: Harper Torchbooks, Harper & Row, 1959), p. 311. Quoted by permission of Harper & Row, Publishers, Inc.

2 *Ibid.,* p. 313.

children fortunate and refused to accept condolences or sympathy from the priest.[3]

Teilhard's earliest memories as quoted from his diary are the following:

> A memory? My very first! I was five or six. My mother had snipped off a few of my curls. I picked one up and held it close to the fire. The hair was burnt up in a fraction of a second. A terrible grief assailed me; I had learnt that I was perishable. . . . What used to grieve me when I was a child? This insecurity of things. And what used I to love? My genie of iron! With a plow-hitch I believed myself, at seven years, rich with a treasure incorruptible, everlasting. And then it turned out that what I possessed was just a bit of iron that rusted. At this discovery I threw myself on the lawn and shed the bitterest tears of my existence![4]

It is not surprising that a little boy with this touching childhood history might become concerned with searching for a world with other than fearsome changes, and would become interested in durability, deathlessness, and perfection.

CONCLUSION

I believe man is driven to seek perfection because it seems to offer a magical protection from his basic anxieties: helplessness, loneliness, unlovableness, and body destruction. Guilt, the turning of aggression onto the self, is the single most important factor behind these anxieties. The greatest hindrance to man's greater development is his inability, up to the present, to deal better with his aggression and destructiveness. I believe that for man to survive he must learn to curb, tame, channelize, and sublimate his aggressiveness and destructiveness. To do this he must first face more

[3] Claude Cuenot, *Teilhard de Chardin, A Biographical Study,* trans. Vincent Colimore (New York: Helicon Press, Inc., 1958).

[4] *Ibid.,* p. 3.

honestly his greed, his envy, his hatred and fear of the stranger and his hatred and fear of change. Only then can unconscious destructive guilt be changed to conscious guilt, which can be controllable and useful. If we do this, man will have made a giant step forward, even if it is not to Point Omega.

REFERENCES

Cuenot, Claude. *Teilhard de Chardin, A Biographical Study*. Translated by Vincent Colimore, New York: Helicon Press Inc., 1958.

Fenichel, O. *The Psychoanalytic Theory of Neurosis*. New York: W. W. Norton, 1946.

Freud, S. *Beyond the Pleasure Principle*. Standard Edition, vol. 18. London: Hogarth Press, 1920.

———. *The Future of an Illusion*. Standard Edition, vol. 21. London: Hogarth Press, 1927.

———. *Civilization and its Discontents*. Standard Edition, vol. 21. London, Hogarth Press, 1930.

Teilhard de Chardin, Pierre. *The Phenomenon of Man*. Translated by Bernard Wall. New York, Harper & Row, 1959.

———. *The Divine Milieu*. Translated by B. J. Wall. New York and Evanston: Harper Torchbooks, Harper & Row, 1960.

———. *Human Energy*. Translated by J. M. Cohen. New York: Harcourt, Brace, Jovanovich Inc., 1962.

Politics and a Creative Citizenry

Mark F. Ferber, Ph.D.

For the newcomer to Teilhard who is expert in neither theology nor the natural sciences, an immersion into his works is one of those rare intellectual adventures. The breadth of his subject matter—all of the world's past and speculation about its ultimate future—the vision and audacity that illuminate his thought, the boldness of his speculation, the unbridled optimism that he brings to his writings, and, finally, the play of the poetic soul on essentially scientific data—all these combine to provide a veritable feast for the novice. His effort to synthesize the conclusions of the natural and biological sciences and to make them compatible with,

---

Before becoming Vice President for Student Services at the University of Santa Clara, Dr. Ferber was a Special Assistant to the President of the University of California. He represented the University in its dealings with the executive and legislative branches of government in Washington, D. C., and later was responsible for effecting a greater university involvement in urban affairs. He has held a number of community and legislative appointments in both New Jersey and California, including membership in The Executive Committee of Industry/Mexican American Action Committee and The California State Advisory Committee to the United States Commission on Civil Rights.

and relevant to, Teilhard's view of Catholic theology, represent an undertaking of the first magnitude.

That he succeeds in pulling and stretching this immense amount of data into a coherent and systematic theory—and one of great power for forcing others (whether in agreement with him or not) to face up to the cosmic questions that face mankind—is, in itself, tribute to the genius of the man. Disagreement over specifics, be they major assumptions or minor points, should in no way detract from the significant effort that went into the great body of work, nor should it diminish the awe and respect for the reflective being who "saw" the relationships embodied in the theory and succeeded in illuminating these relationships with an eloquence rarely found in comparable works dealing with essentially scientific data. What emerges is an image of a soul deeply at one with the universe and profoundly in love with the whole of mankind—present and future. This shines like a flame in his writings and literally reaches out to embrace the reader in warm light.

In discussing Teilhard, I should like to make a few observations at the outset so that you will at least understand some of my assumptions.

First, in broad outline, his sense of evolution as a process fits well with contemporary social theory. It is not merely a broad statement about a set of "facts," but an entire outlook that sees all things in a state of flux and seeks to place these things (be they inanimate matter, living organisms, or humanly created institutions) within a framework wherein change is a constant factor. This, certainly, is congenial to the study of politics, societal relations, economics, and the subject matter of the other social sciences. While earlier social philosophers spent a vast amount of time seeking to establish "ideal" states or modes for a permanent and unalterable sense of nature, of man, and of his institutions, this is no longer true today. The whole milieu in which social scientists work is permeated with the notion of process and the correlative concept of change. That different disciplines utilize different time-frames for their focus is uncontested: the psychiatrist, obviously, and the developmental economist are concerned about differing periods of time and differing manifestations of "change," but both work within a process- and change-oriented frame of reference.

Similarly, Teilhard's sense of the centrality of man as the focus for study is bound to find favor with the social sciences, since man is, after all, the basic unit for our disciplines. While the biologist may find rats or spiders equally fascinating, and while the physicist may spend a highly productive lifetime with the atom or the impersonal forces that affect matter, the sociologist and the political scientist must, perforce, focus upon man and his institutions, his habits and his interactions with other elements within the environment.

Finally, Teilhard's insistence upon reflection or consciousness as the distinguishing characteristic of the man/animal, his felicitous notion that man is unique because "he knows and knows that he knows," strikes me as the only acceptable doctrine underlying our continued studies. I shall, in a few moments, take exception to some of his notions of consciousness, but I certainly agree that our capacity to reflect is that factor which defines humanity. This focuses upon what is central to all men and to mankind in general, and casts aside the superficial differences that, with far greater potency than we like to admit, divide us into nations, races, and tribes: the whole of the "we-they" syndrome.

In summary, then, Teilhard is at one with modern social science when he postulates mankind as the result and ever-changing product of a process (evolution), in which man is unique as compared to other elements by virtue of his capacity to reflect: to think about and alter both his environment and the very evolutionary process that led to his emergence as a sentient being.

At a step beyond the fully developed individual, our paths begin to diverge. For Teilhard, collectivities of individuals, be they tribes, races, nation/states, are not only the next logical, but the *inevitable* evolutionary step. According to his theory of complexification, if I understand it correctly, the same laws that govern the construction of molecules from individual atoms and complex organisms from single cells also govern the construction of societies from single, discrete individuals. Beyond this, he further postulates that this process *must* continue until all mankind is bonded together into a single conscious entity. This, obviously, is the stuff of politics, and I shall return to the point later on. Here, let me merely suggest that the inevitability of Teilhard's formulation—which I gather is contested by Teilhardian scholars—poses a real problem. While none of us would contest the notion of the social nature of man—the necessity of interaction with other men in order to become a true "human"—it seems to me that his hypothesis does not take adequate account of differences between physical matter and social systems.

At this point the theologian takes hold and creates a systematic vision of the future that poses fundamental evidentiary and methodological problems for me. For it seems to me that, carried forward by the logic of his evolutionary theory and illuminated by his theological vision, Teilhard posits a directive force for the past and a clear-cut goal toward which the entire evolutionary process has been pointed—namely, Point Omega, or a total conscious oneness with Christ. Thus, it becomes necessary to stress the clear direction of evolutionary activities and to impose a determinism upon man's journey. We have not simply emerged by dint of the evolutionary process, nor is the future one of possible alternatives which, I insist, must include the self-induced or natural demise of man as a species. Rather, Teilhard says that man is irreplaceable, therefore, however improbable it might seem, *he must*—and the emphasis is Teilhard's—*reach his goal,* not necessarily doubtless, but infallibly. This concept, it seems to me, is central to Teilhard and, in turn, allows for the unbridled optimism that we find so terribly attractive in his writings. It is an optimism that flows naturally from his long-range vision on the one hand and his theological orientation on the other. It is, in short, a natural consequence, I believe, of his heroic effort to synthesize religion and the natural sciences.

Without getting into debate on whether or not it is inevitable, and certainly I am not qualified to discuss the theological implications, let me merely suggest that I am far less sanguine than he about the infallibility of our continued presence as a species. What follows, in fact, makes sense only if this possibility of our demise is accepted; for it seems to me that the reason for contemplating political life in the context of a symposium like this is to suggest that species survival may well be at stake and that we cannot escape to our laboratories, our classrooms, or our seminaries secure in the knowledge that life will go on. Choices made now, through the political process, will affect future generations and may well determine whether or not the human animal will survive.

This leads to an additional comment about Teilhard's view of the world. Emerging clearly from his writings is the notion of a "progressive" science, largely defined, I think, as the natural and biological sciences. This, I believe, flows again from his more basic views. Placing, as he does, his emphasis on man's evolving consciousness, Teilhard sees in science a constant thrust in the direction of increasing our awareness of the world we live in and a step toward noogenesis. As such, any discovery is viewed as an act of consciousness, and, per se, good.

Today, I believe such a view must be seriously questioned. Man's consciousness is not unidimensional but rather, as was so brilliantly pointed out, like a multi-faceted jewel in which reason, emotion, reflection, notions of beauty, and ego are all arrayed and affected by perceptions. Within the same mind, these elements do not unfold as part of a single process but rather in different and varying patterns against the background of the individual's total environmental and experiential base. Thus, we owe Watson a great deal, not only for his work on DNA but for so clearly indicating that a single mind can be working at the very frontiers of science—so much so as to be in Nobel Prize contention—and, at the same time, be engaged in rather petty and malicious behavior. Example could follow example of the brilliant (hyper-conscious) scientist whose relationships with people (family, peers, strangers) were at the level of the most primitive and superstitious of aborigines. We have all had them as teachers, I suspect. For many of us who have matured since Hiroshima, the nineteenth-century notion of an unlimited progress through science and technology simply rings false. The imbalance between our capacity to unfold and understand the secrets of nature and our incapacity to understand, at this point, our own destructive impulses is sufficient to give serious cause for concern.

Lest I be accused of anti-intellectualism or trying to thwart science, be assured that such is not the case. I am, in fact, arguing that we need greater concern and greater systematic attention devoted to the behavioral sciences as related to man. The fetters that bind men's minds can be as real as those that bind the slave, and I am opposed to both. We must reorder our priorities and vastly increase the resources, both physical and psychological, that we devote to understanding man in his social context, for I think we stand on the brink of potential destruction. We must, I believe, see the advances in science that have been made to date as but one facet of the phenomenon of man. Man's behavior must now occupy increasing amounts of our time and thought and become the next breakthrough in our accumulating knowledge of the world.

It is here that perspective becomes so crucial to any discussion. Dominated by a world view that encompasses millions of years, and illuminated by a vision that postulates an ultimate goal, Teilhard can view the events of today as epiphenomenal, secure that the forces of evolution directed toward a divine goal will unfold in a pattern set in motion by the very act of creation. For those of us focusing upon the present and with a less enlightened view of the future, the comfort of such security is denied. We must deal with alternatives whose outcomes we cannot predict, in situations both threatening and unknown. It is here that politics plays such a crucial role and where creative citizenship takes on such singular importance. Somehow, and in ways not yet fully understood, we must seek to master the secrets governing the process of governance and social control, and articulate this knowledge into the political life of our society and of the world in ways that will affect the policy-making processes in a wide array of vastly differing social systems. The task is staggering, and yet, the stakes are so high!

I would like to discuss just briefly what seem to be three alternatives that do face us. Let me suggest these to you.

1. I do believe that, at least as a possibility, we do face total destruction as a species. There is at least a possibility, however remote, that we shall, through some act, destroy humanity as we know it. The megatonnage already stored in Soviet and American arsenals is more than sufficient to do the job and new advances—and how insane the word even sounds in this context—in chemical and biological weaponry have certainly moved the state of the art to levels that are more than adequate for destroying us. I am not Cassandra-like about this, for I do not think it a likely outcome. Yet, to ignore this possibility is, I feel, ostrich-like and I am, by training and inclination, unable to accept Teilhard's notion of our inevitable infallible continuation as a species. I wish this were otherwise.

2. A second, and in some respects more dismal, possibility lies in the nightmare visions glimpsed by Orwell and Aldous Huxley. It is this possibility that lies at the root of the deep concern and pessimism expressed by many of the brightest

of our students and accounts for a good deal of the articulated anti-intellectualism that occasionally surfaces within the current student movement. Premised upon the projection of existing imbalances between our knowledge of the physical and biological sciences on the one hand and humanitarian social institutions on the other, this dark vision posits a world governed by "rational" technocrats and "stabilized" by drugs and social controls to prevent emotion or affection from creating instability. While details may be somewhat blurred, this seems to me not an unreal possibility. We are, after all, only a few years away from 1984.

We have made such phenomenal strides in the physical and biological sciences that, if anything, Huxley and Orwell seem outdated. Molecular biology is probing the very heart of subcellular matter and can only be inches away from creating something called life within the laboratory. Artificial insemination is already widespread among other mammals and clearly the "baby factories" of the brave new world are well within the realm of the nearly possible. At the same time neuropharmacologists are experimenting with new drugs that will reduce pathological hostility to normal bounds and that give promise of raising intelligence. Can anyone here doubt, given these strides, that the possibilities of reducing normal aggressive tendencies to low levels of passivity have not been thought about by some military genius or some think-tank expert? If we are able to establish that intelligence can be raised chemically, do we not also have a potential key for lowering it? Yet, where is any serious discussion of the moral or legal implications of these new breakthroughs? Where is the questioning that would subject such breakthroughs to some public discussion and scrutiny? Nowhere—and this is precisely the point. We are presently so caught up, particularly at policy-making levels, in the fabled faith in science, that we are sorely neglecting the social sciences, humanities, and moral philosophies—those areas of systematic thought that might, just might, provide us with possible solutions to the problems being concocted in the test tubes and the laboratories.

The essence of the Orwellian view turns on our inability to place scientific advances within a framework of humanistic values in such a way as to insure, or at least make relatively certain, that not only mankind but individual men will grow in an environment calculated to increase individual potential and creativity while restricting the manipulative potential of groups within the collective. This is, of course, the role that political institutions ought to play, but I believe they have failed to respond. In short, the challenge has not been met and we grow in separate directions.

3. A third, and for me the most attractive, alternative turns on the possibility of focusing our consciousness upon the problems facing mankind and infusing the policy-making arena with the insights, however imperfect, derived from the physical and behavioral sciences in ample time to allow for a far more rational dialogue than now exists. This, I believe, is profoundly Teilhardian in that it would hopefully bring a meaningful sense of evolution as a process into the forum of public policy-making, rather than restricting it to gatherings like this—however challenging and exhilarating they may be.

For, like Teilhard, I believe that our consciousness does contain the seed for improving the quality of life here on earth and for greatly expanding the sense of oneness that must ultimately dominate our relations with each other if we are not to destroy ourselves. I differ, if at all, only in my conviction that thought and action must both be seen as aspects of consciousness and must be joined together if effective and understood change is to take place. Without this, I am not certain that we shall choose correctly.

The following, then, are put forward as some of the attitudes that might move into and dominate the political arena. This, after all, is the meaning of creative politics—to accomplish rather than to just talk; to work for what we believe to be just and sensible, not merely because of ego gratification or the thrill of the game, but because of our increased realization that choices made or not made can affect the entire evolutionary process and, perhaps, our very existence and that of our children and our children's children.

As you will see, there is little here that is new or revolutionary. Many of the ideas have been around since the Greeks began contemplating the nature of man and his need to live together in societies. What is revolutionary is the emerging consciousness of the potential disaster and the necessity for facing up to the fact that we can and may well eliminate ourselves. The attitudes must begin to seep into our political consciousness and govern our political behavior on a worldwide basis. If they do not, I think we face an increased risk of total obliteration or the prospect of a void and dehumanizing brave new world.

The first, and overriding, attitude comes directly from Teilhard's notion, and that is that we must begin somehow to work on the premise of the oneness of the human condition. Every great religion has set forth this seemingly self-evident proposition and every great civilization has behaved in ways to deny its validity. As we survey the world about us today, this division seems patently clear. Buttressing the moral position of religion, the proof at the level of science is abundant. We are a single species capable of mating and reproducing with others of our species wherever we encounter them, and are subject to similar laws of growth, physical health, learning, and decay.

Yet, we see the world divided into artificial collectivities dedicated to their own self-perpetuation and protection of those living in their borders against harm from "outsiders." Far from the growing unity on a worldwide basis that Teilhard saw as a natural consequence, the last three centuries have witnessed the continual fragmentation of the world into more and more nations and states, each viewing its neighbors with suspicion and seeking to assure its place in the sun. If anything, the pace has accelerated during the last fifty years.

As Karl Deutsch has pointed out in a recent article, by 1970 the majority of the world's adults were older than the political systems under which they were living. This could well signal the bringing together of smaller groups into the greater collectivities envisioned by Teilhard but, as we all know, this is not the case. The end of World War II saw the breaking up of most of the colonial empires of the world and the emergence of countless new states. Yet, this has not led to increased harmony within diversity, or to greater awareness of common humanity. Biafran and Nigerian, East and West Pakistani, Arab and Jew, Irish Protestant and Irish Catholic—the period has simply been filled with continual conflict. Looming as a grim background is the polarization of the United States and the Soviet Union, with its overtones of balance of terror and atomic annihilation.

Yet, against this grim scene, some hopeful signs appear, however dimly, on the horizon.

First, I am deeply impressed with the growing force and strength of the anti-war movement in this country. I do not want to debate the precise degree of insanity of our continued involvement in Southeast Asia, but I do not think any of us would deny the weight of the data that are emerging regarding attitudes about that involvement. One President was toppled and another feels compelled to keep assuring us that the conflict is "winding down"—whatever that might mean—as a result of these attitudes and their manifestation in the political process. While the underlying bases for these attitudes are varied and complex, some consequences are inescapable.

Most clearly, the vast majority of an entire generation have grown up in an environment that is questioning a specific war and that, I believe, is likely to question war in general as a mode of collective behavior. At the policy level, surely no administration in the near future is likely to commit troops to some highly questionable adventure in support of our so-called treaty obligations when to do so would be to court revolution at home, and when the treaty organization seems to consist of little more than the paper on which it was written. What the consequences of this will be for Soviet and Chinese policy-makers obviously remains in the clouded future. But isn't it just possible that a policy based on an evolutionary sense may in fact decrease levels of tension among our real or imagined opponents?

As a second straw in the wind, I would suggest that the test-ban treaty of a decade ago and the current SALT talks, while hardly earthshaking, do pose the possiblity of the two superpowers agreeing to minimal steps in the reduction of arms, which may, in turn, provide the basis for larger steps.

Also, on the domestic level, we find an increasingly heightened awareness of the need to perceive each other and to perceive each of our own citizens—be they black, Chicano, Native American, and, yes, women as well—with a sense of oneness and equality. I do not minimize the barriers that still must be overcome. Working in the field, one can only be frightened by the callousness that has all too frequently governed the attitudes of majority Caucasian men toward those of a different color or sex. But this, I believe, is slowly changing and is precisely what creative citizenship is all about. We must not merely talk. We must engage in the political process, mobilizing support for those who share a sense of our total potential.

The continued existence of the United Nations, while unmentioned here and hardly newsworthy in the press is, in fact, an expression of potential unification. Those who criticize the UN for not solving the Soviet/American impasse simply show a lack of understanding for its basic assumptions. Founded upon the hoped-for premise of big-power consensus, it cannot function when such consensus is absent. Yet, in its specialized agencies dealing with social, cultural, educational, health, and a host of related problems, the UN is a model of worldwide consciousness that would, I feel, find great approval from Teilhard.

Following from the notion of a single world community in the process of unification, it seems essential as well as scientifically accurate to postulate the need for reducing both internally and internationally the unbelievable disparities in resources that exist among the human elements of the world. Increasingly, in this country, voices are being raised about the costs of space exploration or defense, when malnutrition, poverty, foul housing, and abysmal ignorance are the daily lot for far too many of our citizens.

In a world constantly shrinking by virtue of advances in transportation and telecommunication, the current situation seems to me most serious. William Sloane Coffin of Yale has pointed out that if, for the purpose of grasping the problem, we reduce the world's population of some three billion people to a town of 1,000, only sixty of these people would be Americans, while 940 would be all the rest of the world's population. Yet those sixty would enjoy fifty percent of the town's resources. Those sixty would enjoy an average life expectancy of seventy-one years, while the rest of the 940 would, on the average, be dead before they were forty years old.

If we do, in fact, seek a world based on a stable peace, such disparities simply cannot be tolerated, for our own well-being as well as for the rest of the world's. Comparative standard-of-living statistics, which I think used to fill us with a smug kind of pride, should now be viewed with more than a little foreboding in a world linked instantaneously by satellite TV and only hours away from any spot by jet aircraft. The luxury of growing affluent quietly in a pre-electronic environment is no longer ours; and the revolution of rising expectations, whether in Watts or Nairobi, Detroit or Havana, must be dealt with if we are to avert extended violence and bloodshed.

Third, it seems to me that we must begin to perceive and seek understanding of the entire world as an ecosystem, "a spaceship earth," to use Buckminster Fuller's term. While there has been a vast outpouring of literature on this subject during the past five years, it is extremely difficult to see the results on the domestic, let alone the international, scene.

There are a number of questions here that need to be explored: First, the whole set of problems associated with the so-called population explosion. It seems crystal clear to me that this area is rapidly moving into the public arena and away from merely a question of private choice. Yet, we seem singularly ill-prepared for the discussion which should precede this movement. Surely the matter is more complex than merely planned families. We must undertake, and quickly, studies that would bring together not only food and health experts but philosophers and those concerned with ethics as well, in order to understand the full dimension of the problem and the moral choices involved. We must seek to establish some reliable data on levels of food potential and the levels of population they can support; and, if tentative agreement can be reached on this kind of data, what the consequences of various social policies will be. Here, the synthesis of the sciences and moral philosophy is desperately needed for fundamental questions of life and death—and also of life or death for whom and at what point.

Likewise, pollution has moved from being a matter of nasty inconvenience to one of potential public policy, wherein our very survival may be at stake. I do not need to reiterate the horror stories that all of you are familiar with. Suffice it to say that we are literally poisoning the water we drink, befouling the air we breathe, and killing the soils upon which we depend for sustenance. Furthermore, this phenomenon is hardly limited to the industrially advanced nations of the world. As science and technology spread around the globe, the likelihood of ever-greater and more massive pollution becomes more and more real.

What I have tried to suggest this morning is really rather simple. We are at a crossroads in our development as a species. Like the prehistoric monsters that roamed the world, we have grown large and powerful, but there is some question as to whether or not our brains are up to adapting to the next step. For us, the decisions will be made in collectivities, and will be based on choices we make. This, I would argue, is precisely what politics is all about. But to effect those choices we must come out of our studies and out of our classrooms and engage in the process. It is this, I think, that young people demand of us, and we cannot—while counseling them not to drop out—drop out ourselves.

Like Teilhard's magnificent effort to reconcile religion and science, we must try. To have tried and to have failed, can be heroic; to have failed to try is ignoble.

Law in the Age of Planetization

Pearce Young, M.A., L.L.B.

When Teilhard de Chardin discusses the continuing evolutionary process of both man and the universe, he brings to his subject many disciplines, including those of the scientist, the philosopher, and the theologian. His excursions into the law are seldom, and the terms he uses to describe the evolutionary process of man would be foreign to the average judge or practicing attorney. Likewise, I am confident that Teilhard would have found no enlightenment in the lawyer's world of statutes, precedents, and *stare decisis*. Central to Teilhard's system of thought is his belief in the perfectibility of man. This is why the title of this symposium, *In Quest of the Perfection of Man*, is such an appropriate one.

The Honorable Pearce Young, Judge of the Superior Court, Los Angeles County, initiated his multi-faceted career as a teacher of English at Stanford University, where he was the recipient of many literary prizes and a Fulbright Scholarship to Oxford University. He later served two terms in the California State Assembly where he was chairman of the Judiciary Subcommittee on Domestic Relations, the Governor's Commission on the Family, and the Assembly Committee on Criminal Procedures. Judge Young has also served as vice chairman of the California Arts Commission.

Other philosophers and theologians have shared this view of man's perfectibility, but in different contexts. To some, the quest for perfection was a drama within man himself, acted out in terms of reason, will, and appetite. To others, perfection was a process of achieving a "oneness" with nature or of surrendering oneself to nature's laws. For many mystics of both East and West it has been in terms of union with pure "being"—a nirvana of the spirit. Also, there have been many methods advanced for attaining perfection. Some have advocated the exercise of reason; others, faith and revelation; and others, self-denial.

Unlike those philosophers, metaphysicians, and theologians, Teilhard's system of thought is based upon observations of what he believes to be a natural phenomenon. I have paraphrased a few of those observations and conclusions, which I would like to discuss within the context of law and social justice:

1. That within man are two evolutionary processes: one that moves toward individualization, and the other toward interrelation and cooperation.

2. That man fulfills himself, or achieves his evolutionary future, only in association with other men.

3. That the present crises that we see, both within our society and throughout the world, are the results of our yet imperfect knowledge of the evolutionary process occurring within mankind and the universe.

4. That man's attention must be focused upon his inherent potentials, which are both material and spiritual.

5. That this evolutionary process is occurring on a universal scale and will result eventually in a stage he calls "planetization"—a state of universal self-awareness—a period in man's history when there will be cooperation and social organization on a worldwide scale.

These are lofty thoughts concerning the future of man. At first hearing, they evoke old concepts of "natural law"—of immutable principles at work in Nature herself, which man might discover by the exercise of reason. At the same time, they seem to suggest a certain amount of determinism at work in man's destiny. How do these thoughts square with realities as we see them today? In seeking answers, a series of questions arise. Is man really engaged in an evolutionary process toward the "better life"? Is the world really moving toward a government of nations held together by principles of international law? Does justice have a moral basis that is constant for all men and all nations? Is there not an irreconcilable conflict between liberty and authority—between the individual and the power and authority of the state? How would justice between individuals and nations be achieved in an "age of planetization"? Would a higher tribunal in the "age of planetization" have sustained the results of the Nuremberg trials, or the conviction of a Lieutenant Calley? Teilhard does not answer these questions. In his own words he states that he is concerned with man as a phenomenon—that he does not intend to give an explanation of the world, but only an introduction to that explanation. He has left it to others, including ourselves and this symposium, to discuss the more finite aspects of man's behavior.

When we look at society today through one set of binoculars, the picture we see does not seem to justify Teilhard's optimism. Indeed, the world we live in has become a series of crises—the crisis of war, housing, race relations, free speech, and now the environmental crisis. Our laws and our institutions seem geared to respond to crisis rather than to anticipate or prevent it. Everywhere about us, we see the capacity of man to destroy his environment. He can do it by the use of nuclear weapons, or he can do it more gradually by overpopulation or by the pollution of his air, land, and sea. He can do it by acts of violence and rebellion generated by the desperation of those alienated from the affluence of society.

On the other hand, assuming that man can survive these major crises and thereby preserve and perpetuate his species, the forces at work within society today indicate that he may destroy the very quality of life that centuries of human history and sacrifice have made possible. He may, for example, reject individual liberty in the interest of collective security. In his desperate loneliness within a mass society, he may find that conformity is easier and more convenient than individuality. Finally, out of contempt for traditional values, or out of his inability to find moral precepts that give meaning and identity to his life, he may cast aside our legal system which, faulty though it may be, is the one institution that has guaranteed his individual liberty and security. It is to this latter possible tragedy that I wish to direct the majority of my comments. First, however, let us examine the present state of man and the conditions under which any legal system must operate.

Ramsey Clark has said that the two dynamics in our society are population increase, and science and technology. Both of these dynamics have drastically altered human existence. It is a simple fact that change in our society—change generated by science and technology—has sped up the human time clock. This phenomenon of change due to science and technology has been many times greater and more profound in its effect upon the individual and his institutions than the changes brought about by the industrial revolution of the eighteenth century.

Today, for example, man's knowledge of his physical world more than doubles each decade. Yet, in the midst of this intense technological change, man in his biological sense remains essentially the same as he was thousands of years ago. I am confident Teilhard would have agreed that man has not undergone any significant biological evolution since the stone age. His genetic endowments are the same as those of his prehistoric ancestors. His capacity for violence and compassion are determined by the same genetic laws that affected the conduct of primitive man. In other words, organic evolution is no longer relevant to his future survival.

As I read Teilhard de Chardin, it appears that the real

question to which he addresses himself is as follows: Assuming that man's biological evolution is no longer relevant, is there an evolutionary process going on within man as a thinking and conceptualizing organism that ultimately will result in greater unity within himself, with the universe, and in his relationship with others? Teilhard was confident that this process is taking place and will result in a state he terms the "neo life." He said that "thought might artificially perfect the thinking instrument itself; life might rebound forward under the collective effect of its reflection." Again, he says, "the dream upon which human research obscurely feeds is fundamentally that of mastering, beyond all atomic or molecular affinities, the ultimate energy of which all other energies are merely servants; and thus, by grasping the very mainspring of evolution, seizing the tiller of the world."[1]

To Teilhard, this process of evolution was a clear, observable fact, and inevitable in the nature of man. Although this sounds like the voice of the ultimate optimist, there are moments in which he reflects on man's capacity to abort the evolutionary process and perhaps destroy himself and his environment. In *The Phenomenon of Man* we find the following passage:

> The two-fold crisis whose onset began in earnest as early as the Neolithic age and which rose to a climax in the modern world, derives in the first place from a *mass-formation* (we might call it "planetization") of mankind. Peoples and civilizations reached such a degree either of frontier contact or economic interdependence or psychic communication that they could no longer develop save by interpenetration of one another. . . . Modern man no longer knows what to do with the time and the potentials he has unleashed. We groan under the burden of this wealth. We are haunted by the fear of "unemployment." Sometimes we are tempted to trample this superabundance back into the matter from which it sprang without stopping to think how impossible and monstrous such an act against nature would be. . . .

1 Pierre Teilhard de Chardin, *The Phenomenon of Man,* trans. Bernard Wall (New York: Harper Torchbooks, Harper & Row, 1959) , p. 250. Quoted by permission of Harper & Row, Publishers, Inc.

In order to avoid disturbing our habits we seek in vain to settle international disputes by adjustments of frontiers—or we treat as "leisure" (to be whiled away) the activities at the disposal of mankind. As things are now going it will not be long before we run full tilt into one another. Something will explode if we persist in trying to squeeze into our old tumble-down huts the material and spiritual forces that are henceforward on the scale of the world.[2]

I have quoted this somewhat lengthy passage for several reasons. First, it indicates Teilhard's awareness of the phenomenon of change and that the gap existing between material progress and our social ability to cope with it is one of the central problems of our time. Second, that our failure to develop a social understanding—to bring our knowledge of the physical world together in a working relationship with our social knowledge and institutions may well spell disaster for society.

If my interpretation of Teilhard's thinking is correct, then, indeed, he has made profound observations. It means that man must rework his social institutions in such a way that they will anticipate and adapt themselves to the phenomenon of change. Certainly, the law is one of those institutions most fundamental to man's survival. This is as clear a fact as any scientific observation. Indeed, it is as clear and observable as organic evolution itself, since without the rule of law no individual can survive in his society or realize his full potential. Likewise, without an international rule of law, no nation or culture can hope to preserve its internal integrity or realize its potential as a part of world culture. The problem is both individual and collective, national and international in scope. Without a formulation of the law that will embrace individuals and nations, the "age of planetization" may never be realized.

It is unfortunate that Teilhard did not write about the law. He might have provided us with many valuable insights. However, I am confident that he would have agreed

2 *Ibid.*, pp. 252–53.

that the law, like all other institutions, must address itself to social change; that the rules of law that govern human conduct must have a moral and ethical content or, at least, find their derivation in values that express the aspirations of man; that laws that are based upon force and fear rather than reason, persuasion, and common consent can only achieve temporary and superficial obedience; finally, that a new ethic and a new jurisprudence, which address themselves to men and nations and their interrelationships, are long overdue.

All of us have heard the expression that "law is the glue" that holds society together. There may be a small amount of truth in this statement but it says very little that is significant. A law administered by despots may hold society together, at least temporarily. What is needed are laws that are directed to and enlist the support of the whole human being and achieve equality and justice. Teilhard would have been correct in asserting that the law must have a moral and ethical content before it can become a living thing responsive to the needs of people. How and where do we find those ethical and moral standards?

For centuries, man has searched for objectivity and uniformity in the rules that govern human conduct. In that search he has turned frequently to the concept of "natural law." In its strict construction, that concept asserts that inherent in nature is a body of ideals or principles with uniform application to mankind; that by the exercise of reason these eternal and unalterable principles may be discovered and, once discovered, become the standards of morality and justice. The many legal theorists who have accepted this construction of the natural law have argued that the laws that govern human conduct—the everyday laws of our courts—derive their validity from the principles of natural law. Laws that do not conform to those eternal and immutable principles found in nature are unjust; those which do conform are, of course, just laws.

Such a limited and hermetically sealed concept of natural law has little validity and has been rejected by most modern legal scholars, including the late Jerome Frank. In his book *Courts on Trial* Judge Frank points out such a view can give support to causes that are diametrically opposed. While it has supported revolutionary causes, it also has served the purposes of tyrants and despots; while it has supported freedom for the individual, it has also supported slavery. The defects of the theory lie in the ambiguity of its terms. When we refer to "nature" do we mean all of nature or merely human nature, and if human nature—which aspect of it? When we refer to "reason" do we mean God's reason or man's and, if the latter, the reason of which men? Also, there are two additional flaws in this limited concept of natural law:

First, to argue that human conduct must be ordered in terms of "nature" in a cosmic sense runs contrary to man's social history. Although primitive man was closest to nature and free of the State, he was never truly free. With his primitive technology, his slavery to nature was infinitely greater than the slavery of man today. In other words, human achievement often comes from resisting or combating the forces of nature. John Stuart Mill said that nature impales men, breaks them on the wheel, casts them to be devoured by wild beasts, burns them to death. Again, in a passage from Thomas Huxley, cited by Judge Frank, we find the following:

> Let us understand, once and for all, that the ethical progress of society depends not on imitating the cosmic process, still less on running away from it, but in combatting it. . . . The history of civilization details the steps by which men have succeeded in building up an artificial world within the cosmos. Fragile reed as he may be, man, as Pascal said, is a thinking reed; there lies within him a fund of energy, operating intelligently and so far akin to that which pervades the universe, that it is competent to influence and modify the cosmic process. Law and moral precepts are directing to the end of curbing the cosmic process, and reminding the individual of his duty to the community, to the protection and influence of which he owes, if not existence itself, at least the life of something better than a brutal savage.[3]

[3] Jerome Frank. *Courts on Trial* (New York: Atheneum Press, 1963), pp. 354–55.

The other flaw in the strict natural-law theory is that it gives little or no recognition to what is unique in the human personality. With its emphasis on universals and absolutes—upon uniformity rather than diversity—it is contrary to the concept of human dignity, which requires a high respect for the differences existing between human beings.

If, then, a strict construction of the natural-law doctrine fails to provide a satisfactory basis for a legal system, what ethical norms can we discover to establish that basis? Are there moral values that may, though recognizing diversity, still give some degree of uniformity, certainty, and predictability to the law? Here, I would join with Teilhard in saying that I cannot give a complete explanation of those values. The most I can provide is an introduction from a very personal point of view.

Earlier, I paraphrased five observations that Teilhard made concerning man's evolutionary process. The first three of them asserted that man achieves his evolutive future only in association with other men and that our present crises are the result of our imperfect knowledge of the evolutionary process itself. Such imperfect knowledge can only be cured by greater social awareness and understanding. However, to be acceptable and workable, social understanding cannot be based upon myths or dogmatic morals. To the contrary, it must be based upon a scientific philosophy that understands social needs and is capable of predicting change. Such a social understanding must recognize that the only goal of philosophy is the individual and that the goal of society is to provide the means for his self-expression. Further, it must recognize that any state or social institution that is founded upon false concepts about human nature can only be repressive. What qualities can we find that are unique to man's nature?

Man, unlike other creatures, has a curious awareness of his own destiny. Unlike other creatures, he is able to conceptualize. For centuries, he has questioned the meanings and the aims of existence—has desired to become more than just man—perhaps, in Teilhard's vocabulary, to become "neo-man." Older generations found the answers to their questions in traditional ethics and religion. Today, it is difficult to accept those answers at their face value; it is difficult for the scientist in his laboratory or the sociologist in his study of human institutions. The important thing about man's nature is that this search—this quest for meaning and aims of existence—goes on, particularly among young people. Indeed, the young people of our society are seeking new levels of consciousness and awareness, sometimes to their own destruction when they turn to drugs, and sometimes to their enrichment when they turn to religion or philosophy, no matter how esoteric it might be. Their deep sense of alienation from the older generation is due in part to the injustice they see around them. It is difficult, for example, for them to justify a man-on-the-moon project costing 40 billion dollars when they see the poor starving and their cities decaying. It is difficult for them to accept the wealth technology has created when they see that wealth becomes an end in itself rather than the means for self-realization. It is difficult for them to accept a pious lip service to law and order when they see corruption in government and their parents cheating on the income tax. It is difficult for them to respect the will of the majority when they learn it was the silent majority that tolerated child labor and supported slavery.

When young people act out their frustration and alienation in civil disobedience and violence, their conduct is certainly self-destructive and self-defeating. Fortunately, this is not the conduct of the majority. Most of them seek to expand their social knowledge and awareness. They seek moral and ethical values that will give a richer meaning to their existence and their relationships with their fellow man. They seek a society and a system of laws that respond to change rather than crisis. They seek justice between men, between man and his society, and between nations. Indeed, their search would seem to be an affirmation of the very evolutionary process that Teilhard observed. In response to that search, let us return again to a discussion of "natural law." Let us see if we can find within that concept, or in an expanded version of it, some moral basis for a system of laws.

Lon Fuller, in his book *The Morality of Law,* distinguishes between two kinds of morality—the morality of duty and the morality of aspiration. It is his view that the morality of aspiration goes to the heart of jurisprudence and social conscience. It is the principle that laws and government should have as their fundamental purpose the realization of man's highest capacities; that law and institutions exist to provide a framework within which the individual may seek and achieve his fullest capabilities.

Moral duty, on the other hand, sets down basic rules of conduct, without which it would be impossible to live in an ordered society. These rules are the legal imperatives—the "thou shalt nots." Such laws do not convict a man for failing to realize his fullest capacities but only for failing to respect the basic requirements for living in an ordered society.

Fuller refers to the morality of aspiration as the "internal morality of the law." His view differs from the strict natural-law theory in that his conclusions do not involve a chain of reasoning involving the perfect and the imperfect or the absolute and the particular. In his words, to conclude that one cannot know what is bad without knowing what is perfectly good contradicts human experience. When the law says "Thou shalt not kill," it embraces no picture of the perfect life. It rests only on the obvious truth that if men kill each other, no morality of aspiration, no opportunity for the individual to fulfill himself will be possible.

This view is somewhat similar to the Thomistic version of natural law, which sees man as a rational being with an intuitive awareness of certain universal principles of justice. To St. Thomas of Aquinas such a universal principle would be "seek the common good." This would mean living in society without doing harm to others. From this universal principle, laws are derived such as "Thou shalt not kill," or "Thou shalt not steal." These are the positive laws that hold society together. The important thing about Fuller's and St. Thomas' view, as contrasted with strict natural-law theory, is that it is based upon a sociology that regards the preservation of human integrity and human dignity as the ultimate objectives of society. It asserts that if man determines which of those positive laws and institutions are violating the integrity of the human being, he will be able to change those laws and thereby work out the problems of liberty and justice. I feel that Teilhard de Chardin would have subscribed to such a view because it is consistent with his statement, mentioned earlier, that man only fulfills himself, or achieves his evolutionary future, in association with other men. It is a realistic view of human nature that takes into account that which is common as well as that which is unique in the human personality.

Even though laws and government must exist for man's fulfillment and must recognize what is unique in each human personality, we are still left with the problem of how to preserve individual freedom. Are not society and the individual mutually exclusive terms—entities that are inevitably in conflict with each other? I have said before that primitive man is not truly free—that as he becomes more aware of his material and social environment he expands his personal freedom. But does he not at the same time increase the power of the State? We know that a society preserves itself and insures its own survival by being concerned with the majority. Even though the individual's liberty is guaranteed by society, is not his existence always a compromise with the State? In other words, does not the law itself set the bounds of individual liberty?

This polarization of two abstract goods—liberty and authority—is certainly one of the great dramas and dilemmas of our time. Indeed, the problems it poses should occupy the minds of every lawyer, judge, and thinking citizen. Out of this apparent conflict between liberty and authority arise such immense moral issues as the Nuremberg Trials, the My Lai incident, and the rebellion of youth. It involves such questions as whether or not man has a moral conscience, which the State invades at its own peril; whether it is right for one to violate what he feels is an unjust law if he is willing to accept the consequences. It raises the argument that if the State sets the limits of individual liberty, it can also deny liberty entirely. Therefore, every state or nation is totalitarian to a greater or lesser degree. Finally, assuming that mankind can develop some kind of world government of nations, would not the same issues of conflicting liberty and authority be transposed on an international scale?

Teilhard does not give us the answers to these questions and it would be more than presumptuous to suggest that I have found them. During a recent symposium at the Center for the Study of Democratic Institutions, some very learned men discussed these problems of liberty versus authority. Common consensus seemed to be that the conflict is inevitable and that the solution lies in achieving a balance.

I would like to suggest, however, that if we see nothing but an irreconcilable conflict between freedom and security—between liberty and authority—then we may miss a great opportunity to expand *both* freedom and security; that if our social science and our laws are designed to achieve a balance between freedom and security, we may miss that balance entirely. I would suggest that the only way to achieve a balance and establish equilibrium is to expand social knowledge. If we fail to do this, then social ignorance will determine the balance point for us.

Now that I am at the conclusion of this speech, I feel that I have posed many problems but provided few solutions. Some of these problems may never be solved. Others, if not solved, may mean catastrophe for mankind. I have said that the conflict between liberty and authority must be resolved on an international as well as a national scale. With your indulgence, I would like to direct my few final comments to the international aspect of that problem.

If you agree that man's evolutionary future lies in expanded social knowledge, then also you may agree that one's view of social science, or cultural anthropology, may affect drastically the conclusions to be drawn from observing social phenomena. Indeed, there have been two major approaches to the study of social phenomena, both of which admit to an evolutionary process. One is the naturalistic or deterministic view, which sees man as molded and shaped by his cultural environment—which finds within society's growth and development a process of natural selection. To this school of thought, sociology and cultural anthropology are purely scientific studies similar to physics or biology. The derived laws of social and cultural development are the natural result of scientific observation. Such is the approach of Neitzsche or Karl Marx. Under such a view, man's destiny, together with his ethical and moral values, is determined by socio-economic factors that are beyond his power to control.

Contrasted with this is the humanistic approach, which regards the evolutionary nature of man as one of human achievement and discovery. By this view, culture, ethics, and moral values are not the products of brute economics but are shaped by man's creativity—his free will and capacity to alter his environment. To the humanist, the study of sociology reveals certain consistent patterns of human development, but unlike the determinist he does not regard his study as an exact science or even as a natural science. Both views admit the existence of an evolutionary process or a scientific method of observing human history and behavior. To the humanist, however, the mind remains free to reflect on the evidence of nature and thereby change its course. If Teilhard de Chardin does not belong to this latter humanistic school of thought, he at least uses it as his departure point.

What kind of a world legal order would Teilhard have

envisaged in the "age of planetization"? I doubt that he would have predicted a super-state to which all nations will surrender their sovereignty. Rather, he would have recognized that in spite of the economic interdependence of nations, there are vast differences that exist in terms of culture, language, literature, and religion. He would have recognized that while we must preserve what is unique in the individual, we must also preserve the unique in society, and that the genius of mankind often lies in its cultural diversity. At the same time, he would have recognized that in every nation there exist certain ethnocentric attitudes based upon mythological and unscientific views of nature and the cosmos; that when those attitudes become the dominant political attitudes of a nation they can result in bigotry and tyranny. Dean Roscoe Pound has said that uncritical acceptance of a picture of things as they should be, by which unconsciously all things are measured, is a chief source of intolerance, social misunderstanding, class hatred, race antagonism, group hostility and religious animosity. A reduction of intolerance and hostility cannot be achieved, as Teilhard said, "by an adjustment of frontiers." It can be achieved only by expanded social knowledge based upon realistic views of human nature. It can be achieved only by laws and institutions that both adapt to the dynamics of change and preserve and advance that which is unique in the human spirit.

In a recent speech given in Santa Barbara, California, at the Center for the Study of Democratic Institutions, Lord Richie Calder discussed man's capacity to destroy his environment. Great civilizations, he said, have been born, reach maturity, and then die. However, in the great cycle of civilizations, this may very well be the last. The leaders of older civilizations spent some of their precious resources on creating monuments to their own magnificence, such as the great pyramids of the ancient Pharaohs.

> Modern man [Lord Richie says] can throw his pyramids into space where they may orbit, through all eternity, round a planet

which died of his neglect. For in world affairs today, the meaning is absolute. This is the last civilization. Other civilizations rose and flourished and died, but there were others to succeed them. Today, ours is a global civilization. It is not bound by the Tigris and Euphrates, nor by the Hellespont and the Indies; it is the whole world. It is a close community so interdependent that every mistake we make is exaggerated on a world scale. With wisdom, which is knowledge tempered by judgment, we can apply our science to a common purpose and enhance the well-being of the whole human race.

To expand human knowledge and social understanding requires a respect for the dignity of man and a reverence for life. Teilhard de Chardin possessed both of these essentials. Once they become the common property of mankind, then the "age of planetization" may become a living reality.

Conflict, Cooperation, and the Collectivization of Man

Robert T. Francoeur, Ph.D.

There is a very creative caldron of questions seething today in the minds of more and more people around the earth. To my mind, the prime appeal of Teilhard de Chardin's grand synthesis lies in the fact that he tackled these fundamental questions about the nature of man and his future which so concern the professional philosopher, educator, youth, and man in the street. In these areas where definitive answers are impossible and we are reduced to living with "working hypotheses," Teilhard accepted a series of *options,* which many today find not only psychologically and emotionally comforting and inspiring but, more important, convincing—even with our limited evidence.

Dr. Francoeur, a married Roman Catholic priest, holds master's and doctorate degrees in biology and a master's degree in Catholic Theology. As founder, past president, and now chairman of The American Teilhard de Chardin Association, he has written articles and books not only on Teilhard, but also evolution, human sexuality, and process theology. His most recent book, *Utopian Motherhood: New Trends in Human Reproduction,* focuses on the controversial impact of reproductive technology on our understanding of human sexuality and the structuring of family life. He is now an Associate Professor of Experimental Embryology at Fairleigh Dickinson University.

These options begin with the question: "Is the Universe utterly pointless, or are we to accept that it has a meaning, a future, a purpose?"[1] Teilhard obviously opted for a Universe with meaningful purpose and a future, only to face a second option: if we have a future, then what is its direction and character? More precisely, have the decisions and actions of men, past and present, cast us and future generations into some definite channel of development? Are we already committed to a specific future by the past evolution of life and man? Teilhard was firmly convinced from his fifty years of reflection and study that we are committed to a specific future by our past.[2]

Among the wide variety of possible futures, Teilhard found empirically the most acceptable choice to be a process universe that converges on a central cosmic (personal) focus —an "Omega Point." This convergence involves passing through several planes of complexity/consciousness. On each of these planes a dialectics of divergence/convergence/emergence is played out in the birth of new and higher levels of complexity/consciousness. On the subatomic, the atomic, the molecular, megamolecular, cellular, and animal planes, reality diverged to explore (by chance and groping) all the possible forms of existence on that level, only to plunge into a phase of convergence in which certain unspecialized and creatively unstable forms focus on the advent of a new and higher form of reality.[3] Most crucial for us today, this same evolutionary dialectics is now being played out on the human level. Having invested a million or two years in exploring

1 Pierre Teilhard de Chardin, "The Grand Option," *The Future of Man*, trans. Norman Denny (New York: Harper & Row, 1964) pp. 42–44. Quoted by permission of Harper & Row, Publishers, Inc.

2 *Ibid.*, pp. 45–52. Also in the same volume: "The Directions and Conditions of the Future," pp. 227–37.

3 Pierre Teilhard de Chardin, "Outline of a Dialectic of Spirit," *Activation of Energy*, trans. René Hague (New York: Harcourt Brace Jovanovich, 1970) pp. 141–52; Robert T. Francoeur, *Perspectives in Evolution* (Baltimore: Helicon Press, 1965), pp. 128–42; 252–53; *idem, Evolving World, Converging Man* (New York: Holt Rinehart & Winston, 1970), pp. 34, 40, 45, and 176–77.

the rich possibilities of races, cultures, and subspecies, mankind has since the dawn of the Neolithic Age nervously edged toward a united mankind with all the conflicts and cooperative tensions this convergence entails.[4]

On several occasions Teilhard compared mankind's present situation to a boiling point, a critical threshold which, once crossed, would bring into existence a totally new form of human consciousness and being—the "ultra-reflective superhuman"; a differentiated union of all men in a loving, personal, humanizing life drawing its strength from contact with the center of the cosmos, Omega. In *Man's Place in Nature* (1948) Teilhard spoke of the curve of corpusculization evident in the growing complexity of the inorganic world, which leads to the gradual emergence of new, higher, and more flexible forms of freedom, spontaneity, and the ability to respond to an environment evident in the evolution of the central nervous system of animals (cerebralization), and culminates in the social and cultural convergence of mankind.[5] Written in 1936, Teilhard's *An Essay on a Personalistic Universe* approaches cosmogenesis and anthropogenesis in terms of the personalization of individual men and of a convergent mankind: our future lies in the direction of the more personal; in developing and expanding new, deeper, more conscious, and more loving relations among individual human beings and between men and the other elements of our universe; in bringing to birth a personal synthesis and union of the fragmented cosmos through personal and transcendent love.[6]

Centrology (1944) pictures cosmic and human evolution

---

[4] Pierre Teilhard de Chardin, *The Phenomenon of Man*, trans. Bernard Wall (New York: Harper & Row, 1959), pp. 237–53; *idem*, "A Great Event Foreshadowed: The Planetisation of Mankind," *The Future of Man*, pp. 124–39; *idem.*, "From the Pre-Human to the Ultra-Human: The Phases of a Living Planet," in *ibid.*, pp. 289–97.

[5] Pierre Teilhard de Chardin, *Man's Place in Nature*, trans. René Hague (New York: Harper & Row, 1966).

[6] Pierre Teilhard de Chardin, *Human Energy*, trans. J. M. Cohen (New York: Harcourt Brace Jovanovich), pp. 53–92.

as a system and process of ever-enlarging and more conscious centers reaching out to embrace and unite the fragmented atoms of the world. Many of Teilhard's essays touch on love as the basic energy force at work in the universe. The creative tensions of conflict and cooperation appear in each of these essays, but always on a fairly theoretical basis.[7] In Book Four, "Survival," of *The Phenomenon of Man* (1940), for instance, Teilhard discusses the impersonal forces already at work in nature and society, which are forcing all of us into convergence, and which we must recognize, accept, and reinforce (transform) by our love for the Universal All and for each man. But even in this *Meisterwerk,* the discussion of conflict and cooperation in human convergence is quite theoretical.

THE FUTURE OF THE SEXUAL PERSON

In 1936 Teilhard projected the future convergence of individual human (sexual) atoms in these words:

> In what direction may we expect this further evolution of love to be realized? It will lead, without doubt, to a gradual decrease in what still [in 1936], necessarily, constitutes the admirable but impermanent reproductive side of the [human] sexual relationship. Life propagates itself not simply for the sake of doing so, but only in order to accumulate the elements necessary for its personalization. When, therefore, the earth approaches the maturity of its personality, men will have to recognize that their problem is not simply the control of the birth-rate; the really important thing will be to allow full development to the quantity of love released from the duty of reproduction. Under the pressure of this new need, the essentially personalizing function of love will be more or less completely detached from what has hitherto had to serve as the instrument of propagation; in other words from "the flesh." Without ceasing to be physical—indeed in order to remain physical—love will become more spiritual.[8]

7 Teilhard de Chardin, *The Activation of Energy.*
8 Pierre Teilhard de Chardin, "An Essay on a Personalistic Universe," *Human Energy,* p. 77.

This statement from "An Essay on a Personalistic Universe" has accumulated new meaning and much greater relevance in the 35 years since it was penned in China. The social birth of women as legal and economic persons (woman's liberation in its broadest dimensions), the advent of a contraceptive culture after the Second World War, our growing concern with population and pollution, a leisure-oriented culture, the explorations in new forms of human relations among our youth—these and many other factors Teilhard might have foreseen in a very vague way, but obviously he could not appreciate their impact with the detail and perspective we enjoy today.

> The two-fold crisis whose onset began in earnest as early as the Neolithic age and which rose to a climax in the modern world, derives in the first place from a *mass-formation* (we might call it a "planetisation") of mankind. Peoples and civilizations reached such a degree either of physical communion or economic interdependence or frontier contact that they could no longer develop save by interpenetration of one another. But it also arises out of the fact, that under the combined influence of machinery and the super-heating of thought, we are witnessing a *formidable upsurge of unused powers.* Modern man no longer knows what to do with the time and the potentialities he has unleashed. We groan under the burden of this wealth. We are haunted by the fear of "unemployment." Sometimes we are tempted to trample this super-abundance back into the matter from which it sprang without stopping to think how impossible and monstrous such an act against nature would be.[9]

Many of the political, economic, sociological, and cultural aspects of this key statement from *The Phenomenon of Man* are explored elsewhere in this symposium. I want to apply this statement of Teilhard's on leisure and the preliminary elements outlined above, to the more fundamental, more personal, revolution we are involved in in the convergence, personalization, and hominization of the basic human sexual relationship and its coordinate synthetic union, the family.

---

[9] *The Phenomenon of Man,* p. 252.

TEILHARD'S OPTION: A VIRGINAL UNIVERSE

Teilhard's premises as outlined above are almost self-evident in their validity, but I am afraid his vision as a prophet suffered from the myopia of a French biologist-cleric.

Teilhard's premises, I repeat, are solid and valid; it is only his interpretation and extrapolation of them that I seriously question. The future he chooses for the sexual human contradicts his own basic premises, which rest on the statement that:

> The energy that feeds and elaborates our interior life is originally passionate in nature. Like every other animal, man is essentially an urge towards the union that brings out completeness; he is a capacity to love. Plato pointed this out a long time ago. It is from this primordial impulse that the rich complexity of intellectual and emotional life develops and builds up and assumes different forms. However lofty and widespread the ramifications of our spirit, their roots still reach down into the physical. It is from man's deep reserves of passion that the warmth and light of his being arise, transfigured. It is in them that is initially concentrated, like a seed, the highest and most subtle essence, the most sensitive motor, of the whole spiritual development.[10]

In the same "Essay on a Personalistic Universe," Teilhard emphasizes that the "mutual attraction of the sexes is so fundamental a fact that any explanation of the world (whether biological, philosophical or religious) that cannot find for it a structurally essential place in its system, is to all intents and purposes ruled out."[11] More important still is the fact that Teilhard's vision of a cosmic system based on union is, of all the known Christian visions, the most accommodating to and compatible with a realistic appreciation of human sexuality as coextensive with the human personality.

10 "An Essay on a Personalistic Universe," *Human Energy*, p. 71.
11 *Ibid.*, p. 72.

Teilhard's prognosis for the basic human sexual relationship can be paraphrased in two sentences: As men and women, and mankind in general, become more fully human and conscious as individuals and as sexual persons, they will realize that their mutual attraction and fertility transcend not merely the need to reproduce, but even the need to unite physically in sexual intercourse. Men and women will become more sexual, *but in a "virginal" way.*[12]

> Not in flight (by suppressing them) but in mastery of (by sublimating them) the unfathomable spiritual forces that still lie dormant beneath the mutual attraction of the sexes—there lie the hidden essence of chastity and the grand task it will have to face.[13]

Hominization, for Teilhard, entails and requires:

> a gradual increase in the spiritual function of the sexes, accompanied by a gradual cutting down of the "reproductive" aspect and of the physical acts that lead up to it; as mankind is gradually transformed in nearing its maturity, the multiplication of the species will simply be limited to the optimum demanded by eugenics.[14]

CRITIQUE OF TEILHARD'S VIRGINAL UNIVERSE

We would hardly expect a biologist-philosopher-theologian as dedicated as Teilhard was to the reality of human sexuality and its passionately fundamental role in cosmic evolution to come up with a projection of a virginal humanity and universe. But it was precisely Teilhard's biological training that triggered him to this projection.

---

[12] *L'évolution de la chasteté* (unpublished essay to appear in vol. 11 of the *Oeuvres de Teilhard de Chardin,* Editions du Seuil, Paris); Henri DeLubac, *Teilhard de Chardin and the Eternal Feminine* (New York: Harper & Row, 1971).

[13] Pierre Teilhard de Chardin, *Le Coeur de la Matière* (unpublished, 1950).

[14] Letter of 11 November 1934, cited by Emile Rideau, *The Thought of Teilhard de Chardin,* trans. René Hague (New York: Harper & Row, 1967), p. 131.

> Look quite coldly, as a biologist or engineer, at the *lurid* sky over a great city at night. There, and indeed everywhere else, the Earth is constantly dissipating, in pure loss, its most miraculous power [human sexual attraction, sexual energy].
> How much energy do you think is lost to the Spirit of the Earth in one night [through physical sexual unions that are nonprocreative]?[15]

"His very love of biology and of nature recoiled from the wastefulness and insufficiency and degradation so prominent in the use of sex around us."[16] But maybe it was just this biological myopia which prevented Teilhard from seeing the obvious. As mankind matures, we are indeed transcending the biological necessity of procreating; we are effectively liberating the sexual union from reproduction. The "union [of a man and woman] for this child" is indeed giving way to a more fully human and personal relationship of "union for an idea, work, for mutual growth, for personalization."[17] The problem is that Teilhard jumps from reproductive-oriented sexuality to virginity without allowing for the possibility that co-creative sexuality need not be limited to the intellectual sphere—Teilhard's virginal union of man and woman for intellectual fertility and growth. The male/female relationship can be just as creative and intellectually fertile, perhaps more so, when it includes nonreproductive sexual intercourse.[18]

Teilhard's unswerving defense of his own life as a celibate Jesuit, and his evident complete satisfaction with that life,

---

15 Pierre Teilhard de Chardin, "The Spirit of the Earth," *Human Energy*, p. 34.

16 Robert North, *Teilhard and the Creation of the Soul* (Milwaukee: Bruce, 1967), p. 280.

17 Pierre Teilhard de Chardin, "An Essay on a Personalistic Universe," *Human Energy*, p. 73.

18 Abel Jeanniere, *The Anthropology of Sex*, trans. Julie Kernan (New York: Harper & Row, 1967); Charles W. Freible, "Teilhard, Sexual Love, and Celibacy," *Review for Religious* 6, no. 2 (March 1967):282–94; Daniel Sullivan, "Psycho-sexuality: The Teilhardian Lacunae," *Continuum* 5, no. 2 (Summer 1967):254–78; *idem*, "Oraison: Clerical Freudianism," *Continuum*, 5 no. 1 (Spring 1967):160–66.

undoubtedly complemented his biological myopia. In his essay "The Evolution of Chastity" (1934), Teilhard writes that "By its spontaneity and universality, the call to chastity is too close to the infallible instincts of Life to be a dated value."[19] This may be a valid statement but does it mean, as Teilhard concludes, that we, the human race *in toto,* are headed toward a virginal universe? Any more than the spontaneity and universality of marriage (and nonprocreative sexual intercourse today) mean that humans in the future generations and in the life after death will all be married?

A colleague of Teilhard's and a prominent moral theologian, Stanley de Lestapis, has carried Teilhard's projection to its blunt conclusion in commenting on the population situation: "This challenge can be met *only* by the practice of continence in marriage, inspired by the virtue of chastity, and controlled by an appreciation of the optimal population-level required for the common good."[20] Teilhard was far more poetic, and perhaps thus more deceptive when he wrote:

> It is really the universe which, through Woman, is advancing towards Man. If Man fails to recognize the true nature and the true object of his love, the disorder which follows is profound and irremediable. Desperately striving to appease upon something too small a passion which is addressed to (the) All, he inevitably tries to cure a fundamental disequilibrium by constantly increasing the number of his experiences, or making them more material in character. . . . Man must, instead, perceive the universal Reality which shines spiritually through the flesh. . . . Woman is put before him as the attraction and symbol of the World. He can only unite with her by enlarging himself to the scale of the World . . . can only reach Woman through consummation of the universal Union.[21]

---

[19] Pierre Teilhard de Chardin, *L'évolution de la chasteté,* unpublished, 1934.

[20] Stanley de Lestapis, "Défi demographique et avenir de l'humanité," *Revue de l'Action Populaire* (April 1962), pp. 389–403.

[21] Pierre Teilhard de Chardin, "The Spirit of the Earth," *Human Energy,* p. 34.

Robert North, noted Jesuit biblical scholar and convinced Teilhardian, finds in all this extrapolation to a virginal universe:

> an element of the mystic dreamer to which neither the biologist nor the theologian is apt to subscribe. . . .
> Even the scientific insights of Teilhard would seem to have converged on a restoring of biology and bodily matter to a share in the life of the spirit [the fully human sexual embodied person], not only for "second-rate-citizens" in the Kingdom of God but in those who are called to be its leaders and examples. Yet he never for an instant saw it this way.[22]

In projecting *The Evolution of Chastity* to a universal role, Teilhard did acknowledge that his prognosis was not completely satisfactory, either in theory or in practice.[23] I suspect that even with his French clericalism, Teilhard's basic devotion to and respect for the fully sexual human person allowed him to find basic deficiencies in the practice and theology of celibacy in his day as well as in the theology and practice of marriage. In the former, the essence and value of celibacy was expressed in the negativism of "lack of sexual intercourse"; while in marriage, relations between the sexes were kept to a minimum except for procreative purposes.[24]

Teilhard's virginal universe contradicts his premises in yet another major sense. The "differentiated union" forms the underlying structure of his evolutionary synthesis. The elements and components united in any evolutionary centraliza-

---

22 North, pp. 280–81.

23 Pierre Teilhard de Chardin, *L'évolution de la chasteté* (unpublished, 1934).

24 North (p. 282) sums up the defective marital theology prevalent in Teilhard's day, and from which he could not completely escape: "Our practice is based on the dated formula that except for procreation all relation between the sexes is to be kept down to a minimum. By its animal raptures and swooning of the personality, sex is fringed in human instinct with a *horror* combined with animality, shame, excitement, fear, and mystery: all summed up in the slogan found ready-made in Apocalypse 14:4, "unpolluted by contact with women." The closing phrase has also been the trigger for a very negativistic understanding of celibacy.

tion are thereby lifted to a higher plane of existence. Their individual integrity remains intact, but the whole new entity is more complex, more heterogeneous, and more conscious. Union, true union, cannot destroy or lessen what it unites. Yet human sexuality (and the sexual union), when properly understood in the authentic biblical context of interpersonal knowing (communion), is an essential facet of human nature. For some humans the life of celibacy freely chosen is a fruitful and fulfilling way of life, but it certainly cannot be universalized as *the* authentically human way of life for all.[25]

Finally, Teilhard argues for a homogeneous virginal human race; but he also argues that the evolutionary process and its differentiated unions transform the homogeneous fragments of the universe into a very heterogeneous complex—an organism, indeed a super-organism, which integrates and perfects countless distinct and different types of human atoms within its system. Herbert Spencer argued long ago that cultural evolution is *from the homogeneous to the heterogeneous and complex*. With this Teilhard agrees in principle. It is just that Teilhard contradicts his principles when he argues for a future homogeneity in a virginal universe.

AN ALTERNATIVE TO TEILHARD'S VIRGINAL UNIVERSE

If Teilhard's virginal universe is inconsistent with his principles, is there another working hypothesis we can offer that is more in keeping with present evidence and with his principles of a convergent personalizing cosmic evolution? I am convinced there is a fairly evident alternative that we can examine here, particularly in the context of *Conflict, Cooperation and the Collectivisation of Man*.

[25] R. T. Francoeur, *Utopian Motherhood: New Trends in Human Reproduction* (New York: Doubleday, 1970), pp. 242–64; and "Morality and the New Embryology," *IDOC-North American Edition*, #8 (15 August 1970), pp. 81–96; and Pierre Teilhard de Chardin, "The Spirit of the Earth" and "Essay on a Personalistic Universe," *Human Energy*, pp. 42 and 64.

To be valid, any alternative to Teilhard's virginal universe must conform to the three Teilhardian principles outlined below:

First, the ultra-synthesis of mankind and the personalization of the individual thus united must respect the requirements of the differentiated union. The further personalization of the individual sexual person must perfect and fulfill the embodied sexuality that makes us uniquely human.

Human sexuality and the relationship of men and women are a serious matter affecting the basic human situation. They are an invitation for the sexual human to break out of his self-centered circle, to live for other persons, to liberate and fulfill himself.[26] Refusal of this invitation to love is tantamount to a fall back into the fragmented and isolated existence of the incomplete individual; self-enslavement, alienation, and ultimate self-extermination.

Second, our alternative must recognize and integrate the fact that the basic relationship of the human male and female is no longer focused on reproduction, but on interpersonal communication. Geneticist H. Bentley Glass had remarked that the total separation of human sexual intercourse from procreation (by our contraceptive pill technology and our new potentials for producing humans via artificial insemination, artificial wombs, embryo transplants and even asexually by cloning) marks a "major perturbation in human history." With procreation and human sexual intercourse now two distinct realities and two distinct human decisions, we must evolve separate ethics to govern each of these areas of human behavior.

Human sexuality and sexual intercourse (the male/female relationship) must be seen in the broadly human and personal context of the ancient Hebrews—interpersonal knowing and communion in the deepest, most personal way. Thus, "those sexual expressions which build up communion be-

26 Pierre Teilhard de Chardin, "The Spirit of the Earth," *Human Energy*, pp. 20–34.

tween persons, establish a hopeful outlook on the future, minister in a healing way to the fears, hurts and anxieties of persons and confirm to them the fact that they are truly loved, are 'truly Christian relations'."[27] The relations nourished between sexual persons should enhance rather than limit their spiritual freedom, express a compassionate and consistent concern for the well-being of the other, build up the creative potential of the persons involved, burst with joyful celebration of our sexual nature, avoid exploitation, and express the playful element inherent in all healthy human eroticisms (such as we find in dance, song, poetry, and other celebrations of life and the universe).

Third, the future of sexual humans must respect the unique personalities derived from a wide variety of cultures. As sexual persons from a wide variety of cultures and backgrounds are drawn together in a mobile world society, heterogeneity will replace homogeneity. Boundaries that in the past isolated homogeneous islands of people will be replaced by an ever-tightening network of communications and cultural exchanges, which makes homogeneous groupings and behavioral patterns impossible.

The evolution of sexual mankind from isolated, fragmented, and homogeneous cultural islands to a very pluralistic worldwide society has been very well expressed in the recent Task Force Study Document issued by the United Presbyterian Church in the U.S.A. on *Sexuality and the Human Community:*

> We frequently found ourselves challenging the conventional wisdom of the Christian community concerning sexuality, only to find that those conventions were too often the culture-bound wisdom of a part of the community: to wit, the white, Protestant, and middle-class part. But the Christian community encompasses a wide diversity of racial, ethnic, and cultural groups, and therefore a wide variety of assessments of sex-

[27] *Sexuality and the Human Community* (a task force report published by the United Presbyterian Church of the U.S.A., 1970), p. 11.

uality and sexual behavior. The polygamy that is permitted among some African Christians would be unthinkable among the Protestants of Geneva; and the cloistering restrictions upon women in some Latin countries would be altogether unacceptable to most American teenagers. This sobering fact of social and cultural pluralism within the church made it difficult to achieve many generalizations about the appropriateness of specific forms of sexual behavior.[28]

In exploring *The Future of Marriage as Institution,* C. Jaime Snoek, a German Redemptorist theologian, offers a cogent comment on *the necessity of pluralism today in our male/female relationships:*

> It is clear that a multiplicity of cultures will lead to a multiplicity of customs and institutions designed to socialize and institutionalize sexuality. These will be valid to the extent that, within their cultural context, they serve to promote and actualize the idea of humanity in general.[29]

Let me preface an outline of alternate forms of relationships for the sexual person of today and tomorrow, with the challenge issued by the prophetic United Presbyterian statement. In dealing with the problems of senior citizens and with the traditional marriage-oriented ethics, which leave the single person in a type of no-man's land, this marvelously creative (and very Teilhardian) statement asks:

> [Is] abstinence or sublimation the only advice the church will have to give to single persons? Or, will it be able to explore new forms of male-female relationships and, while affirming the primacy of [the monogamous] marriage and the nuclear family as the [ideal] pattern for heterosexual relationship, be able to condone a plurality of patterns which will make a better place for the unmarried?[30]

---

28 *Ibid.,* p. 7.
29 C. Jaime Snoek, *The Future of Marriage as Institution,* ed. Franz Bockle (New York: Herder & Herder, 1970), p. 116.
30 *Sexuality and the Human Community,* p. 35.

What options are we likely to encounter in the decades ahead? As C. Jaime Snoek noted, the churches did not invent monogamy or marriage:

> It is the mature fruit of long human experience, and came into being initially merely to safeguard the continuance of the species through a guarantee of parental care and a certain minimum of economic stability. It has known greater and lesser degrees of flexibility in its history, with more or less pre- and extra-marital freedom.[31]

In human history we can find many precedents that were and are still quite acceptable in different cultures. Some, perhaps all, of these patterns will become socially and broadly acceptable within the purview and experience of Noospheric man.

1. The traditional *monogamous,* sexually exclusive couple marriage, will, I am convinced, remain one of the dominant patterns of male/female relationship despite the increasing tensions of leisure, mobility, women's liberation, our reproductive technology, and an ever-expanding life expectancy.
2. An increasing number of men and women will find an alternate mode of coping with these tensions in a more flexible form of monogamy that allows for comarital experiences, by mutual consent, for both partners. *Co-marital* is a term coined by the Reverend William Genné, of the National Council of Churches, Family Life Bureau, to indicate relationships not extramarital in a competitive and negative sense, but relationships that are co-creative within the context of a stable marriage. This modified form of couple marriage may, I suspect, become the most common form of male-female relationships, since it adjusts to and accommodates the new tensions noted above.
3. *Serial monogamy* or *consecutive polygamy,* which we already have in great measure with our patterns of divorce and remarriage, will in the future resolve the patriarchal inequities of alimony, child support, and custody, and the charge of guilt in the miscarriage of a marriage.
4. *Trial marriages* or *two-step marriages,* advocated by Mar-

31 Snoek, p. 111.

garet Mead and many others, allow a young couple to live together and share personal growth before they reach a decision on whether or not they want to enter into a more stable relationship and begin the serious task of producing and raising a family. This option is in many ways merely an updating of the old Jewish (and current Bavarian) custom of espousal where an unmarried couple tested the girl's fertility. Today a trial marriage is entered into for more humane and serious reasons of mutual growth as sexual persons.

5. *Polygamy for senior citizens* is an option very directly alluded to by the United Presbyterian statement (quoted above). A variety of new factors urge the social and moral acceptability of this option: chemotherapy which extends sexual activity into old age; the economic limitations of single people on social security or retirement; the increasing isolation of the aged from their children's family life; a need for mutual assistance in health care, food preparation, and friendship within their own age group.
6. *Unisex marriages* of two males or two females may soon be legalized in several states. If sexual relations are no longer justified morally in sole terms of procreation, then homosexuality can no longer be condemned as unnatural because it is unprocreative. This would then open the door to a moral and social acceptance of the unisexual marriage.
7. *Single parents,* either male or female, by adoption, artificial insemination, or a more orthodox "affair," is another family option. Of course, there are already thousands of "single parents" resulting from divorce every year in this country.
8. *Group marriages,* which have considerable precedents in American history during the last century: The Oneida Community of upstate New York practiced a very strict religious form of group or complex marriage among its 350 members.
9. *Retirement parents* would mean parenthood postponed to an early retirement age. With more and more union contracts allowing a man to retire at full or part pay after 20 years of service, retirement parenthood is an economically feasible and even desirable possibility. (Of course, the Irish have been doing this for years!)
10. *Contractual marriages* would be renewable at specific intervals, i.e., the recent proposal by two Maryland state

representatives that residents of that state be allowed a legal choice between the customary "until death do us part" marriage and a three-year renewable contract license.

11. Unstructured but stable *cohabitation* is the traditional common law marriage.
12. *Professional parenthood* would limit childbearing to trained couples, as a result of our growing concern with the population problem.
13. *Legalized polygamy and polyandry,* or triangular marriages, or two males and one female, or vice versa, might even include a revival of the Mormon tradition (without the depersonalization and subjection that characterized that practice so often).
14. A freely chosen *single life,* celibate or otherwise, is an obvious and traditional option.
15. The *celibate marriage* is where the co-creativeness of the husband and wife replaces procreation and even the physical expression of sexual intercourse. This model, I should add, is undoubtedly very close to what Teilhard envisioned for marriage of the future.

These are the major options and alternatives we face for the future. They are gropings. They are explorations. And undoubtedly some of these gropings are going to end up in evolutionary dead-ends, as has happened countless times over in the past with evolutionary gropings. There will be among these options some abortions. But the end result of these explorations will hopefully be a more differentiated union of sexual persons, a more fulfilling relationship, and the possibility of the fullest development of the individual human atom if for no other reason than that the necessity of squeezing oneself into some predetermined role is now replaced with a free, human, and reasoned choice among many options.

This, it seems to me, is the creative potential and promise of a pluralistic heterogeneous noospheric society, as opposed to the restricted (sterile) homogeneity of Teilhard's virginal universe.

CONCLUSION

Many times Teilhard stressed that the pioneering elements

in any critical threshold of evolution are creatively unstable and unspecialized individuals who are unhappy with and ill-adapted to their environment. The men and women today who are exploring and creating new male/female relationships are unspecialized individuals who are unhappy with their environment and ill-adapted to it. Many men and women today are exploring and creating new male-female relationships. These people are certainly unstable, unspecialized, unhappy with, and ill-adapted to, the traditional monogamous culture in which we are born and raised. In rejecting the traditional values of family and parenthood, they encounter considerable psychological tension and emotional conflict in their own painful personal gropings and in their exchange with the more conservative and traditional society they hope to change.[32]

In exploring new patterns, they are creating what our traditional society can only label as "gross immoral perversions." These perversions, however, I think are sometimes creative and prophetic of the new, flexible, pluralistic, heterogeneous culture that mankind is entering into—where human sexual relationships will primarily be interpersonal and only infrequently procreative. We are exploring new patterns and these patterns produce a lot of problems. I believe that they are going to produce a lot more problems for men, emotionally and psychologically, than for women.

In this facet of the painful maturation of mankind, there is evidence of a degree of public cooperation. It is noticeable in mass electronic communications; in the exploration of new themes in motion pictures such as *The Baby-Maker, Bob and Carol and Ted and Alice, The Buttercup Chain, Women in Love,* and others that are beginning to grapple with plural patterns; in the Utopian novels of Robert Rimmer, such as *Harrad Experiment, Proposition 31, Rebellion*

---

32 For some of Teilhard's thoughts on "groping" and "invention," see *The Phenomenon of Man,* pp. 222–23; *Essay on a Personalistic Universe,* pp. 53–88; and *Human Energy,* pp. 146–62.

of Yale Marrat, and in his most recent book, *You and I . . . Searching for Tomorrow;* and in the novels of Robert Heinlein *Stranger in a Strange Land* and *The Moon Is a Harsh Mistress.* And then there is a whole vast, mottled chain of underground newspapers. All of these things and many other factors combine into an ever-tightening, Noospheric network that encourages "perverse" explorations and their initial social tolerance and acceptance in an ever more mobile and increasingly anonymous population.

If we are indeed headed for a heterogeneous world with a wide variety of socially accepted relationships, then our educational system has got to face facts and start preparing for it. We cannot continue to squabble myopically about whether we are going to teach the basic facts of life in our schools while we continue to toss our young people into an already pluralistic culture where they are naïvely unprepared for the pros-and-cons of the many different life patterns among which they are going to have to make a rational choice.

There is a lot of confusion today about what it means to be a masculine- or feminine-oriented embodied person, but I believe that this confusion is creative, because it forces us to take a new look at human sexuality and to get out of the little, simple black-and-white world of genital sex. We must realize that human sexuality and the relationships of sexual persons are, for Teilhard and for us, still very much in flux and process.

My belief is that these are the growth pains: the tensions, the conflicts, the turmoil, the collaboration, and the cooperations necessary for the growth of man and mankind. Increased freedom, increased options, increased consciousness, can only mean more personal, hence more human, lives. Pain and joy are both essential parts of growth—in the growth of the individuals, bodily and psychologically; in the growth of mankind, bodily and psychologically. This is the challenge, I believe, of our future.

Educating Evolutionary Man

Emil Mrak, Ph.D.

Teilhard, unfortunately, did not write extensively about education. Charasteristics of his philosophy should, however, permeate education. Perhaps they did at one time, but I am afraid they don't today—at least in most institutions and the ones with which I am familiar. Uppermost in my mind, of course, are those characteristics of idealism, understanding, breadth of thought, and moral standards. We need to get back to these standards and include them in our educational processes.

I would like to pursue this discussion following the thread of the ideals just mentioned, but first, let us go back to the early learning of man.

Chancelor of the University of California, Davis, from 1959 to 1969, Dr. Mrak is most widely known as an international authority on food technology and nutrition. He has held high government posts (serving both here and abroad) concerned with the improved growth and preservation of foods. Among many awards and honors, Dr. Mrak is recipient of the Nicholas Appert Medal and the Babcock-Hart Award of the Institute of Food Technologists; and the Outstanding Civilian Service Award of the Department of the United States Army. He is co-founder and co-editor of *Advances in Food Research* and *Monographs in Food Science and Technology*.

Through the years and through the ages, by learning and observation, man has made four great "discoveries" that have resulted in revolutionary changes that have benefited and changed him greatly. These discoveries: the use of fire, agriculture, urbanization, and now science and technology, have required a great deal of learning and adaptation by man, who in his early history was basically a hunter—an instinct that still remains with us, as is certainly manifested by the popularity and influence of the American Rifle Association. Fire proved to be very helpful, and certainly made life easier. It was used to cook food, thereby making it easier to eat, and perhaps reduced the time needed for chewing. Even more important is the fact that early man learned something about food preservation—drying and smoking.

It is interesting to note that today we are worried about smoke and foods and the carcinogenic effects of smoke, yet man has been smoking his foods, knowingly or unknowingly, since he discovered the use of fire. I am happy that early man and the many generations that followed him were not worried about smoked foods causing cancer.

A far more dramatic change occurred with the "discovery" of agriculture, which occurred about 10,000 years ago—quite recently, as the history of man goes. Agriculture, of course, offered great benefits, for it enabled a more certain food supply and eliminated, or at least minimized, the necessity for nomadism. It also meant that man had to develop new knowledge and learn how to apply it. It meant the changing of his way of life and, in fact, his whole culture. It certainly involved a change in food habits, with cereals assuming a very important place in his diet along with meat, fruits, and leafy plants.

Charles Darwin pointed out that agriculture and the changes accompanying it had to be acquired by each generation. Many revolted against the tedium and went back, or tried to go back, to the more congenial practice of hunting. But there were many who continued to farm, and these, and those of their sons who inherited this taste, initiated an unconscious natural selection toward an agricultural society. This, to me, is a good example of the evolving education of evolutionary man. (But how simple it used to be to learn about early agriculture as compared with the fantastic multiplicity of subjects related to the agriculture of today!)

At any rate, the "instinct" for agriculture is with us, and deeply imbedded whether we farm or not. There are so many people who derive a deep emotional satisfaction from gardening even when they are in no way driven to it by economic or survival necessities. The "discovery" of agriculture, and all that this implied in societal changes, did indeed involve the early education of evolutionary man, and this was a great step forward in his climb toward what today we call civilization.

The third "discovery" in the history of man, dating back only about 5,000 years and a direct result of the application of agriculture, was urbanization. Here is where the great differentiation of effort, specialization, and skills arose. Accompanying the development of certain areas, both geographical and occupational, there was an understanding by specialists of all fields and all skills other than their own. This, of course, led to complications in the development of man: his education, his way of life, and everything else. This, as I see it, is where we still are today, and perhaps this is where some of the fragmentation of experience, learning, and understanding that confronts us today really may have arisen.

But what about the latest "discovery" of mankind, the one we are living with right now, the era of science and technology? I cannot say that most of mankind has developed a great taste for science. Some may regard it as a disagreeable necessity and, in fact, only accept it for its material advantages. Accordingly, some may even try to escape from it and lean toward the instinctive feeling for the earlier revolutions in man's history. Perhaps this is what is happening to some of our young people today. Nevertheless, the newly acquired characteristics of man as he relates to technology are evident.

There can be little doubt that today's man will follow the same course that took place during the previous great evolutions or revolutions, and will eventually find these new developments congenial—I hope.

While speaking of science, we should not eliminate mention of the arts and humanities—especially art itself, literature, music, drama, and so on. It has been speculated that these might lead to a great "revolution" of their own. Without doubt, there will be new creative endeavors, new types of painting, new music, and additional literature, but it does not seem to me that we can expect from this type of creativity a "revolution" that would be irreversible and alter the way of life of hundreds of millions of people. The "revolutions" previously cited are indeed irreversible and have basically mutated evolutionary man.

The advance of man and his education during the last 75 to 100 years have been closely tied to technology and the developments resulting from technological advances. Man, in applying these advances, has tried to make things better for himself, and to secure the happiness he has been pursuing for so much of his history. This does not mean, however, that he has found it. Darwin points out the basic need of motivation for a great deal of human conduct. But while man's motivation may be the search for a happier state, his responses to this motivation may actually breed unhappiness and discontent. When this happens he seeks to learn more and to do more, and at times finds that he has not only not discovered a solution but has become an unhappy snowball or flywheel of learning. Nevertheless, the advance in technological learning does go on and, as a result, new problems are created. For example, even though man has done much to retard his death rate, he has not been able to control his birth rate. Even though he has increased food production, most of the world is still hungry. He has created the automobile to move more effectively, but he now has environmental problems and so on and on. Hence, when he has succeeded in removing one despair, he seems to develop another. Then once again he seeks more information and more education, until he finds another problem that again becomes the most important thing in the world, with its solutions once again, hopefully, unfolding eternal happiness.

If the premise I have developed—call it motivation, ambition, the drive for education, or whatever you wish—is correct, the target being pursued may very well continue to evade the pursuer.

This brings me to the modern-day philosophy and culture that insist that everyone seek an advanced education. This, to me, raises a very basic question as to whether or not such a view is wise or even biologically feasible. I am inclined to doubt if it is. We cannot necessarily expect the son to be what the father was and, even if it were this way, we could not expect him to start where his father left off, although he certainly should begin at a point above where his father started. One can but wonder if there is any chance of this sort of thing continuing over thousands of years unless there are some intervening periods of disaster to give occasion for completely new beginnings.

I am reluctant to pursue this line of thought any further. We have heard much about disaster and impending disasters already. However, I do hope I have indicated that passing knowledge from father to son through the ages does have limitations insofar as individuals are concerned. This educational premise is further weakened by the fact that simultaneously the accumulation of knowledge has been ascending at such a fantastic rate that we are in danger of becoming so specialized as to destroy even the already weakened bridges of communication, interplay, and understanding between areas of specialization.

In the recent history of education, so very much has been concerned with science. We did not forget the arts and humanities, but our great "advances" have come through science and technology. As a matter of fact, our present-day living is based in great part on the scientific developments of the past 100 years, and from this point of view we are today in what some term "the Golden Age."

Let us discuss one phase of this: it was primarily mechanical discoveries that made possible transportation on a great scale and provided means for opening new areas for agriculture and other activities. This raises the question as to whether or not man could have any other "golden ages" ahead of him. One of the most important factors in such an age involves frontiers over which the civilized world can expand. Since such frontiers have been abolished by the advance of man (unless we think of the moon), it appears doubtful that there will be another such age. Hence, once again, unless there should be a catastrophe beyond all thinking, there has been an irreversible change in man's pattern of living.

The education of evolutionary man must take into consideration this limitation of the land and vacant spaces on this earth, which offer certain opportunities for learning through trial and error. Nevertheless, science will continue to move on. The aim will be toward making a better life by curing and preventing diseases, prolonging life, and so on. But strange as it may seem, the new advances (particularly in communications, transportation, medicine, conveniences of various types) may well, and actually will, lead to new troubles that man never seems to anticipate in advance of the actual disagreeable occurrences. Will there be a new emphasis in the education of evolutionary man so that such situations will be avoided? I certainly hope this will be the case, and in the near future.

Let us consider a few specific examples of critical situations that should never have descended on us so suddenly and with such surprise.

You have heard a good deal about environmental problems. I am involved with these problems in the new "Environmental Protection Agency," which has given me an opportunity to understand not only what the problems are but how limited, fragmented, and unilateral the training and thinking are of many of the people involved in seeking solutions. It's not their fault; I believe it's the fault of our teaching profession. Environmental problems in abundance have descended upon us as by-products of our advances in knowledge and technology. Some, therefore, are pointing an accusing finger at those who were and are responsible for the advances, without, unfortunately, realizing that at the same time the critical individual is and has been receiving benefits all out of proportion to the troubles the advances thus far may be causing.

Then let us consider the great amount of knowledge of diseases, cures, and so on, that man has accumulated through the years. It has been very beneficial to man, saving lives and eliminating much misery on the one hand, but setting the stage for biological warfare on the other.

One can go on and on discussing examples of this type. I must, however, raise the questions of food, population, and death control, which are imposing tremendous problems on the world. Education, advances in science, and a humanitarian desire to help others have brought into being, particularly in underdeveloped nations, death control. This has resulted in an increase in population to the point where people do not have an adequacy of food or proper food. Hence we are confronted with the intolerable question of whether the world is better off with a large number of people dying of starvation, or with a smaller (decimated by the ravages of malaria, for example) but better-fed population.

One of the prideful boasts of recent times has been the great decrease in infant mortality brought about by improved medicine. In days gone by (and here I think of Teilhard's childhood), a mother might bear ten children and have only two survive, whereas today she may bear only three and be regarded as very unlucky if all do not survive. But the difficulty in the world will be that the number of people born is too great for the food supply, so a substantial fraction must die early in life anyway.

Now, we have heard a great deal about the "green revolution." We have not heard that it may very well be a Pandora's box rather than a cornucopia. We have only talked about its potential for success and not about its potential for failure. Here again, in teaching we have not been, one might say, multilateral. Apparently in our educational process over the past many years we have failed to induce our students to think in terms of the *adverse* as well as the *beneficial* possibilities of new discoveries. In other words, our educational processes have been unbalanced. We as teachers need to broaden our thinking and that of the students we are educating. But, contrarily, we have been narrowing and narrowing their perspective by the fragmentation of courses and curricula, and by unnecessary impositions in our curricula, thereby setting the stage for more problems and unhappiness. This is the result of what I term an unbalanced and an incomplete education; the very things that Teilhard talked about—the understanding, the idealism, the breadth of thought—are missing.

Today, in certain areas of the world, enormous sums are being spent for education, and particularly for what we term college education. Funds are being poured into research and the development of libraries. We are accumulating so much information so fast that it has been said that today the average scientific article is not read by more than three people.

This brings me to the problem of communications and the use of our ever-expanding fund of knowledge. We have reached such a stage of fragmentation that the advances in knowledge concerning constructive processes are turning out to be destructive. Recall, if you will, what I said about people working on environmental problems. So often we are confronted with tragic situations because so few seem to have an iota of understanding of what really is happening. Unfortunately, this is why I believe our education, in many instances, has not had the helpful and beneficial effects on our daily lives that it should have had, and, in fact, may have produced harmful effects on all of us and on our civilization, too.

Let me give you a few examples and, if you don't mind, I would like to speak about areas with which I am indeed familiar.

Some years ago, a great scientist received a Nobel Prize for the development of DDT. It was used throughout the war years for the control of certain diseases and subsequently in agriculture with great success. Suddenly we find individuals who place a great onus on DDT because of its accumulation in the environment, its effect on wildlife, and its ostensible harm to humans. Aa a result, our lawmakers have tried to act with dispatch and introduced bills galore to ban this culprit. In a way, this might have been good, for if DDT were denied to certain developing countries of the world, it would reverse the gains made in death control and cause increased devastations by malaria. Actually, this effect has already been well demonstrated in Ceylon, and, to a lesser extent, in India. In any event, DDT is now a criminal and it is on its way out. And just about the time we find it disappearing, new information comes to light we didn't think was ever possible. We convicted it on the basis of inadequate information, misinformation, and the absence of information, without bothering to seek the facts before taking action. We never conditioned the people involved or our legislative bodies to look, or at least try to look, at a complete spectrum. So many of us were inadvertently trained to think narrowly.

Some have argued that DDT is a carcinogen, but new information is evolving to indicate that under certain circumstances it is an anti-carcinogen and will actually act as an inhibitor for certain types of tumorogenesis. There is great concern about the occurrence of DDT in Lake Michigan fish. Now we have information that indicates that what was thought to be DDT in the Great Lakes may not be that substance at all, but rather another, perhaps *polychlor biphenyls,* which comes from industrial sources.

What can we do about this situation? Do we flounder in the inadequacies of our training and education, or do we make an about-face and look for another criminal? What do we do in view of the fact that we may have convicted the wrong product? Should we ban another chemical appearing on the horizon on the basis of limited information or thinking, or should we expand our thinking and secure more information before we act? I hope it's the latter.

Such a procedure is not easy. Many people do not want to have facts because it is so easy to be positive in the absence of facts, and emotions peak rapidly in the less informed. We find editorials in the *Los Angeles Times* insisting that DDT be banned because it is killing humans, even though, believe it or not, there is *evidence* to the contrary.

This is the world we are living in today, and I believe that our educational system is, to a considerable extent, to blame. We accept but we do not seem to question. We certainly do not train or encourage one to keep an open mind and maintain perspective. Neither do we offer opportunities to develop the breadth of thinking so badly needed.

Most certainly the news media do not help in this respect; this is well manifested by a statement made by the Editor of the *Washington Star,* who said:

> Look at what we do with speeches, for instance. Have you ever seen a news story which really reflected the content and intent of a speech? The reporter, doing as we taught him, looks for the one startling and contentious or silly statement, and there is his lead. He backs it up with one or two direct or indirect quotes, adds a couple of paragraphs of background, and there is your story.

In addition, there are scientists—distinguished scientists, but people I term "lay scientists"—who have come forth, with great courage, to make pronouncements and even write books in areas far removed from their field of expertise. In some cases their statements have been in order; in other instances they have been incorrect, erratic, and have done a great deal of harm. A person who has been well publicized, has been awarded honors, and is generally accepted as an expert, is listened to regardless of the subject or the correctness of his statements. Teachers, particularly those in the scientific communities, should be on the alert for premature, exaggerated, over-enthusiastic or unfounded pronouncements in the interpretation of scientific issues that arise from members of their own ranks, particularly those statements which have an important bearing on public health and welfare. I believe that such issues should first be resolved within the appropriate scientific community so that subsequent revelations to the students will be presented in the fullest possible perspective, on the basis of all existing knowledge, and in the light of interpretations by the most appropriate scientific authorities. I believe such a course would assure the fullest benefit to the student or the "evolving man."

The behavior I have cited is, to a considerable extent, the result of fragmentation and the lack of idealism and understanding as an essential part of education. I certainly understand why some students are unhappy. They are fully aware of what is taking place, and many of them who are idealistic find themselves frustrated, see little relevance in or connection between one narrow course and another. Unfortunately, students ordinarily do not have an opportunity to obtain a total view of a broad field. We must find a way to permit them to do this by restructuring our courses and curricula to permit greater flexibility and freedom. Harvard may grant an undergraduate degree in three years. An alternative would be to keep the four-year schedule, but devote the first year to an orientation to modern life and modern man. Broad exposures such as this symposium would be ideal.

Advanced education is really an isolated group of islands or, if you prefer, an archipelago of unconnected bits and fragments of knowledge—a tragic state, indeed. One answer to the problem would be to offer broad connected subjects, with an emphasis on the need to think in terms of short- and long-range implications of each advance or change. We need to improve our teaching and to rediscover its thrills and rewards. We need to devote more time to those we are teaching —to influence their type of thinking, their understanding, ideals, and moral values, and to open their minds and improve their ability to speculate on the future. We need to go back to the days of Horace Mann for an understanding and appreciation of education, and to have proper orientation and inspiration.

Horace Mann, over 100 years ago, made a rather interesting statement. At that time he pointed out that experiments on animals demonstrated that if the nerves from the brain to the stomach are cut and separated, digestion instantly ceases. Bring the separated ends of the nerves together again and the processes of life are renewed. Then he goes on to say: "Just think how many of these nerves a harsh, cruel, ignorant teacher may cut in a day."[1] This is exactly how I feel about our fragmented, disconnected, inflexible education system of today.

At the same time, I do not believe that the present-day attitude that there is need to educate all people at the same level is in order. For some reason or another we have developed a sort of cultural sheepskin-psychosis, which pressures everyone to go to a university. In this connection, George Pettit put it in a rather interesting way when he said:

> The more one studies the enthusiastic campaign for more education at all levels of intellectual capacity in the light of man's past history and contemporary cultural problems, the less easy it is to accept some of the current slogans and shibboleths: The average college graduate makes more money than the average high school graduate and the high school graduate earns more than the elementary graduate. One can readily see the fallacy of imputing differences in earning capacity solely to the number of years of schooling completed without regard to the differences in the average ability of the groups compared. Some people undoubtedly would have gone on with

[1] *Horace Mann on the Crisis in Education,* Louis Filler, ed. (Ohio: The Antioch Press, 1965).

school and made more money, had they been motivated to do so. Others just as certainly could not have increased their job capacities significantly by any given number of additional years of school attendance. People who have intelligence, intellectual curiosity and drive usually want to complete high school and college. But they do not succeed because they go to college; they succeed because they have the intelligence, curiosity and drive.[2]

Finally, in all instances we need leadership. Darwin pointed out there is a great need for the "master." This, of course, means leadership (one of the rarest of commodities), and we do not have a program of education that will bring potential leaders to the surface. This is an area we must stress more and more as time goes on. We must find, nurture, and encourage rare individuals who have leadership potential. We *must* find a way to do it. And what is leadership? This, to me, is the ability and the willingness to take responsibility, to go to the lonely outposts of thought and action, and to persuade others to follow you there. Truly, this ability is the rarest of commodities in the world. We live in a world of tremendous pressures and numbers, mass pressures, enormous forces working for the leveling-out of talent and for conformity of opinion. The only way to keep this a good world and to make it a better one is to ascertain creative and constructive individualism, which is another way of saying "leadership."

Professor Leakey indicated that we have despair, but he is an optimist who looks to the younger generation to eliminate, or at least minimize, this despair. I, too, feel the younger generation can do this, but we must help them by changing our outmoded and antiquated system of education. When this is done, and science has continued its advance in a more realistic and balanced way, we can truly turn to the hope and

[2] George A. Pettit, *Prisoners of Culture,* (New York: Charles Scribner's Sons, 1970).

idealism of Teilhard, which he has expressed in this manner:

> Some day after we have mastered the winds, the waves, the tides and gravity, we will harness for God the energies of love and then for the second time in the history of the world man will have discovered fire.[3]

[3] Pierre Teilhard de Chardin, *Writing in Time of War* (New York, Harper & Row, n.d.), pp. 143–44.

In Search of the Thirteenth Hour: Point Omega

J. Ralph Audy, M.D., B.S., Ph.D.

The title of this talk is from a children's story about a magic thirteenth hour immediately after midnight which the children spend in a wonderland of their own. "Point Omega," Teilhard's quasi-scientific term, is to me hard to distinguish from what Pythagoras some 26 centuries earlier called *homoiosis,* or assimilation to God. Teilhard thinly disguises this fact in his effort to show that point omega is the natural scientific end-product of evolution. But the evolution of man is largely decided by man himself (however frightening that

---

Educated in England in the medical sciences and tropical medicine, Dr. Audy has conducted extensive epidemological research in Africa, Ceylon, Burma, and Malaysia. His academic interests have focused both on the natural causes of disease and the increasingly important question of man-made maladies. As Professor of International Health and Human Ecology, and Director of the Hooper Foundation at the University of California, San Francisco, Dr. Audy's work reflects a broad ecological view of man's place in nature. His extensive writings range from parasitology to sociology, and honors awarded include the Chalmers Memorial Medal from the Royal Society of Tropical Medicine and Hygiene.

thought may be), and it is therefore greatly influenced by goals that man may set himself, however dimly he may see the details. If I read Teilhard aright, he supposes that the goal, point omega, is set *for* man, let us say by that very Godhead which we are slowly approaching. I believe this is a dangerous notion: the goal is rather set *by* man, and his perception of it will govern his progress toward it. Also, if man is confused about his goals, he is likely to lose himself in following confused pathways. I see point omega as a goal set *by* man, in this case, by Teilhard himself—by his vision of a Godhead, about details of which others may differ. With more sound reasoning and an analysis developing over a quarter of a century of experimental work, John Calhoun, from the National Institute of Mental Health, has visualized a particular period of late evolution that he calls the Age of Compassion, an era that is potentially possible for man; and I think it would be quibbling to try to distinguish the goal of Calhoun's hoped-for era from Teilhard's point omega.

Whatever we call it, however much we may be uncertain about exact details, and whether or not we wish to argue about its divinity, we *can* have a realistic goal, and my object in this short time is to make a few practical assessments of prospects and ways of getting there.

I like to place together the ideas of point omega and of the children's thirteenth hour because I believe that it is the unfettered child that is (or was) in us that is the fount of the ultimate happiness, joy, and compassion of our goal; and also that it is our children who have the futures—futures that adults should regard as their own. But happiness itself can never be a goal. It is a by-product. Regarding our futures, which are one with those of our children, I am reminded of Szent-Gyorgyi's comment that politicians must always be thinking about the next election but statesmen think about the next generation. Our present approach to the future is that of the politician and tactician. I hope for more efforts, such as this symposium, to develop the approach of the statesman and strategist. Such efforts might also help us to replace national goals with global ones for humanity.

THE FACTS OF LIFE: THE POPULATION AVALANCHE AND FUTURE PATHS

The brochure announcing this symposium quotes Sir Julian Huxley, who refers to "this central concept of man as the spearhead of evolution on earth." Apart from the fact that many would regard modern man as less a spearhead than a multiple warhead, we may expect that Huxley had a special idea in his mind when he used that term *spearhead.* In the course of evolution of life on this planet there have been several finite and tremendously significant steps, each being followed by an explosive deployment of the emergent newly improved group, or spearhead, into the whole arena of life. The next advance has always come much later, its spearhead being some particular and hitherto insignificant part of the deployed forms.

The last-advance-but-one led to the appearance of the placental mammals, and the most recent was the emergence of man, whose distinguishing feature is the way in which he uses (and does not use) his remarkable brain. Let us consider the mind in that brain. I prefer to believe that in real life there is no such thing as an isolated mind, only isolated brains. Every time there is a meeting of minds, even if one of the brains died a thousand years ago and part of its mind is being gathered from a book, then there is a sort of exchange of grafts. Minds always knit themselves into a network, a nexus within which individual minds move like nodes of activity, together weaving ever-increasingly complex patterns. The small, intensely patterned nexuses knot themselves into a larger-patterned nexus that is society. Calhoun expresses a similar idea differently when he defines *brain* as a generic concept:

> any assembly of interconnected elements which facilitate the acquisition, storage, transfer, condensation, relating, transformation, and evaluation of information, making it available for initiating actions necessary to cope with contingencies posed by the environment.[1]

He thus speaks of the *social brain* of, for example, a small hunter-gatherer group. Calhoun suggests that in the first deployment of man over available space, he still remained an animal until his social brain or unit nexuses carried him beyond the stage where he was bound by the ordinary carrying capacity of the natural environment. We can reach an estimate of that time in the following way. Calhoun has calculated that, by the time bands of hunter-gatherer men had occupied the land available to them and for the first time found no way to accommodate increasing numbers by spreading geographically (between 40 and 60 thousand years ago), the world population would have been less than 4.5 million. Foerster[2] has carefully analyzed world population growth over the last 2,000 years. It has been remarkably and alarmingly reliable. If we extend von Foerster's curve backward, we reach Calhoun's population of 4.5 million about 43,000 years ago. *That,* Calhoun postulates, was about the time when man learned to escape his slavery to the environment. Within a mere 20,000 more years he doubled his population, doubled it again in only 10,000 years, doubled that in only 5,000 years, and so on, until now our world population is doubling itself in only 40 years. Of course we all know that this process cannot possibly continue or we should reach what von Foerster calls Doomsday in the fall of 2026 A.D., only 55 years ahead, when the population would approach infinity.

The next question looks into the future. We must assume

---

1 J. B. Calhoun, "Revolution, Tribalism and the Cheshire Cat. Three Paths from Now." *URBSDOC* no. 167 (January 8, 1971). Unit for Research on Behavioral Systems, Laboratory of Psychology, National Institute of Mental Health (Bethesda, Md., 1971), p. 3.

2 H. von Foerster, P. M. Mora, and L. W. Amiot, "Doomsday: Friday, 13 November, A.D. 2026," *Science* 132 (1960):1291–95.

that we won't commit global suicide by a thermonuclear war, otherwise there would be no point in my continuing—presumably anyone so asinine as to start a thermonuclear war is also asinine enough to make it thorough. We can assume that we are almost certain to overshoot the optimum population. Some would argue that we have already overshot it, but there is evidence that we have only achieved excessive densities in patches; that we have not yet learned to cope with such densities but we could do so very much better; and, very important, that the world population needs to increase a bit more to achieve a sort of critical mass for unification into a world sociopolitical unit. I haven't time to go into reasons for that last statement, but there are sound arguments to support it.[3] Calhoun estimates the optimum world population would be about 3.5 billion *adults,* provided they formed a unified communication network. Only such a network would be able to continually enhance both individual man and mankind.

On the following page is shown the growth of our world population in a chart worked out by Calhoun,[4] to whom I am greatly indebted for much intellectual stimulation. The box on the left takes us from the past to the obviously critical time immediately ahead of us. The scales for world population in billions, and for years in the past in thousands, are both logarithmic. The population curve therefore appears deceptively as a straight line instead of shooting madly off the chart as the population avalanche accelerates. The first part, an evolutionary period of *strife,* takes us through evolution until man has covered available space, and his collective brains, faced with new challenge, start being fully human—about 43,000 years ago. We then reach, on the familiar part of human progress, a period of *exploitation,* when

---

3 J. B. Calhoun, "Promotion of man," *Global Systems Dynamics,* Proc. Int. Sym., Charlottesville, Va., 1969, ed. E. O. Attinger (New York: Karger, Basel; Wiley-Interscience, 1970), p. 53; Calhoun, "Revolution, tribalism and the Cheshire Cat . . . ," p. 6.

4 "Revolution, Tribalism, and the Cheshire Cat . . . ," p. 4.

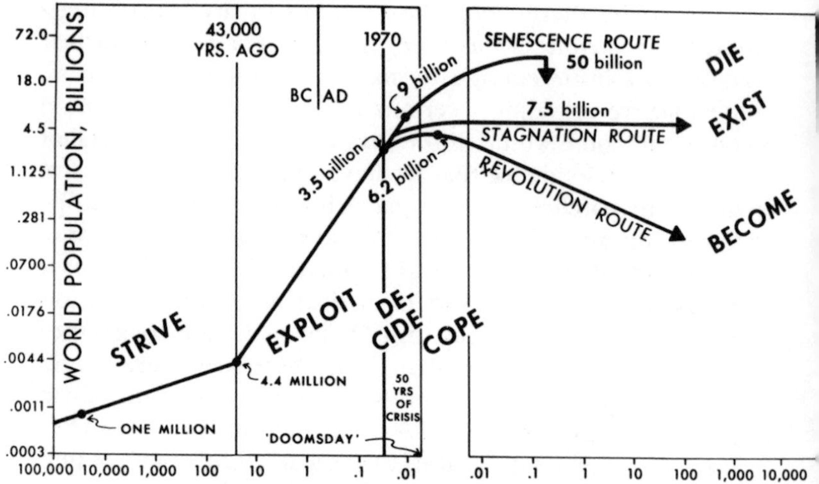

Population history of the human race, redrawn with permission from Fig. 1 of J. B. Calhoun (URBSDOC No. 167, 8 January 1971), whose description (slightly modified) reads: The evolutionary period, STRIVE, covered the emergence of primates to the origin of "biological man" become truly human. The period EXPLOIT covers man's rapid sociocultural evolution and multiplication, an estimated *ca.* 43,000 year span during which each successive doubling of the population required half that of the prior doubling. This period terminates in a brief current 5-year period of crisis, DECIDE, during which we shall by our behavior and decisions determine the future route for thousands of years to come. Its end could be DOOMSDAY if by default we take the route of SENESCENCE. There follows a period, COPE, of uncertain duration, during which adjustments are made to the developing future course. If we elect for the stagnation route, life will be spent in perpetual struggle for mere existence. If by choice we elect the REVOLUTION route, evolution by the environment for increasing human awareness will progress.

each successive doubling of population has required half the time of the previous doubling. We have now reached a highly critical period when we have, say, some 50 years of excruciating *decision*—and decisive action—literally to decide what course mankind will take for the future, perhaps only for some thousands of years, possibly for all time. Broadly speaking, we have the choice of three kinds of paths, according to the way in which we reach the target of 3.5 billion adults *maximum* and how we develop after that.

First, we go on roughly as we are now, and in some 70 years reach our adult target, but with a world population of about 9 billion. On reaching this target, man would fully occupy at least 28 million square miles, leaving only 19 million square miles for all other forms of life in scattered patches and delicate natural balance. But the momentum would carry on and this route would lead to senescence and spoliation of the earth, an era of mega-megalopolises in decay. It would be mankind's tombstone.

If, however, we make a tremendous effort to achieve a *stable* population, the optimum of 3.5 billion adults would be first reached at a world population of 7.5 billion people. At this huge population density, however, man would be forced to revert to a deprived, tribalistic level of existence.

If we set an even more demanding course leading to a steady decline in world population, we could first reach the 3.5 billion adults with a world population of only about 6.2 billion and could start declining thereafter. Although I have mentioned that an increase to some 3.5 billion adults is necessary to achieve a unified communication network, once this is achieved man can start an accelerated development of conceptual space and increased universal awareness by reversing the population trend. Only thus can he approach Teilhard's point omega during Calhoun's compassionate era.

To recapitulate, we can label the world population curve as passing through periods of *strife* and then *exploitation;* we face a very brief period when we must *decide;* then there will be a period, perhaps two to three centuries, while we try to *cope.* But the decision will have been made in *this* century whether we progress to stagnation and *die,* to tribalism and only *exist,* or to an age of compassion in which we *become.*

I emphasize most urgently that the choice of pathway must be made within the next 15 years or so. We must allow for inertia. Also, to achieve the only acceptable path, those actions will have to be remarkable. They will require a revolutionary change, especially in our value systems and social structure. Could it be that the United States might possibly lead the world in starting this? At the moment, it seems that we are set on the wrong course for such leadership.

I now propose to have a quick look at a few neglected facets of our present position. It is impossible to be honest without being merciless.

THE FACTS OF LIFE: THE INDIGNITY OF MAN

We hear much about the dignity of man, and that man differs from all animals because he is the first Rational Being. But man's remarkable brain also allows him to become the first Irrational Animal. The notion that animals are bestial is medieval. We now know what remarkably fine creatures they are, even though some are relatively moronic—such as the noble eagle and the noble lion. Man can be and has been more bestial than any animal. In a challenging historical and scientific review of *The Dying Self,* Charles Fair observes that man, "because of the absolute extent of his neocortex, is unique among animals in being the only one that cannot come to full efficiency, or even to full creature contentment, through a life of pure adaptation. The reason he cannot is that this mode of existence leaves an important part of his central nervous system in a state of functional underdevelopment and the whole consequently in a state of nearly chronic imbalance."[5]

It is the very nature of man's brain that made it necessary for him to invent ethics. Professor Dobzhansky has observed that ethics are characteristically human and not animal. Animals have no need for codes of ethics because they are on the whole extremely well behaved. Their behavior is genetically based, and they have relatively limited freedom. Man's brain, however, has so many potentialities, so many degrees of freedom, and his behavior patterns are so much more complex, that he has need of codes of ethics in order to permit him to form societies.

I resist the temptation to sample a few of the appalling indignities of man, in places from New York to Vietnam, from Pakistan to Czechoslovakia, but instead will comment briefly on some institutions and processes, namely, the city, the church, and what the world has come to in 1971.

The experience of living in cities has been summarized by Stanley Milgram.[6] Increasing human densities increase the load on an individual's capacity to deal with social intercourse. In cities there is a constant need to adapt to overload, and this is done by various forms of disinvolvement. But involvement with others is the essence of being human. Such common techniques of disinvolvement as superficiality, anonymity, shortening the time for social transactions, avoiding other people's troubles, and aggressiveness to protect one's disinvolvement are therefore bound to be dehumanizing.

City life is not the only dehumanizing circumstance. Another is war, especially unusually unclean wars, of which the latest is that in Vietnam. Let me here sound a note of warn-

---

5 C. M. Fair, *The Dying Self* (Middletown, Conn.: Wesleyan University Press, 1969), p. 220.

6 S. Milgram, "The experience of living in cities.", *Science,* 167 (1970), pp. 1461–1468.

ing. Some wonderful flowers flourish on the dunghills of our overcrowded cities, and wars can bring out the noblest elements in a few men most of the time and in many men on rare occasions. But these are the results of man's tremendous variability, potentiality, and polymorphism. Cities and wars are not in themselves noble.[7]

Let us turn to an institution that seems designed to prevent evil from emerging, namely, the church, the great religions of the world. First I must note that there is obviously and always something woefully wrong when people rebel who are specially trained to conform. Since this indicates serious defects in the institution that has trained for conformity, the institution always reacts violently; we find such mutinous uprisings viewed with special alarm in ships at sea and in armed services. But we have recently seen uprisings within the great religions (among which we may include communism; witness Czechoslovakia and Hungary). The more doctrinaire and rigid the superstructure, the more agonizing the unrest. One investigator has reported "that the religiously devout are on the average more bigoted, more authoritarian, more dogmatic and more antihumanitarian than the less devout."[8] However, he measures devotion by the outward appearances of obvious membership in or patronization of the church.

In their book on "wayward shepherds," a group of careful investigators[9] have shown, among other things, how Protestant preachers they had studied generally avoid in their sermons all the subjects that most trouble people's minds and consciences, including the many controversial issues that concern parents and children and that bombard us daily in

7 Incidentally, man's inhumanity to man, and man's "unnatural" (pathological) vandalism of his own natural habitat, have been summed up as a result of his "vandal ideology" by Scott Paradise in "The Vandal Ideology," *The Nation* (Dec. 29, 1969), pp. 729–32.

8 M. Rotkeach, "Faith, Hope and Bigotry," *Psychology Today* 3, no. 11 (1970):33–37, 58.

9 R. Stark, B. D. Foster, C. Y. Glock, and H. Quinley, *Wayward Shepherds: Prejudice and the Protestant Clergy* (New York: Harper & Row, 1971).

the newspapers, as well as universal problems such as that of human numbers.[10]

I have already tried to indicate that the population avalanche is one of mankind's most urgent problems. Boulding[11] observes that if only misery can check population growth, then the population will grow until it is miserable enough to be checked. But will that population, clinging to the last shreds of nature's reserves, then ever be able to improve its lot—or will it only *exist?* Also, following the same assumption, technology can do no more than increase the biomass of miserable humans, the total of human misery. In these modern circumstances, the academic encyclical from the Vatican concerning birth control strikes me as an almost disastrous step backward. (Please note that I say from the Vatican and not the Pope, because the Pope is surrounded by powerful advisors.) The consciences of many fine persons working close to people are repeatedly tortured by inconsistencies between dogmatic pontification and the practicalities of helping sorry mankind in the streets of life. If I may seem iconoclastic, it is because I am opposed to the worship of false images, and I suggest that the undoubted power of the churches to help in the immediate critical years ahead is being seriously reduced by the heavy superstructures and the bigotry they bear.

Good people may do things that can lead to great evil. This comes about most often through remoteness: intellectual detachment and lack of personal involvement—in the picturesque and vigorous language of today's youth, *not being with it.* The intellectual detachment is most obvious when high officers become more concerned with dogma than the rapid changes in the hearts and minds of people, or when teachers in a university lose their sense of proportion in pursuing a special field. By lack of personal involvement I mean not

10 Calhoun, "Promotion of Man," pp. 36–58, Milgram, and Chad Walsh, *From Utopia to Nightmare* (New York: Harper & Row, 1929).

11 K. E. Boulding, *The Meaning of the Twentieth Century: The Great Transition* (New York: Harper & Row, 1964).

personally sharing in the lives, the joys and the sorrows, of people who will be affected by decisions. There is a limit to what a man can suffer for others, and whereas a starving child is a tragedy, ten thousand starving children tend to become a statistic; decisions that affect people must be made by, or at least with, those immersed in the problems.

An important related aspect of sociocultural evolution that receives far too little attention is the social selection of personality types, some of which are psychiatrically recognizable.[12] While it is true that to some extent this means that the fittest fill the jobs, the process has some serious, even alarming defects. If society sets survival value on drive and aggressiveness, what else is being selected with these characteristics? Bureaucracies and the armed services tend to select in favor of obsessive-compulsive personalities. As a result, rigidity increases in those structures that most need flexibility. Some people feel that the turmoil we now observe around us is wholly evil, that their world is disintegrating before their eyes. A priest, Chad Walsh,[13] has studied the change in emergence of popular books about one kind of happy Utopia or another to the emergence of horrifying glimpses of dystopias such as Orwell's *1984*. This change is a very interest-symptom of an illness of society, that nexus of nexuses of minds. Imagine our observing a patient with typhus. Every day his temperature chart goes up one degree and his condition obviously deteriorates as his mind sinks into the cloud from which typhus gets its name. Toward the end of the first week, the trends are obvious. A projection of his temperature chart into the future will show that he must come to the boil in 107 days. But we know that this is only an episode while his health is being challenged by an infection. The week after next he should start rallying. This is how I see ourselves collectively at the moment. The signs of tur-

[12] R. Kuttner, "Cultural Selection of Human Psychological Types," *Genus* 16 (1960) :3–6; H. D. Lasswell, "Political Constitution and Character," *Psychoanalytic Review* 46, no. 4 (1959) :3–18.

[13] *From Utopia to Nightmare.*

moil, deviance, and eccentricity only indicate we are passing through a phase of acute adaptation. Dr. Nathan Adler,[14] citing sixteenth-century equivalents of hippies, has shown how most of what we regard as modern degenerative phenomena are adaptive responses, resembling past responses to throes of social improvement. Many of the signs I see are very healthy: there is an air of realism and honesty about, even while some people are dropping out because they are bewildered and can see no future.

One most unfortunate thing about this reaction of youth is the polarization it leads to when older people become indignant or contemptuous or aggressive, inducing more evocative behavior in the young. There must be more communication. It might help the older intolerant people to remember Father Charles de Foucauld. He was a spoiled brat who became a notorious roué and then a rambunctious soldier before he developed into a splendid person who was a fellow-spirit to Teilhard de Chardin until he was finally murdered close by the sands of Tamanrasset.[15]

In keeping with the attractive mystical air that effuses from parts of Teilhard's works, I want, just as a trial, to approach the idea of point omega from two other angles, one long established and well known, the other more newly emergent. The first is the knowledge that this universe is not simply the 3-dimensional world we can see but is multidimensional: at least 6-dimensional, let us say, of which the man on the street can learn to comprehend only four. It means that we are always seeing only a tiny part, a cross section, of the larger universe. Any instant in our 3-D universe is an instantaneous cross section of the larger universe, and the movement of the succession of the 3-D cross section in the fourth dimension is what gives us the illusion of the passage of time. When light from a star curves around the sun on its way to

14 N. Adler, "Kicks, Drugs, and Politics," *Psychoanalytic Review* 57 (1970): 432–41.

15 M. Preminger, *The Sands of Tamanrasset. The Story of Charles de Foucauld* (London: Peter Davis, and New York: Hawthorne Books, 1961).

us, it is not bending but traveling in a straight line, the shortest distance between points, in a 4-D space-time that is curved by the gravitational mass of the sun. Given such curvatures in 4-D space, our 3-D universe can be of finite volume, so many cubic miles, but with no boundaries, just as the 2-D surface of the earth is finite but unbounded through curvature in 3-D space. Also, an electron here and a positron in Peru may not be two entities at all, but perhaps only one entity in hyperspace that we see passing through our 3-D space twice, and seen, say, as an electron here when it is going out and a positron there when it is entering. My purpose in drawing attention to all this is partly to encourage some humbleness and respect in our thinking, in order to mollify what tends to become arrogant and manipulative thinking among some scientists and among all technocrats.

Phenomena in hyperspace could also be related to extrasensory perception or ESP.[16] As far as I know, the late Whately Carington is the only person to evolve a hypothesis to explain telepathy. The remarkable thing about his hypothesis is that, contrived only to explain experimental findings in telepathy, it nevertheless explains a number of other perplexing things. It is usable, which suggests it may be a good working hypothesis. The basic, mind-boggling assumption you must make, however, is that mental events such as associations not only evoke molecular traces in the brain but have a more lasting existence as what Carington calls *psychons* (simply for convenience), perhaps having more recognizable structure as events in hyperspace than in our 3-D space. (Incidentally, Carington does not mention hyperspace, I am doing it now for fun.)[17] The psychon-system that is my mind

16 L. E. Rhine, *ESP in Life and Lab. Tracing Hidden Channels* (New York: Macmillan, and London: Collier-Macmillan, 1967); W. Carington, *Telepathy. An Outline of Its Facts, Theory, and Implications,* 3rd ed. (London: Methuen, 1946).

17 Since writing this, I have found that Carington wrote about the fourth dimension fifty years ago under the pen name of W. Whately Smith, *A Theory of the Mechanism of Survival. The Fourth Dimension and Its Applications* (London: Kegan Paul, Trench, Trubner; and New York: Dutton, 1920).

is remote from the psychon-system that is yours only in degree. In its nature, it does not differ from the various psychic distances that separate parts of my own mind from each other. If Carington is only partly right, it may be true that gradual identification is possible among minds, literally into a functioning collective mind rather than the nexuses I spoke of earlier.

HOPE FOR MANKIND

I regret that I would need at least an extra eighteen minutes of speaking time to describe exactly how to solve all the problems of mankind. I agree most wholeheartedly with Dr. Leakey's advice, and would recommend the writings of such as Gavin, Stent, Szent-Gyorgyi, and Barbara Ward. I must content myself with noting that we must do what so many young people have been begging us to do: strip off at least some of the humbug, hypocrisy, and bigotry that encourage the appalling blocks to vigorous rational action. A neurosis is essentially cured simply by getting the individual to face more honestly, aided or unaided by others, the garbage in his makeup. Nothing can be dealt with unless it is brought out into the open. Very much malpractice is unconscious or unintended. Therefore hypocrisy and bigotry and malpractices must be brought out into the open. Much advice to this effect has been published lately, but the people who most need help may avoid it, just as a neurotic may avoid revealing his basic problems.

I am simply advocating realism, an essential element to progress and adaptability. The question arises whether mankind is capable of the rationality and goodness to create an improving and internally compassionate society. Those who look into the collective brains or nexuses of minds, about which we know too little, have no cause for jubilation. Some, such as Charles Fair,[18] have produced evidence of cycles in

---

[18] *The Dying Self,* p. 220.

the history of man in which the collective Id has alternately come to the fore and been suppressed, producing what we can see as ages of unreason alternating with ages of reason. He fears we may now be entering another age of unreason, differing from all others (such as the Dark Ages) in that we face the vertical exponential slope of world population and possess vast stocks of nuclear weapons. I would add that we also have too many ordinary people possessing extraordinary power, and an utterly damnable imbalance of wealth in our lopsided world.

Perhaps there is only one secret to the future, that it always belongs to the young who grow into it. Therefore, man's prime concern should be to those basic things, genuine love and personal attention among them, that improve the quality of the individual; improve the quality of the child, who will later become the adult. The ingredients of adulthood are added in the earliest years of childhood. We must—now—invest most heavily in the youth that is on its way!

In his article cited previously, Adler points out that having been dismayed by youth's dropping out in various ways, we are now getting even more dismayed because they are coming in, demanding to participate. I quote him:

> Given the choice, I am afraid that there are too many of us who prefer the docile drug user to the rude political activist. We are unprepared to come out from behind protocol and procedures, to make a relationship with people who are challenging our basic values, to listen, to talk, and to change. We have failed to understand that the issue is not People's Park; it is not the Free Speech Movement or the Filthy Speech Movement, nor is it even drugs. The issue in each of these confrontations and in those that inevitably lie ahead is the demand for a relationship, for an unswerving allegiance to human values above those of the marketplace and the military, and for a commitment to their future. And in the end, their future is the only one *we* have.[19]

---

19 *"Kicks, Drugs, and Politics,"* pp. 432–41.

Panel Discussion

Moderator:

Carl O. Sauer — Professor of Geography Emeritus, University of California, Berkeley

Panel Members:

Ralph R. Greenson
Mark F. Ferber
Pearce Young
Robert T. Francoeur
J. Ralph Audy
Emil Mrak

DR. SAUER: We will get around to the written inquiries from the floor very shortly. The first thing we should do is have the six panelists each take two minutes to offer an afterthought or something in addition to what they said earlier. I think this is an interesting idea. I have never made a talk without being sorry that I didn't have a chance to add an afterthought.

The order of speakers would put Dr. Greenson first.

DR. GREENSON: I think I would say a few words that I was hesitant to say before about the very conception of perfection. I thought the whole notion of having a symposium, of people spending all this time talking about the quest for perfection, futile, unless we really asked ourselves what is perfection in terms of living. Perfection at best is a fleeting moment; at worst it is a state of death—it is inert. I think we would have been much better off talking about perfecting, improving, rather than *perfection,* which I consider a static term, an inert term, and a deadly term.

MODERATOR SAUER: This is interesting. I think Dr. Greenson is like our fellow citizen, S. I. Hayakawa—a person who is concerned with the meaning of words. And this real meaning of words is, I think, one of the rather weak spots in a good deal of Teilhard's writings.

DR. GREENSON: Well, you know, I earn my living with words. I am a psychoanalyst and they are terribly important material; important not just in their definitional meaning, but on whether they are living or dead. The difference between using a living language or dead words is terribly important. For example, the word *scared* is living; *apprehension* is dead.

MODERATOR SAUER: Now, Professor Ferber.

DR. FERBER: Just very briefly. I think I would have liked to have talked a bit about organizations, not necessarily political, because some of the work in the social sciences dealing with large organizations is interesting for us and has relevance for political life as well.

I have a sense, again, as I do with most things, of a dualism here. On the one hand many organizations—ecclesiastical, educational, industrial—simply have gotten too large. Once again our body has outgrown our brain.

I think this has relevance for politics because I think this leads to much of what was talked about yesterday regarding the *angst* of not knowing one's place in the total universe. This terrible depersonalization that takes place within large organizations is, I think, very much involved with the lack of the sense of efficacy facing our people today.

I think, conversely, that there are counter trends. For example, at the level of the university and, I think, perhaps appropriately extended down to the high school, we ought to welcome, rather than create barriers to, requests from students to take part in governance. This is much more than just a sharing of power. I think it is an important part of the educational process. I don't think we ought to merely say, "Come in." Our role ought to be—and I suspect this would be true in other organizations as well—to suggest how complex current organizational patterns are; to suggest that students can, in fact, learn with us as we struggle through the organizational maze that makes up our day.

DR. SAUER: I take it that you are encouraging conference rather than demands in this matter.

DR. FERBER: I am not sure one has a choice any longer.

DR. SAUER: Judge Young will be the next speaker.

JUDGE YOUNG: Thank you very much.

If you invited me to speak here again, I hope it would be on the subject of politics and Teilhard. I do not feel that politics has been sufficiently emphasized during this symposium. Indeed, I found myself agreeing with much of what Dr. Ferber had to say: that the possible future survival of the race depends upon political decisions and that, of all of the decisions that are made in public life, probably the most significant, the most important, are political decisions.

For example, much has been said about reshaping our social institutions. Of course, that can only be done through learning and knowledge. But here again, the funds to supply the Universities come through politics. So many of the problems that have been discussed during this symposium will find their answer, if answers are to be found, within the political process itself.

The tragedy, however, particularly for one who has served in political office, is the enormous amount of public apathy. An apathetic public cannot develop statesmen. But let me state again that solutions to many of the problems that we have discussed today can be found only through the political process.

DR. SAUER: And we move on now to Professor Francoeur.

DR. FRANCOEUR: I have to talk about perfecting man in the

sense of opening up new options for human living; new options for individual people to choose; new options for individual sexual persons to express their own drives, their own potential, and to develop their potential to the fullest. What I have been very much amazed at and very pleased with, has been the recent appearance of a very prophetic, creative, and totally new attitude among many theologians and among many official church groups.

For example: the Presbyterian Statement I mentioned earlier; the number of very interesting stands on plural patterns taken by Methodist theologians; a number of Roman Catholic theologians and the former Episcopal Archbishop of Canterbury came out in favor of trial marriages just recently; Jewish theologians, Borowitz and several others, have jumped into the fire. Thus I am very optimistic that the monolithic thought pattern of the churches in the past (where sexual relations and procreation were tied together inseparably) is now being broken; and this means that we can expect, at least from religious leaders, some kind of creative approach to two new ethics—one for procreation and one for sexual relations.

DR. SAUER: Do you think there is significant advance over the Decameron and Hepcameron?

DR. FRANCOEUR: I don't know whether it's a significant advance. We talk about progress, but I never expected, for instance, the Presbyterian Church, with its very, very traditional stated morality and sexuality, to come out on plural patterns as forcefully as they did. I realize that there are still many years of immobility, particularly in the Vatican and elsewhere, but there is movement.

DR. SAUER: Now I am happy to introduce friend Audy again after that magnificent and wise talk that he gave earlier. Do you have a little more that you can throw in now?

DR. AUDY: Well, I think that there is a goal that we could call Point Omega, although man will strive for it only if he sets it for himself. But it is a very remote goal, and nobody is going to keep working toward something that's too remote. And I think many of us in this symposium have been breaking it down so as to set the necessary steps, the short-term goals.

One of them that I don't think has been mentioned is the need to work really heartily for world unification. The young people are among the most important soldiers for this—I was going to say "struggle," but it's not that; it is an effort to meet challenges. Life is not worthwhile without challenges, so don't just drop out; unite and get cracking! Dropping out is least permissible when the odds are bad—and they are bad.

Also, one very little thing: in order to improve communication, which will be vital in the time to come, all efforts at communication should be met more than halfway by both sides. And I would add, to some of the righteously indignant young people, and to some primly contemptuous older ones: think sometimes about your manners—at least let's try to maintain the level of manners of a really nice animal.

DR. SAUER: And now once again, Dr. Mrak.

DR. MRAK: One think I hoped would have been more discussed at this conference is the biological nature of man. Some mention was made of the book *Territorial Imperative,* but not of *Hidden Dimensions.* I personally believe our reactions have an awful lot to do with space and our closeness to others in the sense of space.

When I helped to design the Davis campus, I insisted that we have ample space so people weren't crowded together as they are on some campuses and in most cities. I learned, at least I thought I learned this, from what has happened in so many of our cities. At Davis we have enough space so that students can be and are dispersed, and the tendency is to gather only in small groups. They seem to get along better under such conditions.

My second thought relates to the possibility of continuing education for our legislative bodies. We require our teachers to attend teachers' institutes as a means of continuing education. I feel there is a need for our legislators to be regularly exposed to up-to-date information, especially those serving on Committees concerned with the very complicated areas of modern life. I know that some of our legislative leaders have expressed an interest in acquiring this continuing education. But how to do it? Perhaps they should spend a month or so each year at an institute. I have been exposed to their thinking in connection with the environment, and it indicates a need for up-to-date information. I must add that I have found most legislators very open minded and hungry for information.

DR. SAUER: And now we are supposed to talk to each other briefly before we get around to the questions to be answered.

Something that struck me in particular (and I must use the first person, because I can only speak for myself) was the extent to which Father Teilhard served as a catalyst for many people with many different interests and many different interpretations. This symposium has been a very interesting experiment in that an individual, a somewhat controversial individual, served as a basis and a valid basis for a great, great range of serious discussion.

To me personally, another interesting thing about this conference has been the extent to which we are ethnocentric. We make attempts to escape from putting ourselves at the center of the universe. But to a curious degree, we have become so much concerned with our relation to problems of ourselves and other countries that we take a rather strange stance as Americans looking out onto other cultures and parts of the world.

I have been wondering if a panel of half women might not have been an interesting experiment. I think it would have been an interesting thing, in such a symposium as this, to have had several representatives of quite different cultures. We have, after all, not universalized our culture, or our religion. If we had had, for example, a Brahman and a Chinese scholar and a Zuni Indian, it would have been a rather interesting spread of horizon and development of alternatives.

DR. FRANCOEUR: One of the things that really disturbs me in a conference like this is the monologues without dialogues. I wish there could be more time for discussion.

DR. GREENSON (to Dr. Francoeur) : I would like to ask you a question.

DR. FRANCOEUR: Go ahead.

DR. GREENSON: I am a psychoanalyst and I hardly said anything about sex at all. You got up there and talked on and on and you had these 16 options . . .

DR. FRANCOEUR: I only gave 15, actually.

DR. GREENSON: Well, I am quite willing to leave him one secret. But the reason I mention it is this: I think there is a great danger in confusing plural varieties of sexual freedom of all kinds and the thought that this increases pleasure. I believe there is something to be said for the very fact that sex is not easily available, that one has to struggle to get to it, which makes it all the more precious. If you make it too available and you make everything permissible, you are going to lose a great deal of the pleasure in sex.

DR. FRANCOEUR: Okay. When I was talking about these 15 or 16 options, I wasn't talking about a totally free society. I think one of the things that I would have liked to go into was the responsibility that is involved in this situation. If you have multiple options and you have the relationship, the serious relationship of two sexual persons, there is a tremendous responsibility involved in this relationship. If it is creative, if it is celebrational, if it is joyful, if it is everything, then it's got to be serious.

DR. SAUER: This is a dialogue, gentlemen, and the clock is upon us.

I shall refer the next inquiry to Judge Young. The question is: "How can civil disobedience be treated as self-destructive?"

JUDGE YOUNG: I am very grateful to whoever posed this question since it also troubles me. To frame the question of civil disobedience another way: Should one violate what one feels are unjust laws if one is willing to accept the consequences?

If we look at the history of this nation, we see many examples of individuals who have violated what they felt were unjust laws and have accepted the consequences. As a result of this, certain social changes have occurred within society.

What troubles me is what we mean by civil disobedience. Should one be able to break any law if he is willing to accept the consequences? For example, I am certain that no one would argue that he should be allowed to commit murder as long as he is willing to accept the consequences. There is a point, I assume, where it is proper to disobey certain laws that you feel are unjust if you are willing to accept the consequences. Where that point is, I am frank to admit that I don't know.

DR. MRAK: Were you ever forced to make a decision that implied that the law itself was not right, and decided to let a person go even though he had broken it? I don't want to put you on the spot.

JUDGE YOUNG: I think any judge should attempt to achieve equity under the law. I preside in a criminal court and deal mostly, of course, in criminal law. If I have a decision to make, I apply what knowledge I have of life and people in arriving at that decision. The law is there to assist you, possibly to minimize error that you might make in reaching that decision. But this problem of civil disobedience and whether one should not obey what he feels are unjust laws is a very, very difficult one.

DR. AUDY: This process of civil disobedience, isn't it always preceded by a long period of criticism and dissent, and so on? That's the time when these things should be changed.

JUDGE YOUNG: Usually that is true. In other words, you see the reflections of it in society before it is acted out by the individual. Very true.

DR. SAUER: And there are two questions for Professor Audy. The first one I will let him pass up: "Where is Point Omega?"

But the second one I think . . .

DR. AUDY: Well, this question is: "What dimension of time will the thirteenth-hour stage of man's evolution be placed in? Will it be in the fourth time dimension or not?"

Well, you see, all events in this universe take place in the multidimensional thing, and nothing takes place in the third dimension of the universe that isn't already represented in higher dimensions. The point is that what we see and know must be a that-much-smaller part of reality, and the passage of time is wholly an illusion in three-dimensional space. "What dimension of time" in the question is meaningless, since if the passage of time is the way we perceive the movement of our three-dimensional universe in four-dimensional space-time, "time" can very loosely be regarded as the fourth dimension (although I don't think that view is particularly helpful: it is better to conceive of the three-dimensional universe as an instantaneous cross section, and at the same time a *process* evoking changes, moving through four-dimensional space-time). An object in our three-dimensional part-universe is represented in the four-dimensional larger universe by what is called its *world-line* extending into what we would call its past as well as its future. If (and it is a big *if*) mental events have their world-lines, then we can conceive of the building up of four-dimensional group-minds, into which future minds in our world might be drawn operationally. My purpose was to suggest that such notions are by no means idle and unscientific. They should be scientifically explored in the course of studies of ESP.

DR. SAUER: Now for Dr. Mrak. If he wants to talk about DDT and the brown pelicans, he may do so.

DR. MRAK: By the way, I have no objection to restricting the use of DDT, but I hate to see it done by pushing a panic button. The other question I have been given asks: "As society has become increasingly interdependent, isn't it necessary for our education to also be increasingly multidisciplinary rather than, as you say, have "issues settled within the proper scientific community?"

Well, I couldn't agree with you more, and when I said

"within the proper scientific community," I certainly didn't mean to rule out the interdisciplinary aspect. But when people appear on the television or radio or are quoted in the news media by reporters before becoming involved, it bothers me. Remember what I said about the Editor of the *Washington Star* and how his people react to stories? He summarized my concern very well.

DR. SAUER: Our members who have really stirred up discussion are, as you may suspect, Professors Greenson and Francoeur. This is one question among several along similar lines that were addressed to Dr. Greenson: "You stated that Teilhard did not account for the human drive toward aggression and that evil results from the misuse of this drive. How do you react to Francoeur's statement that sexual experimentation can create new forms of human relationships, in view of the fact that the drive toward love is often a disguised drive toward aggression?"

DR. GREENSON: I will answer to the best of my ability. First of all, let me say this. I will respond to the last part of it. How did I react to Dr. Francoeur's statement that sexual experimentation can create new forms of human relations? I think that there is a great danger in taking this question too superficially.

DR. FRANCOEUR: Agreed.

DR. GREENSON: And I don't think what you were trying to say was that various or different forms of sexual behavior between two people is going to result in new kinds of people emerging.

DR. FRANCOEUR: Right.

DR. GREENSON: What I wished you had said, and hoped you said, was that in sexual relations between two people there is great room for experimentation and creativity. I think even Teilhard says this, by the way. He has a beautiful section in *The Phenomenon of Man* on sexuality. Even he said that sexuality is not merely for propagation or just for one another's pleasure, but that you should experience a certain intimacy with one another in spontaneous, free, unfettered sexuality like that of a child (I am using a phrase Dr. Audy used, "the unfettered mind of the child"), but these unfettered instinctual drives of the child ought to come out in sexual relations between people who *know* each other and *care* about each other, and *talk* to each other, and even know one another's names.

DR. FRANCOEUR: Definitely. I certainly wasn't advocating the playboy mentality of "Let's jump into bed, but let's not get personally involved. I don't even care to know your name."

When a new technology forges a new world (as we are doing now with our reproductive and contraceptive technology), a whole new culture emerges in which our traditional language increasingly fails to express what we are trying to say. Teilhard himself had this problem in shifting from a fixed cosmology to a process cosmogenesis. A good example of this problem of terminology comes up in your question, Dr. Greenson, about "sexual experimentation." Does the question refer to simple "genital experimentation" *à la Kama Sutra,* or does it embrace a much broader scope of human sexual development? The term "sexual experimentation" appears also in the question Dr. Sauer gave me in the context of my remarks about the "celibate" or "celebrational" marriage. This option has been strongly advocated by Robert and Mary Joyce of St. John's University in Collegeville, Minnesota. They feel that the sexual relationship of husband and wife can and should be co-creative without being procreative. They go even further and argue in a very Teilhardian vein that the husband/wife relationship can and should be co-creative without being ever expressed in sexual intercourse. I disagree with the philosophical and theological premises of this position (as I indicated in my paper), but this is definitely one among many options open to the human sexual person seeking his own perfection and growth in a social context.

Another question that was thrown to me was: "If we spend

the amount of money on finding the source of true universal love (per Father Mooney) that we spend on flights to the moon, then wouldn't all 16 of your options be opted, and then would man have reached the perfection that Teilhard was alluding to?"

Man will never reach the perfection of Dr. Greenson's comment about perfecting man. We won't find the source of true love, but we can constantly seek it.

DR. GREENSON: That's the fundamental.

DR. FRANCOEUR: That's the challenge of life.

DR. GREENSON: Exactly.

Appendix

PIERRE TEILHARD DE CHARDIN, S.J. (1881–1955)

The surname of Pierre Teilhard de Chardin is Teilhard, pronounced Tay-yahr. He signed his name Pierre Teilhard. Because we always think of the last name as the surname, it is not surprising that some people refer to Father Teilhard as Chardin or de Chardin, and have even coined the adjectives Chardinian or Chardinesque. But this designation is incorrect. The name is always Teilhard or Teilhard de Chardin. The adjective is Teilhardian. The name Teilhard has been traced back to 1325. An ancestor was ennobled in 1538. When Pierre Teilhard's grandfather, Pierre Cirice Teilhard, married in 1841, his wife's family name, de Chardin, was appended to his own, a custom not uncommon in Europe, and one which helps to distinguish different branches of a large family.[1]

Pierre Teilhard de Chardin was born and raised in Auvergne, France. He developed an interest in natural science in his youth, which he maintained throughout his lifelong membership in the Society of Jesus. Although his university studies were diverse, including physics, chemistry, geology, and paleontology, it was in the latter field that he

[1] Courtesy of The American Teilhard de Chardin Association, N.Y.C.

later specialized professionally and in which his scientific reputation was established.

He traveled widely as a representative of his order, which gave him the opportunity of making *in situ* studies in natural history and the origins of man. Among the countries in which he did field work are Tibet, Somaliland, Yemen, Malaya, Burma, Java, India, and South Africa.

During the First World War, he served in the front lines as a volunteer stretcher bearer and received both the Military Medal and the Legion of Honor.

Following the war, he lived for many years in China, and while there was a major participant in the recognition and classification of Peking Man. Collaborative work such as this, as well as his own contributions in paleontology, led to many academic distinctions. These included a professorship in geology at the Catholic Institute of Paris, and directorships of the National Geographic Survey of China and the National Research Center of France.

His extensive list of publications includes technical scientific works, as well as his more famous writings in philosophy and religion. Of the latter, perhaps his most widely known are *The Phenomenon of Man, The Appearance of Man,* and *The Future of Man.*

Teilhard was a frequent visitor and lecturer in the United States, and following the Second World War he was a more or less permanent resident of New York City. It was here that he continued his philosophic work under the auspices of the Wenner-Gren Foundation until his death in 1955. He is buried in the small graveyard of St. Andrews on the Hudson, the Jesuit Seminary in New York.

* * *

In Teilhard's system of thought, the origin and development of both man and the universe should be understood in terms of a continuing, and as yet uncompleted, evolutionary process. The natural history of man and the universe should not, he believed, be interpreted as a linear progression in which atoms, molecules, and cells have made their final combinations into disparate species, including *homo sapiens.* Such a sequential movement toward fragmentation is the exact opposite of Teilhard's view of natural history.

At the heart of Teilhard's cosmology is what he sees as a clear pattern of increasing unity and coalescence of man and matter, rather than growing separateness and divergence between them.

In attempting to explain this point of view, Teilhard made extensive use of neologism and metaphor. Very often, quite different neologisms are apparently used to refer to the same concept, e.g., *noosphere* and *biosphere.* Some of the more frequent and representative of these terms are used here in quotes.

According to Teilhard's reading of paleontological and other scientific findings, the evolutionary process has been "convergent" or "reflexive." That is, all matter is, so to speak, turning in on itself toward a state of "complexification." In this process, matter is achieving more and more complicated forms, of which man is presently the most complex example—he knows and knows that he knows.

However, the "complexification" of matter will continue until a state of "noogenesis" is reached (Gr. νοῦς, mind: γένεσις, generation). By this he appears to mean the development of a new and higher level of consciousness, self-awareness, self-understanding. This "noogenesis" will be manifested on a universal scale ("planetisation"), both in individuals and in human institutions.

At this stage of evolutionary development—metaphorically termed "Point Omega"—man will have arrived at the "biological perfection of himself." Individual men will then be characterized by "cerebralisation" or "superhominisation"; as such, they will have achieved a totally new level of fulfillment or "super-creativity."

This realization of the evolutionary process at "Point Omega" will also become manifested in human institutions.

With "noogenesis," mankind will have achieved a new and superior type of social organization, characterized by cooperation on a worldwide scale.

Teilhard was a formally trained scientist and a reputed paleontologist. He was also a wholly committed member of the Society of Jesus. As such, he believed that another phenomenon paralleled (or was implicit in) the process of "convergence"-to-"noogenesis"-to-"super-creativity." This process is "Christogenesis," which in his final testament Teilhard synthesized for himself as *in omnibus omnia Deus,* ἐν πᾶσι πάντα θεός: God is everything in all things.

A. Bernstein
—compiled from
the Symposium Program